PENGUIN
DESERT

Mary Weijun Collins lives in Auckland and is married to
Ian Collins, a Professor at the University of Auckland. Mary
left China in 1995, moving to New Zealand to join her oldest
daughter, Enya. The next year her mother and her youngest
daugher, Nini, also came to New Zealand.

DESERT ROSE

Mary Weijun Collins

PENGUIN BOOKS

PENGUIN BOOKS

Published by the Penguin Group

Penguin Group (NZ), cnr Airborne and Rosedale Roads, Albany,
Auckland 1310, New Zealand

Penguin Books Ltd, 80 Strand, London, WC2R 0RL, England

Penguin Group (USA) Inc., 375 Hudson Street, New York, NY 10014, United States

Penguin Group (Australia), 250 Camberwell Road, Camberwell,
Victoria 3124, Australia

Penguin Books Canada Ltd, 10 Alcorn Avenue, Toronto,
Ontario, Canada M4V 3B2

Penguin Books (South Africa) (Pty) Ltd, 24 Sturdee Avenue, Rosebank,
Johannesburg 2196, South Africa

Penguin Books India (P) Ltd, 11, Community Centre, Panchsheel Park,
New Delhi 110 017, India

Penguin Ireland Ltd, 25 St Stephen's Green, Dublin 2, Ireland

Penguin Books Ltd, Registered Offices: 80 Strand, London, WC2R 0RL, England

First published by Penguin Group (NZ), 2004

1 3 5 7 9 10 8 6 4 2

Designed by Mary Egan
Typeset by Egan-Reid Ltd
Printed in Australia by McPherson's Printing Group

ISBN 0 14 301937 6

A catalogue record for this book is available
from the National Library of New Zealand.

www.penguin.co.nz

This book is for my father who loved me dearly;
for my mother who created me.

ACKNOWLEDGEMENTS

To my husband Ian, without whom I wouldn't have the serenity to think and to write.

To my daughter Enya, who has offered me invaluable emotional support and unconditional love.

To my daughter Nini, who has contributed her computing expertise and unconditional love.

To my friend Daphne De Jong, who offered her invaluable writing experience and sound advice.

To Russell Lewin, who helped me with his knowledge about writing.

To Lesley Marshall, who helped with the birth of the book.

吃苦并不难，

难的是懂得，

怎样以苦换甜。

Hardship is invaluable,
it teaches you how to seek happiness.

CHAPTER ONE

The traditional culture of China was a jar of degeneration.

BO YANG
(A FAMOUS WRITER FROM TAIWAN)

I was in no mood to talk to my playmates. Sparkle and Snow were chatting and laughing on our way home but I was quiet. Head hanging, heart sinking, I found it difficult to be sociable, even to smile. The year was 1955 and I was ten years old. The autumn wind blew bitterly, tearing off the brown leaves and flinging them on the ground, each fall of leaves causing me further sadness. The dream I'd had the previous night had cast a dark shadow over me.

Six months earlier, my father, together with thousands of other intellectuals in my home town Qingdao, had been taken to an isolated place, escorted by security guards, to confess the 'sins' in their past. They were to tell the government in detail what they'd done for the previous government, the National Government led by Jiang Jieshi (Chiang Kai-shek). Many of them were then arrested or killed either for what they'd done at that time or for what they said about the past.

I missed my father terribly.

In the dream of last night, I had seen a small window open in a pitch-black ghastly place. I recognised it as the front building of the Teachers' College where both my parents worked. The dense plants underneath the window seemed to be crying. Two mysterious figures, tall and dark, were hiding there. Someone whispered an order and my father's head appeared through the window. He looked frightened, his body was shaking. Two pairs of big hands like iron pincers took his upper arms and he was pulled out through the window, the buttons of his clothes dragging on the

9

concrete window sill, making a clear, gentle sound, so incongruous in the homicidal atmosphere. I then saw my brother and me kneeling in front of a coffin, where both my father's and my mother's bodies were lying inside, motionless. My brother and I, both kneeling beside the coffin, were crying bitterly. Many people were there, standing and watching, indifferent.

I was woken by my own sobbing. My pillow was soaked wet by my tears. What a horrendous dream. It seemed so real. The story and the picture were haunting. My heart was racing. My body was shivering, even though I was in bed, and a terrible question kept haunting me: would my father ever come back?

After I said goodbye to Snow and Sparkle, I unlocked the door into our single-room home. It felt depressing in the twilight but I decided to stay in and wait for my mother to come back from work. Somehow I had a sense that I needed to see her as soon as she came in. I was in a weird apprehensive mood and I could do nothing else but look at the door where Mother would come through.

As time passed, it became dark and gloomy. I stood at the door, waiting, fraught and agitated.

At last my mother stepped in. She looked ten years older than she had that morning when she left to give lectures in the college class. The expression on her face was sad and cold. She was holding a small pot with some leftover food in it. It was my father's pot. He'd taken it with him when he went to take the political movement of Clear Up the Historical Reactionaries. Mother walked towards the double bed, which was the main furniture in the room, sat down on it, and said: 'Your father was arrested.' So Father had gone, just as the dream had foretold. I don't know how I could see the future event in my dream, but I knew it even before my mother told me. I began to cry uncontrollably.

The political movement of Clear Up the Historical Reactionaries was just one of many mass political movements since 1949. To maintain his power Mao wanted to be like the fisherman in the well-known Chinese story. In this tale a heron was picking out a mussel inside a shell and the shellfish caught the heron's beak. The fisherman then picked up them both. Mao had learned the lesson well from this story. He wanted people to fight against each other so he could benefit from the disquiet. He divided the public of China into two groups depending on what you, your parents or your grandparents did before 1949. The families of factory hands and peasants were the proletariat and they belonged to the good 'red' class, while the people from rich families were the evil 'black' class. He emphasised that landlords, affluent farmers, business families, political dissidents, bad characters and right-wing thinkers were the entire 'class enemy' — 'black elements' — and their children and grandchildren were 'the children of black elements'. He initiated the theory of class struggle and inspired the red class to accuse and attack the black class. He could watch the two classes fight and enjoy his power untouched.

Both my mother and father had tertiary education, which was rare in those days. My mother had graduated from Guang Hua University of Shanghai, today's Fudan University of Shanghai. My father was one of the first graduates from Shandong University. Both of them majored in Chinese literature.

My mother came from a high-ranking official's family. She was one of two girls in the whole province of twenty-five million people who had the chance to go to university. Her parents owned a mansion, which became a museum for Shandong province after 1949. However, my mother didn't have a civilised life until she was twelve years old. She lived in a remote poor village of Shandong, a northern province. When she was eight years old, her mother had her feet swaddled. She screamed and begged her mother not to: 'Please, Mother, leave my feet free. I will do all the heavy labour in the fields for you.'

'No. If you have a pair of unbound feet, no man will marry you.'

'I don't want to marry; I want to live with you forever.'

'You silly girl, it's not up to you. Pity you were born a girl. Every woman has to serve a man and get a living.'

With her mother watching, she screamed while two strong peasant women used a piece of white cloth, fifteen centimetres wide and five metres long, to wrap her small feet: the biggest toe stuck out untouched, the other four toes were to bend down underneath the soles. Tears filled my grandmother's eyes but she didn't make them stop — she couldn't. She knew how painful it was from her own experience when she was a little girl, but the only thing to blame was the misfortune they'd had to be born female, the very unlucky sex. When the terrible process of binding

11

was over, she gave her daughter a piece of cornflour bun and some stir-fried bean sprouts to console her. My poor mother smiled, with tears still in her eyes, when she saw the bean sprout dish. It was a rare food.

The swathe around Mother's small feet stayed there all the time, like iron teeth constantly biting her skin. She was allowed to loosen the wrapper for only a short time in the evening, when she could put her feet in warm water to soak for a little while. Then the wrapper was tied around the rotting skin again. For half a year she was tortured by the pain and inflammation, until the skin and flesh died off and the four toes were fixed under the sole permanently.

In 1949 when many people from affluent families fled to Taiwan, my mother refused to go: to start with, she distrusted the corrupt Jiang Jieshi's government, but more essentially the pain of her feet made her shiver even at the thought of taking long trips. Thus my parents' ill fate was sealed.

In 1918, my maternal grandfather, a scholar who was read and wrote all the time in his tiny, shabby study, passed the state examination with top results. It was the way for the poor to climb up the Chinese social hierarchy in those days, which was called *xue er you ze shi*, being a Mandarin by studying well. My grandfather became a high official of the province and the whole family became rich and noble. It offered my mother the chance to go to school and her feet were 'liberated', the swathe was taken away and she could wear ordinary shoes, but the bones of toes were broken and her feet were ruined. She could never get rid of the pain from her broken toes, even though they were bound only for four years. Her painful feet were the curse of her life.

In 1926 she went to Shanghai for university education when this great city was under the influence of Western countries as well as the Communist movement from Russia. My mother was a bold person by nature, radically minded and adventurous. In 1927 she joined the newly established Chinese Communist Party. She was active in fighting for the poor and the exploited against the corrupt ruling class. One day in 1930, when she was walking along small, quiet lanes in a poor area of Shanghai to put announcement papers on the wall for a revolutionary strike, a hostile fellow student saw her and followed her to her living place, a small attic in the centre of the city. The next day, during the early hours, she was pulled from her sleep and taken to the police. She spent two years in prison and then her family paid some big gold coins and bailed her free. Her parents and brothers were so angry at her 'naughty behaviour' that they sent her to a poor and backward place in Shandong. There she became a teacher in order to making a living.

Her boyfriend, Ye Lin, was the leader of the Chinese Communist Party's underground organisation at the time and he had tried his best to save her from prison but failed. Later he was in danger too and had to flee to Yanan, the centre of the Communist movement from 1928 to 1936. My mother was told that Ye Lin was killed during the fighting by the Communists. She realised, then, that cruelty was the nature of the Communists' cause and she never tried to join the Communist Party again. This would become a black spot in her personal history: she was labelled a 'traitor of the Communist revolution' by the authorities.

My father came from a wealthy landlord family in Changle of Shandong. His grandmother was a heroine in the local area carrying the name of Guanyi, Buddha the Kindness. She was generous and sharing. When the harvest was bad and people suffered from starvation, my great-grandmother set up two huge woks outside their house and cooked millet porridge from dawn to dusk. Hungry peasants from four directions came and took the free, life-saving food.

My great-grandmother had established the family tradition of being kind and generous to those in need, which had a great deal of influence on my personality.

In 1935, my father met my mother in Juxian County of Shandong, where they both were teaching Chinese literature at the only high school in the county. They fell in love and got married soon, even though my father couldn't divorce his first wife from a marriage arranged by his parents and the matchmaker. There was no such thing as divorce in those days, and his first wife had to live in my father's home until her death. It was a common practice in those days for a country woman abandoned by her husband, which was known as *li hun bu li jia*, to remain in his house.

When the Japanese war broke out, my parents did not escape to the peaceful southern part of China, as most intellectuals did. The reason was unusual but reasonable: again, my mother simply could not bear the long and hard wartime trip with her ruined feet. Instead they moved to my father's home town Changle and settled down there.

Before I was born, my mother had lost three of my older siblings. They died from lack of nutrition and medicine during the Japanese war. In those days, once a child fell ill, even if it was with only an ordinary cold, it would be enough to kill them. My mother must have been very brave and strong to bear the terrible trauma of losing a child again and again.

When I was born, I only had one sibling, my brother Main, who was five years older than me. My parents were so happy that they had a girl again. I was my father's darling and he liked to gently caress my small, elegant fingers and say, 'They look exactly like mine.'

During the Japanese occupation, my father couldn't keep his teaching job and he was sent to be trained as a junior government official. The three months' training time — short but unfortunate — was to determine my father's tragic destiny. It was later to be seen as his historical error by the subsequent Communist government.

So, my family was amongst the blackest of the black. But we ordinary people didn't know this until the tragedy came.

In 1948 Father left our home town Changle when the civil war between Mao and Jiang Jieshi became intense and the Communists began killing the rich. He went to the city Qingdao (Tsingtao) and found himself a teaching job in a girls' high school.

Back in Changle, the rest of the family — my mother, my brother Main and I — nervously watched the civil war situation become turbulent and chaotic.

One day a group of soldiers of the People's Liberation Army moved into our house. They were sent by the newly established Communist government to lead the 'land reform movement' — taking land away from the rich and dividing it up to distribute it to the poor. There were eight of them, and we were to offer them free food and accommodation, according to the authority orders. Other rich families in the village were told to do the same and they complained a lot. My mother didn't — she was always a generous person and was happy to share what she had with the soldiers.

Amongst the soldiers there was a young boy of sixteen who was grieving over his parents' recent death and my mother was kind towards him. She showed him how to play the harmonica and presented the precious German-made harmonica to him as a gift to encourage him to be strong.

The young soldier and the rest of the team were deeply touched by my mother's kindness and generosity. Before long the whole team billeted in our house became friends with her.

One night the head of the group took my mother out of everyone else's earshot and told her, 'We are going to crack down on the rich families soon. I want you to know.'

That night my mother didn't sleep. First of all, she went to see Cloud, my stepsister-in-law from my father's first marriage. Her husband, my older stepbrother Fu-chin, who was a high-ranking military officer, had left for Taiwan with his army. 'Dear daughter-in-law,' my mother told Cloud, 'we have to run away, otherwise we'll get into big trouble. The Communists are well-known to be brutal to the rich.'

'Run away?' said simple-minded Cloud. 'How could we leave the whole property and run?'

'We have no option. For our life's sake, Cloud, we must leave our possessions behind and run for our lives.'

'I cannot do that. Let's wait for a little longer. I might decide to run away if the situation turns out to be really bad.'

Poor Cloud, she didn't have the chance to watch the situation change since very soon afterwards the Communists looted her house, confiscated her assets and tortured her. She was hung up on a tree, arms tied behind her back, dangling in the air. She was whipped and struck so hard that she lost consciousness, whereupon cold water was poured on her head to wake her up for more lashings. She was ordered to tell them where her husband was, but the poor woman had no idea. Actually her husband and the army had run away in such haste that almost nobody had had the chance to say goodbye to his family. Everybody thought the soldiers would be returning home a short while later and no one realised it would be a separation of nearly half a century. The whole family, Cloud, her mother-in-law and her two little daughters, Pure (four years old) and Phoenix (two years), were thrown out of their home to live in a shack, a half-room, no more than twenty-five square feet. They stayed there for decades. Pure developed heart disease after the horrendous events.

When Pure grew up, she had difficulty finding a husband: no decent man wanted her because of her sick heart and black family background. Her father being in Taiwan, the enemy's side, didn't help. When she was twenty-four, an age at which a woman is regarded an old spinster in the rural areas, she finally had a suitor, a young man who also had difficulty in getting married, for his family before 1949 had been land owners and therefore a black family. The young man and his family told Cloud that he didn't mind that Pure was black nor that she was sick, so long as she could bear children for him. Poor Pure, how could she give birth to a child since she was so ill? Two years later when she was still not pregnant, her husband beat her up and her mother-in-law berated her. She died when she was only twenty-six.

My mother did not sleep a wink after she came back from Cloud's place. Early the next morning, she put all the household bedding out in the sun, opened the windows wide as if she would be back home soon, and with a woven basket over her arm and ten-year-old Main and four-year-old me in tow, off she went. Nobody suspected that she had abandoned the whole property, leaving behind all her assets, even gold and silver treasures. Since roads were blocked and everyone was checked, those carrying valuables would be arrested.

Later on, whenever my mother recalled this brave event, she would sigh and say: 'Poor Happy, I hope she didn't have a bad ending. I am so sorry we couldn't take her with us.' Happy was our dog.

After all sorts of adversity on the way from Changle to Qingdao — roads were blocked and everyone was checked (many were killed or arrested if they were found to have money with them) — my mother, with Main and me in tow, finally made the trip and we joined my father in Qingdao. My mother soon found a teaching job and later both my parents became Chinese lecturers in the Teachers' College of Qingdao. We had a few years of happy life.

Qingdao is a coastal city between Beijing and Shanghai. It has beautiful beaches and Westernised buildings. The Germans, British, Americans and Japanese were all there at different times, and they had all left their marks. The famous Tsingtao beer, for example, was first brewed by a German company in Qingdao.

The Teachers' College of Qingdao was located in Licun town, a suburb twenty miles away from the city centre, which was surrounded by rolling fields and dense groves of trees — poplars, cherries, peaches and apples. The Teachers' College was on a quiet road beside an agricultural Scientific and Research Institute with its vast experimental lands that grew roses, tomatoes, radishes, turnips and rows of pine trees. It was a paradise for children to ramble, hiding and seeking, exploring and adventuring as well as stealing the fruit and enjoying the Eden-like setting.

We lived in the residents' section of the college, where fifteen families shared a long brick building. Behind the building was a little stream, clear brisk water flowed with groups of small carp swimming and tiny crystal shrimps jumping. Each family had a room as a bedroom, lounge and dining-room, plus a tiny kitchen separated by a public courtyard on the other side of the main room. The spacious courtyard was a perfect playground for us children.

There were eight girls of similar age to myself in the neighbourhood. Every evening after dinner, one of my playmates would knock at the door and put her head in, calling: 'Weijun, let's go to the toilet together, shall we?' I would stop eating and jump up from the seat, ignoring Mother's scolding, grab a piece of toilet paper, holding it by its corner, and shoot out of the room. Outside in the public courtyard, a small team of seven girls would be standing, each holding a piece of paper, and then we headed

Me as a new student at No. 5 Middle School of Qingdao, aged twelve

towards the public toilet with the paper dancing in our hands like butterflies. Six of us would dance and sing outside the toilet while the other two sang inside, since the toilet could hold only two persons.

We'd learned the songs and dances from the college students. The college students held festival ceremonies every year on May 1, Labour Day, on October 1, the National Day, and the New Year Day. During those days, the students would perform all sorts of entertainment, such as choirs, solos, short plays, witty talks, rhythm talks, folk dances and instrumental music. There would be a prize-giving for the best performance so the students took rehearsal seriously. We children would watch the rehearsals from the beginning to the end. No matter how many times they rehearsed, we would be there, standing at the door, crawling on the window sill, eyes open wide and watching attentively and then in the moonlight, we would copy the songs and dances learned from the students in our public courtyard in the evenings.

In summer evenings when the heat was fading away, my parents would go to the wheat field behind our house. They always took me with them. I was the only child living with my parents at the time. My brother Main was staying at his school during week days and only came home on Sundays.

I enjoyed the evening walk with my parents. The sunset was pink and purple; the wheat fields were golden in the harvest season. Cool breezes blew the wheat stalks, making gleaming waves far into the distance, forming a glittering ocean. My parents chatted quietly about literature and their lectures but I would interrupt them every now and then: 'Look, Baba, Ma, I can make the flower sing.' I would hold a flower called Evening Beauty that opened in the evenings with its red, yellow, white and apricot petals sending a subtle fragrance to the air. I would nail the stem, cast the stamens, and blow across it to produce a whistling sound. Every time, hearing my call, my parents would stop their chatting and listen patiently to my 'singing flowers', and smile kindly.

On some Sundays my parents would attend a conference in the central city on educational or political issues, and they always took me with them. We would have a picnic in Zhong Shan Park, shop in fancy stores, and go home with packages of snacks and pretty dresses.

In October 1949 when Mao won the civil war against Jiang Jieshi, he exclaimed on the balcony of Tienanmen building, 'The People's Republic of China is established, China is liberated and the Chinese people are standing up.' But actually the only person standing was Mao himself. The Chinese people started a time of suffering worse than ever before.

After the 'liberation', Mao and his government carried out all sorts of mass political campaigns one after another, first in 1949 the Land Reforming Campaign resulted in all rural residents losing their land to the government, then in 1951 the mass movement of Reforming the Capitalists closed down private businesses and confiscated the owners' properties to revert them to state ownership, and in 1953 the Pressing Counter-Revolutionaries led to thousands jailed or killed, they were the ones who were suspected of being Jiang Jieshi's followers or 'spies against the Communist cause'. Two years later came *su fan*, Clear Up Historical Reactionaries. By this time everyone realised Mao's was crueller than any previous government and everyone was as scared and terrified as a cicada in the late-summer evening wind.

Mao's government ruled the country by controlling the media. No individual opinion was allowed to be expressed, even in private, and only the Party's voice was heard through the media. As a result, the Party's voice — virtually Mao's personal opinion — became the mind of the whole nation. Any individual who dared to express his own ideas would end up either in a labour camp or ruthlessly and suddenly executed.

As well as the media, Mao's government controlled all personal details. They established a tight system to control every individual's privacy — the system of dossiers and *hu kou zhi*, controlled registered residence. To gather the details of every individual, the government sent numerous people travelling all over China to investigate each person's past. Every year a report was added to the original one by the person's employer, and no one was allowed to look at his own dossier. The dossier was like a shapeless noose tied around the neck. No matter where you went or what you did, you were watched by the secret eyes of the Party. It was a prison without walls. As for the *hu kou zhi*, it confined one to stay and live in one place and nobody could move away since housing, food, fabric, fuel were all rationed and no one could survive in a place without their registered residence.

In August 1955, my parents, like all the educated people in China, were ordered to attend the campaign of Clear Up Historical Reactionaries and they were detained in secret premises and confessed their 'sins' in their history while the Party sent heaps of men to various places to check their histories. It was a long process and the atmosphere was murderous. Every participant, like a suspect waiting for his sentence, was interrogated and some were executed.

I was half-nervous and half-excited as I watched my parents packing up sheets and quilts and mosquito nets ready to attend the 'political study'. I could see my mother was worrying and my father was distressed. As my brother was at school, I was going to stay at home by myself which made me excited. I was looking forward to an independent life without Mother around to tell me what to do or what not to do. I had little idea that my life was going to change forever.

After my parents left, I had meals in the students' canteen of the Teachers' College and in the evening I locked the door of our home and went to my playmate Snow's home for company. Snow's parents were also in the political study and she and Swallow, her younger sister, were home alone. Later I fell ill, lying in bed at Snow's home. Both Snow and Swallow were at school but I was too ill to get up. I had developed a severe stomach pain and was extremely weak and sick. I didn't have any energy to go to the canteen to eat and for the first time in my life I experienced the terrible feelings of loneliness and homelessness, something that was to become so familiar in my later life. I missed my parents terribly. When would they come home?

Months passed. I had no idea where my parents were or when they would come back, but some teachers, mainly younger ones, gradually returned and the school started again, though with fewer teachers. I kept hoping to see my parents at any moment.

One day I asked a classmate of mine whose father was a teacher in a primary school, 'When will our parents be back home, do you know?'

'Why? Haven't your parents come back? My father has been back for a long while. Your parents must have historical problems. They are anti-revolutionaries!' I was horrified.

I remembered a song we learned to sing in early 1955, which I enjoyed and sang cheerfully with innocence:

Hold the hoes tightly, hoe the weeds absolutely;
Off their heads go, for they are bad elements.

I now realised we'd been singing about my father, a father I was going to lose because he was a 'weed' and 'a bad element' and he was going to be beheaded.

One day I was home by myself, lonely and scared, when a guard from the college came in. He said, 'I suppose you want to see your father? Come with me.'

I followed him to the front courtyard of the teaching area, where I found the corridors blocked and two guards walking to and fro. There was an eerie air hanging about the once-pleasant place. After a short while I saw my father coming towards me. His tall thin figure was even more willowy and his face twitched with a mysterious nervousness. One of the guards brought a wooden bench for my father and I leaned my body against him. I felt a warm feeling that I'd missed for a long time. How nice it was to see Baba again. I looked up at his lovely gentle face, wishing I could see it all the time. Stroking my hair gently, he lowered his head and asked me, 'Has your mother come home?'

'No, I haven't heard anything about Ma for ages.'

Father gave a sad sigh. 'How are you getting on by yourself?' he asked carefully.

I burst into bitter tears, 'I am starving. The Teachers' College gives me very little money. I don't even have money to buy enough cabbage.' With a sad face, Father put his thin hand into his pocket and took out a two-yuan note and handed it to me. I couldn't believe my eyes. A two-yuan note, the biggest money I had even seen. I stopped crying and gazed in gratitude at the note and at my father's face, and he looked back at me with a sad, thoughtful expression.

This was the last time I saw my dear father.

Quite a few weeks later, my mother's personal history was at last cleared up and my terrible orphan life finished, but our happy domestic life had disappeared. Sighing and worrying, my mother was depressed; I was nervous and scared.

I missed my father dreadfully. Each morning I thought he might be back, but then the day would be just another disappointment. His departure became something of a nightmare. I didn't believe he could disappear just like that, and I missed him too much to accept the truth. Every day after school as soon as the bell rang, I would jump up from my seat and shoot out of the classroom and run along the street frantically. One afternoon my shoelace came loose and I stepped on it and fell to the ground. When I got up with a bleeding knee, I wept, reminding myself that there was no father at home. I refused to accept this, and thought, 'No, Father is at home this time.' I ran to him so hysterically that I forgot to buy the sanitary paper for my mother that she had asked me to buy after class. When I arrived home empty-handed, my mother was cross with me. She had to tear up an old notebook for her period. I didn't care what she said. All I was concerned with was seeing if my father had returned. But once again, Father was not there. Weeks passed but I could not forget him. As if under a spell, I stubbornly believed he would come home one day. Each afternoon I ran wildly home, pushing myself hard, believing that if I wasn't quick enough Father would be gone again. I would imagine Father sitting in front of the stove with a gentle smile on his face. The fire would be roaring and the room would be warm and cosy. Father always knew how to make the stove work well. The steam from the heat would be spreading over the glass of the door and the window making the room warm and cosy. How much I wanted Father home. I wanted to see him, even just once again. Yet each day his image would vanish like the steam vapour, leaving nothing but air.

I couldn't believe it. One day I would catch the hem of his clothes like in the past when he took me to the market, letting me hold onto his clothes if his hands were occupied by food. So every afternoon I would open the door of our home and be just about to shout out 'Baba!' when I realised there was no Father. Mother would be sitting in front of the desk marking her students' papers with red tearful eyes. Our iron stove was cold and frightening, with a wide opening like a huge mouth laughing mockingly at me. Its steel coldness pierced me to the bottom of my heart; sadness wrapped me in its dark cloak. I was crying inside. I dared not cry out loud in case I made Mother cross or sad again.

My father's 'crime' was, as we were told later, that he had once joined the Three Youth League of the National Party led by Jiang Jieshi. But because he was only in the League for three months, and couldn't remember it many years later, he had failed to 'confess' it in the movement of Clear Up the Historical Reactionaries. He was declared disloyal to the Party, an historical anti-revolutionary. He was rated as a dangerous person who did not trust Mao's government.

Snow's father was cleared at the end of the movement and recovered his teaching job because he was cunning enough to guess the Communist Party's intention and told them a lot of false crimes of his history. When the crimes he confessed were found out not to be true, the officials didn't mind his lies but believed he trusted the Party very much, even too much, which was in line with the direction of Chairman Mao's doctrine: being 'an obedient tool of the Party'.

My father was sentenced to ten years in a labour camp at Yellow River Farm Camp, in the northwest part of Shandong province, a very poor area. The day before he was sent to the labour camp, my mother was allowed to visit him in detention. He was totally beaten and submissive. Standing in the windowless room without even a seat, his tears kept on streaming down his face. He used one of his hands to wipe his tears, the other to hold his trousers up. His belt had been taken away by the guards, which was a common way in the detention centre to avoid suicides. Sobbing bitterly, he lamented: 'I will not survive ten years in prison. I can't see our children any more.'

Mother decided to appeal my father's case. A few weeks later a new sentence was announced. Instead of ten years, his sentence was converted to three years, which was great news for both my mother and my father, but not for me. I was too little to understand the difference between three months and three years. I was just feeling I had lost my father for ever and the loss was too huge for a girl of ten years to bear.

Unfortunately, isolated in prison, my father didn't realise how much the political climate had changed. By the time it was nearly the end of his prison term of three years, bad news came. He had committed a 'new crime': he had once talked about Soviet Russia in a friendly way, not knowing that Mao had had a big quarrel with the Russian leader Nikita Khrushchev, and the relationship between China and Russia had become bitter. My father was reported by one of his prison inmates. This practice was always encouraged so that the inmates would not become friendly, which made the prison life even more hellish. My father was accused of spreading approving words about the Russian enemy, and his sentence was changed from three years to eight.

In 1961, six years after my father went to the labour camp, we received his last letter. It was brief and sad with wobbling handwriting. He told us that he was in poor health, and that he wanted us to go to visit him. He also wanted us to bring him some food: five hundred grams of millet, five hundred grams of red beans and one kilo of rice. This was the first time he had asked us to send him anything, and the first time he'd wanted us to visit him. However we couldn't find any of the food he asked for, since the whole country was starving. Everyone was rationed to four hundred and fifty grams of dried sweet potatoes per day only, and apart from this there was absolutely nothing you could put into your mouth other than salt and cold water. Everybody could hardly stand due to extreme lack of food and malnutrition. My mother's tuberculosis had become bad and I also was too weak to take a long journey. It was decided then that Main would go to the labour camp to visit Father for the family. What a life-long regret my not going has been for me. Millions of times in my later life I have wished that I had taken the trip to see my father at that crucial time.

My brother set off for the journey with empty hands — we could not buy any food in our area. Filled with grief, my mother and I secretly saw Main away on a dark evening. We avoided anyone from the neighbourhood since it was regarded as a reactionary sin to visit a political prisoner family member.

In the gloomy dusk, my brother left home and started the torturous journey.

After a two-day train journey, followed by ten hours in the bus, he faced a small town, poor and remote. To his great surprise, he saw some street vendors selling dried persimmons. It was a miracle indeed, even though the persimmons were old and rotten. This could not happen in Qingdao, for people driven crazy with hunger would tear the vendors into pieces if they dared to sell any food in the street. Main bought five kilos of dried persimmons and he felt a bit more optimistic.

Carrying the persimmons in his travelling bag, he started to walk along the dusty road towards the headquarters of the Yellow River Labour Camp. After eight hours he arrived hungry and exhausted at a small village. He knocked at one of the doors. The villager took him to see the head of the village, who showed Main the village school, a shabby mud house divided into three small classrooms with a few rows of wooden desks and narrow benches in them. Main gratefully stayed in one of the classrooms for the night, half asleep and half awake from the coldness and the hard wooden desks underneath him. Early the next morning, with a hungry belly, he scooped water with his hands from a little stream, drank some, washed his face and used his frozen fingers to tidy his unkempt hair. The idea that he would see Father thrilled him. He wanted to look decent. He prepared some long talks to have with the father he had not seen for six years.

At four o'clock in the afternoon he finally arrived at the Yellow River Labour Camp but he was told his father was not there. Father had been recently shifted to another spot, ten miles away. Main wanted to see Father so keenly that he started to run despite his sore feet. In the dark evening, he reached the camp where Father was confined. The porter in one of the many rows of grey mud houses took him to a room with two narrow wooden benches. After a while, Father was brought into the room by a guard with a gun on his shoulder. As soon as Main saw Father, he burst into tears. He couldn't believe his eyes. He saw a rotten skeleton with a very sick man's dragging step. Father was not the father he remembered. He was decades older, grey headed, grey bearded with a thin, pale face and a numb expression. And how bent his back was! His body was like that of a shrimp, stooped over to the ground, gasping heavily. His clothes were shabby with so many mending patches that the original colour was no longer discernable. Seeing Main, Father asked eagerly, 'Where is your mother? Where is Weijun?' Main couldn't stop crying. Father didn't talk but kept looking at the armed guard, who was big, tall and strong, like a black tower over a dying locust, closely watching the prisoner for the whole fifteen minutes of my brother's visit. Father was silent. Main was crying. The guard spoke: 'The people's government is merciful towards the prisoners. We show great humanitarianism. Isn't this true, No. 1004?'

Father, tottering in front of the guard like a weak sheep, nodded slightly. A while later, the guard stopped talking and said, 'Time's up. No. 1004, go back to your cell!'

Main was left in the empty room by himself. He felt as if he had just had a nightmare. Slowly he moved towards the exit. His feet were painful as if burnt by fire. After three days' hard journey, and with a broken heart, he arrived home on a gloomy evening. His feet were full of horrible blisters, some as big as apricots.

My father never did come home. He died soon after he saw my brother. It was during the Three Starvation Years in the early 1960s. He died from chronic bronchitis with the complications of pneumonia, and he died hard, with plenty of pain, no food, no doctor, no medicine, no freedom, and most of all, no beloved ones around him. The pain was overwhelming when I heard of his death, and I have never gotten over the suffering caused by my father's miserable death.

Many times I've found myself absorbed in painful contemplation, trying to imagine what it had been like for him when he was approaching the end of his life. Was he relieved at the end of his tortured life, or was he pained by the injustice? Was he in agony yearning to see his family, worrying about his little and beloved daughter, or was he numbly and reluctantly accepting his ill fate? What would he have been able to tell me if I'd been with him before he closed his eyes forever? Millions of times I have wished I'd been old enough to visit him before he died.

After Father was arrested in late 1955, Mother became a sour person. Giving frequent long sad sighs, her mind seemed always far away from the present and from me, which frightened me. And for years afterwards, she was never the cheerful, cheeky person she had used to be. I felt that when I lost my father, I lost my loving mother too, just as the fateful dream had forewarned.

The atmosphere at home was so heavy, as if dark clouds were pressing low in the small grim room forever. Sometimes I would try to talk to my mother but she couldn't hear. She would snap at me when I asked her a question. She would say: 'You are a half-orphan now. Don't spoil yourself.'

I would go out of our house, trying to cheer myself up, but the outside world was cruel, too. I remember once when Old Smart, the neighbour's seven-year-old boy, saw me in the public courtyard, he asked me, 'Tell me, Weijun, where has your father gone?'

I shivered and sheepishly answered in a very low voice, 'He is in the meeting for political study.'

Old Smart burst out with a crack of vicious laughter.

Another day at school a fellow schoolgirl pointed at me and said to her friends, 'She is the child of an anti-revolutionary!'

I was shocked. I remembered how sweet that girl had been to me when I had first shifted to this school from the city, calling me 'Little Beauty'.

Humiliation fell cold and heavy over me like non-stop rain.

One Sunday afternoon, to my joy, a boy called me: 'Weijun, we need one more player. Come and join us.'

I stood in the row with the other three team players, trying to avoid being hit by the opposing team with a fabric ball filled with sand. I was supposed to jump when the ball came, but I didn't move quickly enough. My body was tired and sluggish, and I often got hit by the ball, and consequently felt guilty and began to get bored. Finally I said, 'I don't want to play any more,' and started to walk off towards my home. To my dismay, a boy named Big Mountain, who used to be pretty kind to me, shouted: 'Curse you! If I was your father, I could give you good lessons to let you know what to do. Now your old man's in jail, you are running free! A true fatherless anti-revolutionary!' Laughter from other children burst like the claps of falling rocks, attacking my heart.

I was bullied like this quite often. Sometimes I kept quiet, other times I rebelled, depending on my mood. One day half a year after my father had gone, I was sitting on a rock at the bank of the stream, washing my bare feet. My friend Sparkle was washing her clothes while we were chatting away. Another girl from the residential section came over. She was older and not particularly close with us. She walked behind me all of a sudden. She jumped on my back, her legs on my neck and shoulders clasping her hands on my head, laughing away, 'Weijun, you little bastard, I am your father coming back from the labour camp. Call me Dad, call it now!' In Chinese culture, the older you are the more superior you become. Her bottom was pressing on my back and her hands were twitching my head. I became enraged. With my sharp nails, I clutched the flesh on her legs tighter and tighter until she cried. I didn't loosen my nails' hold until she gave in, begging miserably. I suddenly stood up, throwing her up in the air, dropping her moaning on the wet ground. Standing in the middle of the river, I gave out a loud laugh. 'Ha, ha, ha! You little tortoise, remember your lessons from your old aunt of me!' With these rude words, I ran away quickly.

Most of the time, however, I preferred to hide myself at home. But the atmosphere at home was very scary. Mum used to say: 'It is too painful to live on. If I cut the artery on my wrist, I would die within a few minutes.'

One evening after dinner I left home, trying to run away from the hellish pressure of home. It was a cloudy night with no moon or stars visible. I wandered over to the far end of the college, where my playmate Jade's family lived. Pushing the door open, I saw a sweet happy family scene. The whole room was full of the smell of cooked sweet potatoes and corn bread. Jade and her younger brother were setting the table, her mother was carrying the dished-up food, her father was helping and her older sister was playing the violin. A while later they all sat around the square dining table, eating and chatting. It seemed I was absolutely forgotten in the shadowy corner. I felt a piercing pain in my heart. I dragged myself up, scrambled towards the door and retreated back to the cold, dark starless night.

I no longer had friends to play with after school, since all the adults would call their children away if they saw their children playing with me. Nobody ever came again to visit our house. People shunned my mother and me as if they were avoiding the plague. Main would come home on Sunday, stay for half a day and leave abruptly. My mother and I were totally isolated.

The Chinese New Year came for the first time without Father. My mother tried to make it as cheerful as it used to be, but how could she? The contrast was so sharp and I could never forget the misery I experienced during that devastating Spring Festival.

One evening I called on several of my playmates to go to a Peking opera but nobody wanted to go with me. However, I couldn't stay at home since the atmosphere was so depressing and unbearable. I decided to go to the opera house alone. In the middle of the show, tears began running down my cheeks as the actress on the stage cried her heart out, complaining that her official husband had abandoned her and their two children. A terrible picture came into my mind: Mother was lying on the floor with a very pale face and dead-looking eyes, blood was pouring from her artery at her wrist . . .

I jumped up, scrambled through the audience and bolted out into the cold darkness. Despite the chill outside, sweat sprang out on my forehead and matted my hair. When I arrived home I saw Mother lying in bed. With my heart pounding, I moved slowly towards her. Breath stopped, muscles tensed, I put my fingers under her nose and waited. After a while I felt a little warm air coming out of her nostrils. My body collapsed all of a sudden. For the first time, I noticed one of my shoes had gone missing on the way home.

Later my mother told me that the very night when I had gone to watch the Peking opera, she did try to cut her artery open but failed. She said: 'You need lots of guts to kill yourself. Besides, I don't want you and your brother to be orphans.'

A few months later I developed hepatitis A, a rare disease in those days. Maybe my body was trying to help me regain my mother's attention. When the doctor told my mother the bad news, she was sincerely worried. She paid more attention to me. It might sound strange but I was grateful to the disease for it had won my mother's love back for me.

My mother's health deteriorated quickly and soon she was too sick to give lectures in the classroom. She was shifted to work in the college library. What a great joy it was to me! A magic door opened for me to a world of imagination. As a lonely child, ill-treated for something 'bad' I had no idea about, reading was the ideal escape. I dwelled in the imaginary world created by authors, as well as in my own imaginary world which was enhanced by books. I explored the universe in my imagined world and I became a dreamer. 'Dreams make hopes': I became happier.

But reading was not a common passtime in China. For thousands of years, as a feudalist country confined by a rigid mindset, China had been a country of talking and listening. The emperors listened to their ancestors; mandarins listened to the emperors, the inferiors to the superiors, wife to her husband, children to their parents . . . Anybody who used his own mind to provoke new ideas committed the sin of *fan shang*, disrespect of the higher, and would end up as an unforgivable criminal. This custom has made the country stay senile and unable to progress. Such an economic and scientific handicap has caused the people to be rigid, short-sighted, narrow-minded, timid and never daring or wanting to try new things or think for themselves. Book reading was considered a novel thing for the minority of scholars, or as a help in making *ba gu wen*, articles with an extremely rigid style. In the early 1920s, the government started to send bright young boys to Western countries and they brought back books written by Western writers which were translated into Chinese from English, French, Spanish, German and other foreign languages. It was a new thing to the Chinese society and they remained only in the academic élite. I was lucky: Living in the campus of the Teachers' College I had access to those translated books.

My mother encouraged my reading by providing snacks together with the books. She liked to place some peanuts at my side when she offered me a book first thing in the morning. Lying in bed, I read while eating, while Mother laid the fire, cleaned the house and cooked breakfast. Food, the material nutrition, and books, the mind nutrition, were feeding me at the same time. As reading was always linked with the pleasure of eating, I enjoyed it with inexhaustible desire and pleasure.

I went to the library every day after school and dived into the depths of the bookshelves like a rabbit jumping happily into his burrow. I would take tens of copies home and read them in all my spare time. My reading speed became so fast that my head was moving from left to right, which caused disbelief and laughter amongst my classmates. But my class teacher, Liu Xuemao, understood me. He always showed his appreciation and compassion when he saw me reading. He would tell my ignorant classmates to stop laughing at me.

One day I was standing lonely and sad in the school playground when Teacher Liu (a respectful term in Chinese society, which is commonly used) came up to me. He said to me in a gentle voice, 'Weijun, don't be too sad for your father's absence any more. Be brave and enjoy your life.' His sympathy, understanding and kindness might have sounded simple to an adult, but was great to a bullied and ignored child. It was the first time in my life that somebody other than my mother had shown kindness when I most needed it. Gradually I began to recover from the trauma of losing my father, after this event, and I suddenly became aware that I was not always alone. Somebody would be with me when I was in despair.

Reading wasn't considered a proper thing to do in China. Children were expected to work hard on their textbooks and recite them well, but reading books other than textbooks was considered unnecessary. Eighty-five percent of the population were peasants; and a huge proportion of the peasants were illiterate. People hardly understood how important it was to develop a child's mind by reading; books were considered a luxury and to buy a book meant to waste money. I was one of the few children who had the privilege of having so many books to read.

My reading moved from Chinese children's books to international fairy tales translated into Chinese, such as books by Hans Christian Andersen, the Grimm brothers and Aesop's Fables. Children's scientific books attracted me too, and they stimulated my imagination. My adventurous personality was formed at this stage.

Gradually my reading moved from children's stories to Chinese folk legends, then to detective stories and then to Chinese literature, and finally Western literature. My favourite authors were Balzac, Goethe, Hugo, Tolstoy, Jane Austen, Gorky, Chekhov, Dickens, Turgenev, Flaubert, De Maupassant, the Brontë sisters, Dostoevsky, Dumas junior, Thackeray and Pushkin.

Brought up by Western books, Western authors took the role of my mentors, forming my way of thinking freely and independently. This was so different from my contemporaries that I was almost an alien in Chinese society, which was an odd mixture of cruel Communism and narrow-minded feudalism. I became a black sheep in China.

CHAPTER TWO

In 1957, when I was twelve, I entered No. 5 Middle School of Qingdao. There were twelve hundred students, half juniors and half seniors. I stayed there for six years, three as junior and another three as senior, till 1963.

The first day of my middle-school life was a glorious start. My Chinese composition for the enrolment exam was considered the best one, and it was copied into big characters and was put up on the school's Wall of Merit.

When I passed the Wall of Merit, someone recognised me, and then all the boys and girls who were there watching the Wall of Merit made me the centre of attention. Hundreds of appreciative eyes looked at me and I heard expressions of admiration all around. They admired my dress as well as my composition. I was wearing a white silk shirt with elegant sleeves and a sky-blue skirt with a nice cut around my slim waist.

In the afternoon I was chosen to be the representative for the newcomers, to give a speech. Afterwards, my class teacher came up to me smiling and said, 'You made a wonderful speech.' And my classmates told me I was the 'beauty of the school'.

Soon I was selected as a prefect of the class, taking charge of the study aspect as a liaison between the teachers and the students. This meant I had a lot of chances to talk to my teachers, and so I got more attention from them and did well in my studies. However, my good fortune didn't last long. In October 1957, Chairman Mao announced a new policy: to deepen the practice of class struggle, it was ordered that school children ought to be treated differently according to their family background. I lost my position as prefect as well as the admiration of my classmates. Some girls who used to be jealous of me took the chance to bully me and many of my friends were distant from me.

We had classes in the morning but in the afternoon we did manual work on the school vegetable patches or in the fields of nearby villages, which was Mao's doctrine of *qin gong jian xue*, doing for learning. We were supposed to 'learn from workers and peasants' and according to Mao's words 'schools are not places for study books but for learning practical skills'.

Our school became a model school of 'doing for learning' as we had grown a lot of big cabbages. One afternoon when we were working in the vegetable patch, the wife of Romanian president Ceauçescu paid a visit to our school. Our cabbage patches, worked hard by so many students' hands, grew huge and looked vigorous. The Romanian First Lady was very impressed by them and had a snapshot taken holding a cabbage while we students watched her with great interest and envy. She was wearing a sleeveless blouse, the popular Chinese women's fashion at the time. It was called 'saddle', because of its style — very short and tight cut without sleeves or collar, a clever way to save material. To call it a saddle was a vivid way to show its small and meagre shape. The Chinese language is good at giving figurative names for anything from fashion and menus to political slogans.

The Romanian First Lady was from a foreign country, a faraway place. Watching her smiling face and her fine, white skin, I admired her so much that I could not take my eyes off her. She was the first foreigner I had ever seen. Oh, the desire of my heart! How much I longed to travel afar as she did, to a foreign country!

As Mao's power increased, he tried to convince the world that his was the greatest kingdom on the earth. Propaganda was seeping into every corner of the country, in the newspaper, on the radio, in the official speeches, in the classrooms and on the walls. Many singing and dancing troops were inaugurated to help spread the propaganda of Mao Zedong's thinking. The Qingdao Dancing and Singing Company was established at this time.

I was called by our music teacher Wang Jin-xian to his office, where I saw a couple of pretty ladies in their early thirties waiting for me. They were the most beautiful and elegant ladies I had ever seen. One of them was short with a silvery voice, the other was slim and tall with a beautiful figure. Teacher Wang told the ladies: 'This is the prettiest girl in our school. Now you can test her.'

One of the ladies sat in front of the piano and asked me to sing a song. After I'd finished singing, she laughed and said: 'Her voice hasn't matured yet even though she's so tall.'

'Yes, she is,' the other lady said. 'She would be a good dancer with her tall, slim figure.' And then this lady did a few dance steps and asked me copy. The two ladies exchanged appreciative glances, which made my heart leap with excitement. I could tell that they liked me. I had always dreamt of being a performer when I was watching the students' performances at the Teachers' College. Oh, my dream would come true!

Days passed with no word and I became more and more upset. Then one day I heard that another girl who was from a 'red family', a factory hand's family, had been chosen as a future dancer. I could hardly believe it! The shock was so great that I couldn't conceal my tears. While I was crying in my seat in the classroom, I heard a boy mocking: 'She wants to be a performer? Even I am better than she is. At least I come from a glorious peasants' family.'

I was depressed and miserable for weeks. Why was life so unfair to me? Why did I come from a humiliated 'black family'? I became ashamed of my non-revolutionary family background. How much I wanted to have been born to a factory hand or a peasant family. I would give up anything and everything if only I could reborn and be a member of a 'red family'.

Fortunately I was not abandoned by all. Teacher Wang established an after-class club, the Singing and Dancing Troupe. I was chosen as one of the members, and with thirty-odd other talented or lovely-looking boys and girls, I learned how to give performances. I learned dancing; I did drama; I learned to play various instruments — violin, *yueqin* (a kind of full moon-shaped instrument), *qinqin* (an ancient instrument inherited from Qin Dynasty), *yangqin* (a grand flat instrument with many metal strings to be played with two thin and vibrating sticks) and *erhu* (a two-string instrument, common in Chinese music). Unfortunately, several of these instruments were abandoned during the Cultural Revolution and have never been revived, although they were pretty sophisticated and

Me (last row, first on the left) and fellow performers from the Singing and Dancing Troupe. No. 103 Regiment, 1974

unique. These activities — singing, dancing, drama and playing instruments — became my major activities after class, and my spare time was rich and cheerful. My school life was not at all boring.

Every afternoon after two periods of classes, the activity time would start when students could take part in sports, arts, performing and other activities. We, the members of the singing and dancing troupe, would meet together and rehearse for festival days.

One day in 1958 we went to the Grand Hall of Lucun for the annual entertainment festival. There, tens of performing teams from various schools, universities, government bodies and villages crammed at the back of the stage, waiting for their turn. The mood was fervent: there would be a big prize-giving ceremony afterwards, and every team wanted to get the first prize. There were about thirty different performances, including choir, solo singing, dancing, comic talking, rhythm talking, short plays and folk dancing. The one I was in was a folk dance called 'Festival Dance of Laoshan', a traditional mass dance of New Year celebration in Qingdao. The dance had almost vanished after 1949, but teacher Wang took on the important job of trying to revive it. We were sixteen boys and girls of the

35

similar age and good looks. Silk dresses, fancy fans, embroidered scarves and colourful umbrellas were the girls' costumes; hand drums, ringing sticks and silver bells were the boys' accoutrements. When the Chinese trumpet began its exciting, bright and high-pitched music, all the sixteen lads and lasses in glittering dresses glided onto the stage, flinging, jumping, twiddling and rolling. The applause from the audience was thunderous.

Singing and dancing was very exciting; touring around various districts for performances was even more interesting and it offered me chances to meet friends from other schools. It was at this time that I made friendships with my long-term girlfriends, Elegant and Grace. Elegant was a slim and pretty girl who later became a professional dancer. Grace was a couple of years older than me and looked after me like a real big sister.

During my puberty when my hormones were raging I enjoyed a love game created by my own mind. In a country like China, a Communist system mixed with feudalism, a country with dense population and poor housing conditions, individuals had no chance to enjoy privacy. Sex was the major taboo for thousands of years. I did not know how my counterparts managed their love lives but I created my unique one. Inspired by my reading and entertainment activities, I developed a strong tendency towards imagination and created a mental game of romance in the world of fantasy. I would secretly fall in love with somebody and enjoy the mental happiness fervently. Each time it would last a few weeks until I changed my love object to another boy, who could be one of my classmates, my singing and dancing partner, or a movie star whom I had never seen in person. The fact that my 'boyfriend' knew nothing about my affection didn't bother me. I was happy enough just floating in my dream haven like clouds flying in the sky, no fixed direction, no consequences and absolutely contented. I was enthralled by the aesthetics of the opposite sex. The fact that I was only in spiritual love not only offered me happiness but also protected me from the cruel reality.

For seven years, from twelve to nineteen, I dwelt solely in this self-created spiritual happiness. In my later life when misfortune was the keynote, I would recall these happy years and be comforted and encouraged by the fact that at least I was not tormented all the time.

In early 1957, a couple of visitors — political activists — from the Teachers' College, frequently visited our house in the evenings and had long talks to my mother, trying to persuade her to criticise the Party: 'Come on, Ms Zhou, Chairman Mao is initiating a wonderful situation where "one hundred flowers in blossom and one hundred mouths in speech". Our Party welcomes different opinions and wants to listen to criticisms to improve our job. Please answer the Party's call and say whatever you think about the Party's faults.' Nobody at the time realised that it was Mao's trick of 'attracting the snakes out of their holes', which was to make the intellectuals speak first and then condemn them afterwards. Later Mao cleverly played with words and said he was playing *yan mu*, an open plot, not insidious tricks.

My mother was a wise woman with great intuition and foresight. She was upright and straightforward and was ready to say whatever she was thinking, which offended many but attracted those who were pure and honest.

Traditionally, China being a poor, densely populated country with a low living standard, the people had two major hobbies as entertainment: window-shopping and chatting. Both cost no money. There were so many who were just good at talking, and the two political activists who came to our house would talk for ages. My mother could sense there might be some catch behind the deliberately long talks, and she hated long-winded talkers. She preferred reading and wanted to do more of it, so she was annoyed when the activists gave long lectures to her. She would tell them to stop: 'Sorry, I don't have time to listen to you, and I wouldn't want to talk to you even if I did have any criticism. I'd prefer to talk to the president of the college himself.' The president was one of her sincere friends.

The activists left our house without success.

In the summer of 1957 came the second step of the Opposing Rightists Movement — cracking down on the 'rightists'. The ones who had been encouraged to speak out about their opinion of the Communist Party and the government were now called rightists, the Party's enemies. It was almost a miracle that my mother evaded the fate of becoming a rightist considering she was so frank and plain-speaking.

Seven families out of the fifteen in our residential section got into trouble. Snow's father was condemned as an 'extreme rightist' and was sent to a remote coal mine to do physical labour in custody. Both of Jade's parents were rated as rightists and were sent away to different countryside areas. Jade and her younger brother had to live on the income from her older sister who did odd jobs on farms. Big Mountain's mother was forced to do a cleaning job for the college as a 'rightest'. One of my mother's colleagues became psychotic and another two committed suicide. Our residential section lost its previous cheerfulness; my remaining playmates became sad and subdued and we avoided talking to each other. The atmosphere was lonely and eerie; everyone was nervous and cautious. I sank further into my own dream land.

All over China three million intellectuals were designated rightists. They would suffer degradation and humiliation for as long as twenty-three years before they would be liberated by the second generation of Chinese leaders in the early 1980s.

After the Opposing Rightists Movement, Chinese intellectuals became mute. Mao's became the only voice in China after that, and without an opposing voice he did whatever he fancied. In 1958, he initiated the economic movement of Big Leap Forward. He believed that the huge population of his kingdom was the greatest productive force on the earth. He believed that so long as everybody worked harder, China would become the ideal Communist country, in which materials would be ample and the moral level of the society would be superbly high. In this so-called revolutionary romantic Communist mood, he ordered the whole nation to follow his fantasy:

'I order three mountains and five rivers to go, as I am coming!'
'There is no God in the heaven, there is no Dragon King in the sea, I am the God, I am the King.'
'As how much our guts are, how much the land will provide.'

Mao believed the amount of steel production was the measure of how well developed the country was. He was determined to catch up with the United Kingdom and United States by producing more steel as soon as possible. He gave orders to the whole nation to make steel. Rural dwellers were collected up and taken to the city to make steel, leaving no labourers in the fields. Agricultural production suffered tremendously.

We school students stopped class and became steel workers. We built mud stoves in our playground. Locks, woks and any household equipment made of metal were brought in and stuffed into the stove to 'make steel'. To obtain fuel, we burnt anything that could be burnt. All the hills and mountains were bare after 1958.

To please Mao, or to avoid being executed by him, the villagers gave exaggerated figures about products created and Mao liked to believe them. It was reported every day in the newspaper that, one after another, villages in the country had 'made stars' — had produced ten thousand kilograms of wheat from one *mu*. (One *mu* is about 666 square metres. Usually one *mu* can produce at most 250 kilograms of wheat.) When Mao visited a village in Hebei province, the villagers gave exaggerated figures on grain products, and in an excited moment he chanted, 'Well, we have so much grain. We must find ways to consume it.' After that, a mania for consuming food took over the country. Everyone was doing odd things to waste food. Those who didn't do so would be condemned as 'not listening to Chairman Mao', which was a huge mistake and very dangerous.

In 1959, to carry on his mad ideas of the Big Leap Forward, Mao started another political movement, Cracking Down on the Right-wing Party Element, in order to sweep off his rivals. More people lost their freedom and dignity. The president of my mother's college committed suicide to avoid the humiliation of being 'a right-wing element', as he once confessed that he doubted if one *mu* of land could really produce ten thousand kilograms of wheat.

After the crack down on the right-wing party members, nobody dared to say even one single truth. Everyone wanted to please Chairman Mao. Everyone was keen to give a rosy report to the central government, and to Mao. Everyone was deceiving and Mao was deceived. He believed China had become a wealthy Communist paradise and his kingdom was full of all sorts of grains. He initiated a quarrel with the Russian leader Nikita Khrushchev and exclaimed that China should be the big brother of the Communist group of countries. To show he was the number one, he gave orders to return all the grain China had borrowed from Russia in one go. All the state stores were emptied in no time.

Famine started to appear at the end of 1959. Food gradually disappeared from shops and stalls. By the beginning of 1960, virtually everywhere in China there was no food available in markets or fields. The country residents went back to their villages after the steel-making movement, only to find out they were in a desperate situation. The government asked them to supply anything they had to support the city residents. A city resident's food ration dropped to 11.5 kilograms from fifteen kilograms per person per month, which meant that each of us received 11.5 kilograms of sliced dry sweet potatoes every month, which was far from enough, while the villagers had nothing provided from the government. The situation became worse until the end of 1963. This was the Three Years' Starvation as the people called it, or the 'three-year natural disaster' by Mao and his government's statement, during which thirty million people died from hunger. Most were rural villagers.

Hunger is a powerful devil that can drive you crazy. Many times I would go to the fields after school trying to find anything that I could put into my mouth, even though I knew I couldn't. After searching in vain, I would lie on the ground, face on the soil, weeping. I was thoroughly beaten and bewildered from hunger.

One grim autumn afternoon I saw my neighbour's boy Big Mountain wobbling in the fields and stooping to the earth to scratch the soil. His fingers were covered with blood and his eyes were like a hungry wolf's when he saw me. I was so scared that I ran from him. The next day when I happened to pass his home, I saw him sitting on the ground, legs apart limply, head hanging, cheeks sallow, motionless. Before I started to run again I realised that he was too weak to stand up. A few days later he died.

Long before breakfast, I would be waiting in the queue at the open window of the school canteen, holding my bowl. The cook, wearing a white uniform and with the expression of a general, offered us our ration of food for the next four hours: a hundred grams of mouldy, sun-dried, boiled sweet potatoes. They could barely cover the bottom of my bowl. I tugged them into my mouth with my fingers while walking to the classroom. Other students were doing the same — the paths between the canteen and classrooms were full of students whose fingers were moving quickly from bowl to mouth. The dried sweet potatoes tasted delicious — in fact nothing had ever tasted as good, and I wondered why I hadn't realised how nice they were before. The sorrow was that the amount was so little, and my bowl became empty long before I was satisfied.

The disease of dropsy became common all over China. Women went through premature menopause, and in 1962 hardly any babies were born. The villagers died in such numbers and at such speed that nobody bothered to bury the bodies. Later we were told that in Jiangxi, Anhui and Hubei provinces people ate their family members' bodies.

Everywhere people talked about nothing but food. It was exciting to talk about food that you no longer had, but it created a killing pain for the listener. I burst out in a rage once when I heard my mother and brother talking about fish, bread and apples. The words penetrated my mind and stabbed like knives in my tummy. I dashed out of the house, grabbing a hoe in my hand, and ran to the fields behind our house. I dug again and again into the loose earth. Of course it had been dug up many times and everything possibly edible in the soil was gone. Still I wanted to try my luck. Using all the energy I could collect in my hungry body, I hoped I could dig up something. Anything, even a worm. Minutes later, I had to stop, exhausted. There was absolutely nothing I could put into my mouth. I remember it was a bright day. The grass was shining in the golden sun and tree leaves were dancing in the air. Everything in the world seemed fine except the humans. Why was I an ill-fated human? I wept and wept until it was dark. Arriving home I found nothing could soothe my bewildered empty stomach. I drank two glasses of cold water with a pinch of salt for flavour and waited for another hungry sleepless night.

During the three years of starvation, I ate all sorts of things that normally I would never put even near my nose — leaves from willow trees, apple and apricot trees were okay, and so were grass roots, but Guanyin earth was painful. The whitish fine earth could take the hunger away for a short while, but it caused terrible constipation. My mother had to use a spoon to dig out the faeces to relieve me. I didn't have any energy to cry even though it was painful and the spoon was covered with blood.

In 1963, the starvation was finally relieved and we could focus on study at last. I was eighteen, in the third year of high school. Now that the Sino–Russian honeymoon was over, we were ordered to learn English instead of Russian. The problem was that there were no English teachers available. After a thorough search, our school managed to find an old man in his sixties who had learned English in his early years, but he hadn't used it for ages. (His pronunciation was terrible, as I discovered later. I couldn't pronounce a word properly. I then had to try to correct my mispronunciation. I worked so hard on it that it made my tongue swollen.) By the time I finished my high school, we managed to learn from a thin English textbook full of political slogans such as 'Long live Chairman Mao' or 'We believe in Marxist and Leninist ideology.'

In my class there was a bright boy, Wang Du-ji, who was good at his subjects and fond of poems. Seeing the poor conditions people were living in, he became angry, and he wrote some poems to express his disappointment with the Party's leadership. When he showed these to me, I realised that what he had written wasn't suitable politically, and I knew I should report him if I was going to act as an 'obedient tool for the Party', as we had always been taught. But I didn't want to ruin his golden future as he was not only bright but was from a 'red family', a peasant family. He could be accepted by a good university and have an excellent future. On the other

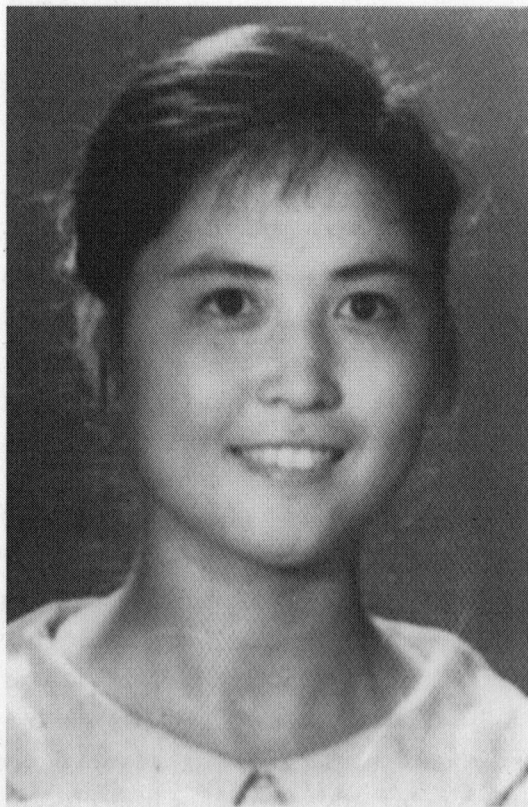

Me, aged nineteen years

hand, I could get some benefit for myself if I acted loyally to the Party — if I reported him to the head of the school Party branch. It would balance my 'black family' background and I could have a better chance of being accepted by universities. I remained in painful indecision for a while. At last I decided to protect him instead of trying to get personal gain. I returned his poem book without much comment. Unfortunately another girl in our class, whose father was a rightist, and to whom Wang Du-ji also showed his poems, reported him and handed in his poems to the head of the school. She was later accepted by a university even though she had a 'black family' background.

Soon Wang Du-ji was placed under house arrest by the school authority and was forced to confess his crime, including whom he had offered his poems to for reading. I, of course, was on the black list. He was cut off from sitting the university exam, and was jailed for seven years during the Cultural Revolution. A couple of months before he had served the full length of the seven-year prison, he was set free and was regarded as one of the pioneers who were brave and sensitive enough to disagree with Mao's wrong policies of the Big Leap Forward, but he had lost his youth, his educational opportunity and his health. His wife had left him. He was a much older, sick man when he stepped out of the prison.

I too was punished for my disloyalty to the Party — a bad mark was put under my name even though I was allowed to sit the examination for university entrance. When the staff from the university which I chose to go to, the University of Shandong, came to ask for my dossier since I did well in the examination, my school refused to co-operate. When the staff from the English Department of the university came to my school again, they were put off since they were told that I 'was not trusted by the Party'. Later, during the Cultural Revolution when the rebellions threw out the school authorities and exposed the historical documents, it was found out that my dossier said that I was a student from a black family with low political consciousness and that I had not drawn a clear line between myself and my black family: I was 'not worth an education in the university'. The university place was given to a boy whose English was so poor that he was often scolded by our teacher — but he came from a peasant family.

CHAPTER THREE

I could not accept the fact that I had failed to get into university since I had done so well in the examination. For many weeks I was depressed and miserable, but I didn't want to give up. With frustration and anger, I picked up my textbooks and prepared for the next year's exam for university entrance. I studied for many days until one day I met my class teacher, Mr Wu, and he told me: 'You know, you failed this year's exam not because you haven't done well in your subjects but for political reasons that are something to do with your family's past, and you will never change it. Don't waste you time.' He was a beloved teacher with amiable manners and was respected by everybody. I didn't want to believe what he said but, at the bottom of my heart, I knew he was right. If I couldn't change what my parents did in the past, I couldn't go to college, simple as that. Absurd but true.

I stopped preparing my lessons and started looking for a job. We school-leavers, especially the ones from 'black families', weren't supposed to have jobs. With little hope I went all over the place begging for jobs, but was refused again and again. One day, my brother Main came back from the school where he was working as a relief teacher and showed me an advertisement which was put up on a power pole at a roadside, a common way to make things known in the time. The advertisement was about employing middle-school English teachers for a community-funded school. 'Why don't you have a try?' my brother suggested. I was not that confident about it. I had learned some English, but my pronunciation was poor and my vocabulary was no more than three hundred words. Still, it would do me no harm to go and have a trial.

I summoned up my courage and went for the interview. I was nineteen, 1.7 metres high, a very rare height for a girl those days in China, even in Northern China where people are taller than in the south. I had a perfect waistline. My sprightly and vigorous character was reflected in my curious and sparkling eyes: it was commented on by many that I looked like one of the famous actresses from the Uighur where the local beauties have impressive dark eyes, long and exquisite brows and thick black hair.

The interview was in August 1963. I was asked to give an English lesson to thirty-odd adults in a big classroom. I was very nervous before I took the lesson. My palms were sweaty and my legs were shaking. Somehow once I got onto the rostrum, I became calm and confident. I felt that my parents, whose life-long careers were teaching, were offering me spiritual guidance, and I was familiar with being at the front of a classroom. Ever since I was a little girl, my mother would bring me to her classes when I refused to stay in the kindergarten. As a tiny little girl wearing a red-and-white dress, I would stand in front of the class while my mother was giving lectures. The rostrum always made me feel at home. So it was as I gave the trial lesson. A piece of chalk between my fingers, I started the first lecture of my life. I was wearing a mauve-coloured sleeveless shirt with an elegant round collar and a dark green silk skirt which dropped freely to my knees. Whether I gave a good lesson or not I had no idea, but I could see that I was liked by my listeners. Three weeks later the good news arrived — I had been accepted as a teacher at the Cangkou Community School.

It could barely be called a school since it didn't have any premises. The classrooms were borrowed from a local evening school and the teachers' only office was a shabby shed that used to be a warehouse. The school did not get funding from the government but relied on donations from the community. The students were those who had failed to pass the entrance exam for government-funded schools. It was not easy for a young and inexperienced girl like me to work with those poor-quality students. But the real problem for me was with the staff.

There were twenty-odd bachelor teachers who had great difficulties finding wives since they didn't have a steady job provided by the government. In those days a job allocated by the government was called an 'iron bowl' — unbreakable and permanent — but working at Cangkou Community School was not like that. It was unsteady and low income, therefore low in social standing. I became a hot topic of discussion amongst the single men and everyone had designs on me.

I became Mainspring's girlfriend for a short while, and then I decided I didn't love him. I was strongly attracted to Pine, my previous classmate at high school and a university student in Beijing now. Back in the early 1960, the first time I set my eyes on Pine, a short but attractive boy with curly hair and smart manners, somehow I had the feeling that I was destined to fall in love with him. He was quiet and good at his studies. He was from a peasant's family so he was red in the political sense, and this made me obsessed by him even more, as if he was a noble. By the time I failed to enter the university, he had been accepted by the Industrial Institute of Peking, a very good university at the time. He became even more attractive to me. In fact, he became a cult-figure to me. My failure to enter university made me attracted to a university student, like a hungry man envying the bread in another man's hand, as if his rank as a university student was, like the diamond crown on the head of a prince, making my desire to be his girlfriend eager and strong. He was, at that time, chasing my girlfriend Flower, but she didn't love him even though he kept writing long love letters to her. However, I was writing even longer letters to him. I had learned a lot from Western romantic novels and my mother was quite free in parenting, so I was headstrong and wayward. My demeanour was open, bold and indiscreet, a bad personality by Chinese standards, since women, especially unmarried girls, were expected to be shy and obedient, with few words.

In the winter holiday of 1963 and summer holiday of 1964, I invited Pine to stay with us. He ate three meals with us but stayed at my friend Grace's place at night to avoid gossip. Still, my romance caused a lot of rumours even we did nothing sexually. I did enjoy his kisses, very sweet and exciting for me. I was desperately in love with him and was blind to his flaws. When Grace told me that he had spread bad comments about me behind my back, I was sad he didn't love me as much as I did him. I wanted to try my best to be better for him.

In 1964, shortly after people's bellies were a bit full with food, Mao called out another mass political movement: the Four Clarifications Campaign. Mao ordered that every work unit must catch 'bad elements' up to a ratio of at least five percent as proof of loyalty to the Party. The targets were those who lacked political understanding, who were corrupting the economy, who were not behaving according to social standards, and who had committed crimes. Two 'wrong elements' were caught in my school: Shen and me.

Shen, one of the unmarried teachers of the school, was caught sleeping with his girlfriend. In Mao's China, romance was considered a bad thing, a bourgeois trait. You were allowed to go out with your boyfriend or girlfriend to walk, talk, shop or to see a movie if you were fully prepared to get married — and that was all you were allowed to do. Anything more intimate than that would cause a scandal and your name would be ruined. If you slept together before marriage, a black mark was written in your dossier. Any affairs outside marriage, or 'improper relations', were huge mistakes and the offenders were humiliated in public, punished by their workplace superiors.

One day after school, the head of the teachers told me to stay. 'There will be a meeting about you,' he said in a stern voice. His face was serious and he refused to look me in the eye, which frightened me. Even though I was still fairly naïve and ignorant about the complicated society, I could feel the intimidating atmosphere of political mania. Later I was to know that the reason why I became 'a wrong element' was that the unmarried men of the school were angry with me when they found out I had taken Pine as my boyfriend, and they wanted to use the political sword to hurt me, a common practice in Mao's China — political brutalities being used for personal revenge. The more essential reason, of course, was that I was one of the 'black children', who were always the most vulnerable to be condemned.

In the denouncing meeting I was attacked by fierce words from my colleagues. The light was dim but the air was hot. Stern-faced, they stood up one by one to accuse me, except my ex-boyfriend Mainspring who was sitting quietly, head hanging down, suffering in agony.

I was accused as a 'stinky pretty bourgeois' who liked to wear colourful clothes, which I was not supposed to do as a teacher. Although I wanted to say something for myself, I wasn't allowed. I had to hang my head low and accept the humiliation. I was confused. It was true that I liked beautiful things and I liked to think I was pretty, but I had no idea what was wrong with that. I had no more clothes than the others — all I had was three colourful shirts and a couple of skirts. I had no more cotton ration than others, which was fifty-five centimetres per year. I had one pair of 'good' trousers made of polyester, which was fashionable at the time and had cost me three months' saving.

The denouncing meeting hit me hard. From that moment, I developed a feeling of loathing about my looks. I wanted to change my appearance; I wanted to reform myself, body and mind, be a good disciple of Chairman Mao, become a peasant, tough and coarse in physique, in order to be accepted by others.

After the meeting, the head teacher told me: 'The decision has been made. You are not suitable as a teacher since your bourgeois behaviour is a bad influence on the students. You are dismissed from the school.'

I was too embarrassed to tell my mother the bad news. So as not to go home, I sat on a wooden bench outside the door of the office for the whole night. In the meagre light I wrote many pages of self-criticism. When the head teacher came early the next morning I bowed down, tears running, sobbed out my words and handed him my self-criticism paper, begging him to let me stay. He received the paper without a word. I did not get a call from the school. My job, I was told later, was taken by a relative of the head of the educational bureau.

I became jobless again. Six months later, when I was twenty-one, I was exiled to the Gobi Desert in the northwest.

Mao had an extraordinary idea about how to solve the unemployment problem in his kingdom — sending city youth to barren areas to do whatever they could to survive. If they couldn't survive, it was all right for him as his was a populous country and he could afford to lose many of them. Once he stated that he could afford for half of the billion-strong population to die without weakening his power. To lure people to leave the cities, Mao wrote a poem which was constantly repeated in the newspapers and on the radio:

> The gigantic sky is vast enough for birds flying.
> The enormous sea is wide enough for fishes swimming.
> The countryside is a prodigious land.
> City youths will achieve high success.

Thus *shang shan xia xiang*, go to the countryside and settle in the remote places, became another big-scale mass movement in China. School-leavers were persuaded to leave their homes and the cities in which they lived. Superficially, it seemed the city youths left their hometown willingly, but in fact few were volunteers. We had no option. We were forced, exiled. Ever since I had lost my job in Cangkou Community School, members of the residential committee of the Teachers' College constantly visited my home and badgered my mother, 'You must listen to Chairman Mao and let your daughter taste the wide world and get educated by the peasants.'

My playmates Sparkle and Snow, after failing the university entrance exam, were sent away to the countryside: Sparkle to a poor village one hundred miles away from Qingdao, Snow to a border area even further away, with her younger sister Swallow. Later they married local men and settled there. I was wilder than them. I made up my mind that if I was to go, I would go afar — to Xinjiang.

Xinjiang, one of the far northwest provinces near Inner Mongolia, is a huge area of high land covering one hundred and sixty thousand square kilometres, about one-fifth of the country. The original name for Xinjiang was Westland, which was changed by Mao's government in 1949. I had heard about Xinjiang through songs and movies, and my heart would jump excitedly when I heard the beautiful Xingjiang folk song:

> Our Xinjiang is a good place
> The scenery is attractive.
> Snowmelt, melons, grapes and many other nice things.
> Come on, come on,
> Come to develop Xinjiang
> Give your lives wonderful meaning.

Movies about Xinjiang showed the local people, the Uighurs, wearing exotic robes and dancing amongst the vineyards. Abundant grapes — the Horse Tits, as they were called for their big size — dangled in the air and beautiful girls danced underneath them. The girls braided their hair into numerous long plaits. The number varied according to their age, with only two remaining for married ones. They wore half-watermelon-shaped caps, decorated with sparkling beads, while the young lads wore striped long robes, high black boots, and played their traditional music instrument, happily dancing and singing. The huge expanse of desert looked romantic and pretty with camels riding into the red and purple sunset, serene and eternal. I wanted to ride on a camel and to sing the romantic folk songs. I wanted to dance with the Uighur lads in the moonlight under the grapes and on the golden desert.

There was a popular documentary movie about life in Xinjiang that looked interesting and beautiful. One of the scenes that was especially thrilling for me showed Zhou Enlai, the prime minister of China, interviewing city youths from Shanghai and telling them, 'Even if you are from a black family, you can't change it but you can choose a revolutionary route as you are doing now — to do physical labour in the fields in a remote place.' Those city youths who were interviewed by Zhou became popular and their photos were printed in newspapers, portraying them as hardworking model youngsters. How much I envied them!

There was another reason why I wanted to join the Production and Construction Corps of Xinjiang. Mao had a theory that 'guns make power' and he always held onto the armed forces tightly. This attitude made anything to do with the army popular and the army itself become a privileged class in Chinese society. A member of the People's Liberation Army of China was envied by all. The army officers married the prettiest girls in the cities, while the soldiers had the beauties from the countryside — by regulation, officers were city residents and soldiers were countryside residents. The army's status became even higher from the early 1960s when it was in the hands of Lin Biao, Mao's closest colleague at the time — his name was even in the constitution confirming him as Mao's successor.

I had a strong inferiority complex about my family background and I was lured by any idea that could draw me closer to the army to lift up my social standing. However, it was impossible for me to join the army as only those who came from red families were eligible for it. When recruiting, the future soldier's family background was checked out, going back five generations, and if anyone in any generation was not 'red' — being a landlord or even a small business owner — the eligibility would be revoked. Of course I would never meet the criteria but I might join the Production and Construction Corps of Xinjiang, which, to me in my innocence, sounded like it was something to do with the army.

Unfortunately there was no enrolment stand in Qingdao and I had to go to Shanghai, Beijing or Tienjin to join the PCCX. Good news came. An old friend of my mother's, Uncle Wang, the vice-chancellor of the

Agricultural Institute of Xinjiang, was attending a conference in Beijing and invited my mother to Beijing for a visit. She sent me instead.

In the West Beijing Hotel, I met Uncle Wang and expressed my desire for Xinjiang. He was friendly with the Minister of Personnel Department of PCCX, who was attending the conference and staying in the same hotel. Uncle Wang took me to meet Minister Young, a tall man in his early forties with confident manners. He was a war hero and had lost one of his legs. Some gunpowder was still in the deep tissue of his skin but the inconvenience didn't stop him from holding such an important job. He was happy to help me. 'We need new blood. There is no problem for you to realise your goal, either to be a performer or a school teacher, just as you like,' he said. I was enthralled by his words. How lucky I was to have such a high-up official on my side.

I left Beijing immediately. I wanted to take action rapidly so that I could arrive in Xinjiang as soon as possible. 'I will be a member of the Corps of Xinjiang soon!' I exclaimed to my mother the moment I returned home. She became sullen and distracted.

Seeing the danger that my mother might prevent me leaving, I became anxious and dreamed about Xinjiang. In the dream, I was walking along a yellowish earthy road in the middle of huge fields of alfalfa in full blossom like a purple carpet stretching to the end of the horizon, kissing the white clouds in the blue sky; a golden sun was shining at the top of snow-covered mountains. A horse-drawn cart was in front of me and I tried to run faster to catch up with it. No matter how hard I tried, the cart was moving farther and farther away, leaving me in despair . . . Cold sweat was on my forehead when I woke up. What a gloomy dream, a bad omen. It seemed I would be rejected by the PCCX.

I must work harder to go to Xinjiang.

Early one morning while my mother was out, I sneakily found the *hu kou ben*, registered residence book of the family, mounted on my bike, and shot away to the residence bureau. The man in charge was pleased to know I wanted to shift my residence away from Qingdao to Xinjiang. A few minutes later I got the paper authorising the change of residence. I didn't realise what a huge change I had made: by withdrawing my right to live there, I had become an alien in my home town Qingdao.

As one's residence was fixed for life under Mao's policy, people were not allowed to remove their *hu kou* from poor and remote areas to cities and towns, where living standards were better; and hardly any city residents would be willing to remove their *hu kou* to the country unless they were forced. Under this system, you stayed where you were born, city or countryside, and nobody was allowed to choose a place to live. Now that I had shifted my residency to a poorer area, it would be almost impossible to shift it back to Qingdao.

My mother was enraged when I told her what I had done. She scolded me, 'What a silly girl! You'll never be allowed to live in Qingdao again. Countless people would willingly give up anything for a Qingdao residence.' To show her anger, she didn't talk to me for days. Other than that, she didn't do much to try to stop me going. She realised that sooner or later I would be sent away under Mao's orders.

'Xinjiang? That is a faraway place. It is dangerous for a young girl to go to a harsh place like that.' Elegant and Grace tried to stop me but I was adamant.

I went to Shanghai by sea. My luggage was a bedding roll with an enamel wash bowl tied up to it, a greenish travel bag and a brown imitation-leather suitcase, which my mother had bought for me. It was a stormy day and the sea trip took three days when normally it was only a twenty-four hour journey. Everybody on board was seasick. They couldn't eat the disgusting meals the ship kitchen provided. As a person with a strong tendency for deference and sympathy, I offered my apples to the travellers; and by the time I arrived in Shanghai my whole bag of apples was gone. I did not mind. I thought I could buy apples everywhere. Nothing was further from the truth.

Holding Minister Young's letter of introduction, I visited one of the collecting stands for PCCX in Shanghai, where my name was put on the enrolment list and my train ticket was paid from Shanghai to Ulumuqi, the capital of Xinjiang province. To my delight, they offered me a dark green uniform as well as a cap, similar to a soldier's, only without the red panels on both sides of the collar or red star on the cap. However, I was too ignorant to tell the difference.

In the railway station of Shanghai, hundreds of city youths were ready to get on the No. 53 Train to Ulumuqi. Everyone was carrying big travelling bags full of shoes, clothes, cooking oil, rice, biscuits, fruits . . .

Their parents, grandparents and siblings were there to see them off; everybody burst out crying when the train started moving. The city youths on the train were yelling: 'Mama! Baba! Nana!' Their families were calling their names in heart-breaking screams while waving their hands madly. The sound of the cries from hundreds of throats was so loud that the whole station was echoing as if it were a thunderstorm. My heart was racing and trembling even though I did not understand why those people were so sad.

The five-day train trip from east to northwest was going to pass six provinces — Hebei, Henan, Shanxi, Shaanxi, Qinghai and Gansu — over a distance of more than ten thousand kilometres. I looked out of the train windows with great amazement and curiosity. The September breeze blew in through the train windows and my heart danced with joy. I was going to Xinjiang, the remote mysterious place. Dreams and imaginings were drifting in and out of my mind. I could hardly wait to see what it was really like.

The land gradually became monotonous. A bored atmosphere permeated the carriages and the passengers dozed off in their seats. They would twist and jerk their bodies every now and then, tortured by their uncomfortable positions. More passengers pushed on board each time the train stopped; many bustled in through windows when there were too many pushing and shoving at the door. Everyone was running frantically as if they were escaping from a fire. The conductors delivered meals on a trolley: rice, noodles, vegetables and a few tiny pieces of meat, poor quality and unappetising but quite expensive. Most passengers ate the food they'd brought with them to save a few cents. After the third day on the train, the supply of water became difficult, and everyone was rationed to one mug of water per day. There was no water in the lavatory; and as more passengers got on, the corridors became overcrowded. To go to the toilet was extremely difficult. The corridor was full of people sitting or squatting on the ground and it seemed a terribly long way to the toilet when you urgently wanted to answer nature's call and had to be careful not to step on people's feet. The toilet was occupied most of the time and sometimes was even full of passengers who were trying to elude the ticket checks.

The northwest climate is famous for its wide temperature ranges. The air in the train was hot and smelled of sweating bodies and the decomposing food wastes in the daytime but became freezing cold at night. The train moved more and more slowly, since it was steadily rising in altitude. We spent two days and two nights travelling along the Hexi Corridor through Gansu and Qinghai provinces. After the Hexi Corridor, the train started to travel on barren land. Grey earth was the only thing we could see, but suddenly a building was in sight. It was Jiayuguan, an ancient border mark where an old-fashioned house stood absurdly in the middle of nowhere surrounded by a brown sandy storm. This point had been the beginning of the Silk Road in the past, and now the lonely building marked the distance from the home we'd left behind. There was a popular proverb spreading amongst the passengers describing the sad feelings of leaving home for the west — *guo le jia yu guan, liang yan lei bu gan*, see the Jiayuguan, tears constantly run.

The aridity I felt when the train was riding along the Hexi Corridor was something I had never known before. The wind from outside was hot and burning. My nostrils were as dry as a windpipe and my eyelids felt as dry as paper. Even the biscuits on the little table would crumble at the slightest touch.

The landscape outside was endlessly grey and empty, with the lead-coloured sky and grim land being all we could see. I heard that the local people lived on very little water, all gathered from the rare rains in the summer season. They stored the precious water in big pottery jars or concrete pools. To own more water meant greater wealth. The same water would be used again and again — washing rice and vegetables first, then washing dishes, then washing face and hands before finally being used to water their vegetables. I could not believe there was a place so dry in the world. I didn't know that Xinjiang was even worse.

During the night of the fourth day in the train, we stopped at a small station called Flaming Mountain. A violent wind came in through the open door like a mad animal, and the rocks on the mountain were red without even one blade of grass. The entire place looked so hostile and uninhabited.

Another day passed as we toiled along the barren land until at last green colour appeared. We had arrived at Ulumuqi.

Ulumuqi was a big, busy city with many grey concrete buildings. The only difference from other cities in China was that the majority Han

54

people were dotted by people of minority nations with their exotic garments. There were altogether thirteen minorities in Xinjiang: Uighur, Kazakh, Tajik, Daur, Kirghiz, Huizu and more. The Uighur women wore colourful robes and the men black corduroy suits. They walked in a different way from the Han people. We walked in an twisted way, copied from our bound-feet mothers, while the Uighurs walked with natural smart steps. They spoke a language like Russian. Actually they were closer to Russian than to Han Chinese. They were angry towards the Han and complained, 'You have taken all our sugar, wool and meat away.' They had never stopped trying to fight to win their independence back.

I got off the train at nine by Xinjiang time, which was two hours later than Beijing time, and I felt freezing cold. Coming from Qingdao in the middle of August, a short-sleeve blouse and a silk skirt was all I was wearing and I had to jump up and down to warm myself up. However, soon after the sun was high up it became unbearably hot. This reminded me of a proverb about the dramatic change of Xinjiang weather — 'Wear a fur coat in the morning and change into silk at noon; eat your summer melons while you sit around the stove.'

I went to visit Minister Young after I collected my luggage, which was transported in a different carriage. However he was away and his secretary, also his wife, met me. She told me that Mr Young had left a message about me: 'It is the political fashion that everyone needs to do physical labour for a while in order to increase the political capital. However, Weijun should stay in the nearer regiment in order to be convenient to shift back to the city.' I accepted this idea happily since I had prepared to 'learn from labourers and peasants to reform the mind', as Chairman Mao had stated.

Mrs Young, a pretty lady in her late thirties with permed curling hair, dark bright eyes and oval face, wrote a letter for me to enrol me into the No. 6 Agricultural Division, the nearest division to Ulumuqi. Many other city youths were sent to the southern part of Xinjiang, five days away by truck.

There were nine agricultural divisions in the PCCX: each division had five or six regiments, each regiment had ten to fifteen teams, and each team had hundreds of workers.

The next day I took a truck ride and set off for my new place, sixty kilometres away from Ulumuqi. Our truck ran quickly towards the suburbs and soon I saw the centre of the division, a small town called Wujiaqu, with shattered mud houses and earth roads amongst a few rows of only one kind of tree, a kind of poplar called 'slashing the sky'. Their trunks, with few branches, grew thin and straight into the sky as if they were trying to stretch their necks to drink the moisture from the air.

After Wujiaqu the truck sped up on a level, empty, huge land, only occasionally passing some vague signs of human residence, and then we reached the centre of the No. 103 Regiment, a muddy village called Caijiahu. After Caijiahu the driver ran the truck like mad since he didn't have to worry about anything on the road. He told me that sometimes he was sent for a long-distance errand and he would doze off while he was holding the steering wheel. The weather became very dry and hot, so the driver opened the windows on both sides. The dust whirling around the wheels was like a brown-coloured storm spraying us in a powder bath; nothing else was visible but the yellow dust. We were covered by it and my nostrils were filled with fine earth. I closed my eyes and gasped with my mouth open, my mouth filling with dust and my teeth becoming gritty with sand.

In the late afternoon after a four-hour bumpy ride, the truck eventually arrived at my destination, the No. 13 Team of the No. 103 Regiment of the No. 6 Agricultural Division of the Corps of Xingjiang province.

Each team worked on a huge piece of land of about two million acres, but most of it was barren and ignored by the locals, who lived in a green oasis. The residents of the PCCX were originally the veterans of the Civil War, and when Mao won the civil war over Jiang Jieshi he ordered the soldiers to stay in the barren land to develop it. That was why the organisation was given a military name. When I received my wages, a month later, twelve *yuan* was deducted to pay for the uniform I had received in Shanghai, which was a shock to me. I now realised that the PCCX was not an army organisation, for you got your food and uniforms provided free in the real army. I was not the only one confused. Many other city youths were too. They complained that they didn't want to be agricultural hands but had come to join the army. But it was too late and there was no way we could go back since we'd lost our city residence.

I was to stay here for ten years from the age of twenty-one to thirty-one years old. Apart from the grey-coloured empty land extending to the far horizon, I saw no construction but pile after pile of firewood. The pieces of wood were dark brown in colour, twisted awkwardly, with rough bark peeling off here and there. I would learn later that each pile of firewood indicated a family living in a cave beside it. This firewood had come from the Gobi Desert bush and had probably been growing there for millions of years. It was disappearing rapidly, though. Only a few years after I was there, there was no more bush around and men had to ride on their bikes for hours to the deep belly of the Gobi Desert to cut firewood. The Gobi Desert bush was so dry that a mere kick could break a trunk as thick as a bowl even if it was alive.

At the far end behind the constructions of the cave dwellers, I saw two lines of poplar trees, thin and small, indicating how raw this place was. A flat-roofed mud house was in the centre of the huge empty place and this was the kitchen for the whole team — about a hundred and fifty men, women and children, made up of veterans, villagers who'd come from all over the country looking for food between 1959 and 1963, and the city youths from Shanghai, Tienjin, Beijing and Qingdao who'd been arriving since 1964.

Now, bewildered by the emptiness and nothingness of the place, I stood motionless for a while. It was not like a real place but a place of my nightmares.

A short man with a weather-beaten face came up to me. He introduced himself as Old Yang, the head of the camp. With a broad smile he shook hands with me. His hand felt coarse. 'Welcome. We need young labour like you. Come with me now. I'll show you the office to buy your ration tickets for meals and the storeroom to get your tools and kerosene.'

'Kerosene?' I was puzzled for a second, then realised there was no electricity; kerosene was the only fuel for light at night-time.

I followed him into the kitchen where I saw two pieces of wooden board and a wok as big as a small satellite. A couple of men were making buns on one of the boards and at the other one some women were cutting marrows. We passed the kitchen and came into a small room — the office and the storage room, which was full of farm tools. A man was sitting behind a table amongst the tools: it was made of a rough wooden board and four narrow twisted sticks into the ground. From a cardboard box on the ground he took out two bunches of tickets, the thicker one black and

57

the thinner one dark red. He counted them for me: 'This is your monthly ration, twenty kilograms altogether — fifteen kilograms of corn buns and five of wheat buns.' The man, Sincere Su, spoke in a Shaanxi province accent and looked confiding and kind. He was too shy to look directly at me and when he talked to me he watched me sideways and blushed. I took the meal tickets, ninety of them altogether, each one for a bun of two hundred grams, which was for one meal. The headman then led me to an area behind the kitchen where there was a small room set up as a shop. A round-faced woman who spoke in a sonorous Gansu accent wrote my name in a notebook and handed me a half-bottle of kerosene. The headman said: 'Be careful using it — this is all you get for the whole month.' He then took me to one of the firewood piles and I saw a hole on the ground. We descended a few earth stairs and came to a primitive door. A strong earthy smell rushed out when the door was open. I sneezed uncontrollably. The air inside was suffocating and there was no window for light except a hole on the roof. The cave was dreadfully dark with only the dimmest of light. The lamp, sitting in a hole on the mud wall, was a small ink bottle with a hole at the centre of the lid and a piece of cotton leading from the kerosene to the lid. The lamp's light was smoky and as small as a pea. The top of the roof was low with unkempt reeds and mud visible.

The headman pointed some pieces of wooden board joining together two narrow benches, and said: 'You can stay in this bed. The owner has gone to her home town to visit her parents. Later you will have to build your own cave.' He then turned to the three other girls in the room, who were staring at me with interest: 'This is Liu Weijun, our new team member.' Their faces looked vague in the dim light and I could hardly see them.

I heard them start to talk after the headman left:

'Well, you are slim and fine-skinned.'

'Why do you come here? Even hares wouldn't choose this place to shit.'

'Look at your elegant hands — can you stand the heavy labour?'

'Have you had your dinner? Here you are. I have saved my wheat bun for tonight. You can have it.'

I felt hungry at that moment, and gratefully took the bun and started to eat. It was dry and tasted bitter. Later on, I learned that the water in the area was bitter, so the crops were bitter too. One girl offered me some salty green peppers and chilli. These were the three kinds of food out of five that I was going to have meal after meal, day after day, month after month for the next ten years: Chinese cabbage, marrow, chilli, corn buns and wheat buns. The wheat buns were considered fine food and were rare. Other vegetables such as potatoes, tomatoes, beans and capsicums were available occasionally. Land was not scarce but water was and it was rationed. We were not allowed to grow vegetables that needed a lot of watering.

When I placed the half-bottle of kerosene on the bare board, Glory, the head of the group, poured it into a bigger bottle and said to me: 'We share the kerosene together. You mustn't stay up too late and waste the kerosene. It's no fun without light if we use it all up before the next month's ration comes along.'

I unpacked my stuff while the girls chattered to each other, sitting on low wooden stools, mending their clothes or making shoes.

'Why did they send you here?' a girl called Bright asked me. 'This is the farthest camp of No. 103 Regiment. Apart from a few rats, antelopes and wild pigs, there's nothing in our part of the Gobi Desert.'

Before I went to bed, I asked where the toilet was. Bright said: 'You don't have to bother to find the toilet. You can help yourself anywhere near the camp.'

I went outside. The moon looked extraordinarily large, alone and absurd above the infinite, empty land. I could see a few thin bushes here and there. They were soso wood and tamarisk, the only two kinds of bush in this area. I squatted down beside a bush and peed. Later I discovered that the toilet for the whole residence was just a big hole in the ground, without even a roof.

The next day Glory delivered me the *can tu man*, a big, metal, square-shaped hoe with a long wooden handle: 'Today's job is to build a channel in Three Thousand Mu.' Every piece of land was named by its size. The smallest piece of land in No. 13 Team was Five Hundred; the biggest was Ten Thousand Mu.

The group of twenty-odd women walked to the field. On the way, I saw nothing but endless bare earth extending to the horizon where the grey-coloured land met the same-coloured sky. Some of the land was covered with a layer of white powder — salt and alkali. Other parts were dotted with small patches of bush and grasses called camel thorn and jiji grass, the only two kinds of weeds in Gobi Desert. Both were greyish-green and looked very dry. The soil was very fine and could actually be fertilised if water was provided, but water was so scarce. Snowmelt led from the Sky Mountain by our man-made channel was the only source for irrigation.

The mountain was visible at the end of the skyline like crystal fish-heads jumping out of the grey sea, and its peaks were covered with snow all year round.

The job was simple but very physical, hoeing the soil to make ditches, and the working hours were very long — from early morning till the dark evening.

I lifted my hoe vigorously, but very quickly began feeling tired. Stopping, I looked around, and discovered the only thing I could see was the horizon — there was not even a single tree. I saw the head of the team was watching me and realised that the other women had worked ahead of me; I had to catch up. I learned that you had to work non-stop except for the fifteen-minute breaks in the morning and afternoon. When breakfast and lunch was delivered, we ate at the end of the field sitting on the ground.

The air was so dry that my throat felt as if it was on fire. How much I missed Qingdao, my mother and the ample supply of apples that were always available. Oh! Qingdao apples, red, green and pink, crunchy and juicy. If I could only have a bite, the suffering from the thirst would be relieved. The dust in the air was as fine as flour and it penetrated my shoes, socks, sleeves and trousers, causing a very uncomfortable feeling as if I were wearing a layer of film made of dirt. And how slow the time moved. It was only early afternoon and I was already exhausted, my arms ached and my back was stiff. All my bones were in agony and screamed for me to stop.

This was the job I would do in August, when the wheat was collected and the maize was not yet ripe, and in winter from October to March, every year, for ten years. The earth was never frozen, even in winter when the average temperature was minus thirty degrees and sometimes even dropped to minus fifty degrees, since it was absolutely dehydrated. Actually, drought was the most horrible killer in the Gobi Desert. Every now and then, we heard of people being lost in the Gobi Desert and dying from dehydration. The temperature was extreme — in summer it could reach forty-five degrees. There was no rain at all in spring, although it was very stormy; summer was hot and dry without rain; autumn was very short, with once or twice a little shower; in winter it snowed a lot and the world became frozen and crystal.

In spring, we worked in the cornfields; in summer we harvested wheat; in autumn we picked up maize ears and cotton; and in winter we built channels. Later on we grew opium.

Time dragged in the Gobi Desert with hard physical labour in the daytime and sewing socks, making shoes, and mending clothes in the evenings in front of the oil lamp. There was no television, no films, and no books — in fact there was no entertainment of any kind at all.

When it was time for me to dig my own cave, the headman, using a piece of stick, drew a square on the ground and told me and another girl Silk: 'This is where you will make your house. You can start work on it now.'

Silk and I set to work. First we dug a hole which was about 1.5 metres deep, and then on one side of this hole we dug out a slope to make a doorway leading down from the ground. On the other three sides of the hole we plastered some mud. Then we put some rough sticks, which were in scarce supply, across our hole to form a roof, and plastered them with mud mixed with straw and reed. We left a one-foot-square hole in our roof, which was where the light could come in. We called it a 'sky window'. To cover the sky window took much begging, weeping and pleading, because we had to get a piece of plastic that was big enough to cover it. Glass was inconceivable. Every now and then the wind would blow the plastic away or a hen would step on the 'sky window' and break it, which would be a real disaster. Sand and dust would flow inside like a waterfall and our heads, beds and bowls would be full of dirt.

So this animal's den was my home. I was lucky as I was young and healthy. Sick and old people or young children could not cope with these inhuman conditions and they either died or developed serious diseases. I shared a space of ten square metres with four other people. Each one had to compromise with a living space of no more than 1.5 by 1.8 metres. We modern cave men learned and developed the science of space management. Every inch of room was used cleverly. In the cave the wall beside my bed was my 'territory of air space' where I hung bags, face cloths, foot towels, straw hats and coats. But nails were extremely precious and I formed the habit of lowering my head when walking and staring at the ground, hoping I might pick up a nail or, if I was in real luck, I might find a needle, which would thrill my heart since needles were so useful but were always scarce. I dug a hole in the wall above my bed and it held my toothbrush, toothpaste, meal bowl, spoon and chopsticks. Holes we dug underneath the bed for storing watermelons and rock melons, if we were lucky enough to have some, to save for the fruitless winter season; and after we had covered them with earth we placed our boxes of off-season clothes and shoes under the bed. For years I had one suit of winter clothes and two suits of summer clothes, no more than that since fabric was extremely precious: every person's ration for cotton was three and a half feet for a year, and nylon was not heard of in the Gobi Desert. Our clothes were always mended by patches with all sorts of colour. The famous saying for using clothes to the full was 'three years as new, three years as old, and another three years after mending'. So each item of clothing should work for nine years before it was retired, and after that we would undo it and use the fabric as mending patches. If it was too worn even for mending, we would use it to make 'fabric board', the material for making the soles of shoes. Shoes were always a headache in the Gobi Desert because the hard and long physical work wore them out quickly and every woman was virtually making shoes all the time. The heavy physical labour in the fields would wear out a pair of shoes purchased from the shop in one month, while the ones we made by hand could last for three months. The winter shoes sold in the shop were not only expensive but also never warm enough for the open air, so we all made our own winter shoes by hand: the top was thick padded with sheep wool and the sole was fabric board, called 'thousand layers' and sewed up densely and thickly with hemp. I cannot remember how many hours I had spent beside the kerosene lamp sewing up shoe soles with sore fingers.

CHAPTER FOUR

Autumn harvest season came soon after I arrived in the Gobi Desert. The main job in that season was to reap maize ears for one and half months. There were ten thousand *mu* of maize fields in No. 13 Camp, and the job was always for women only. Actually all the hardest jobs in the Gobi Desert were done by women. The men's job was to look after the channels and it was a day and night job, not suitable for women. It could become extremely stressful if the bank of the channel was broken. At the vital moment when the flood was roaring and running, it would need very strong arms to hold a bulk of clay as big as a little hill to stop the water.

At six in the morning the headman banged a piece of steel — a bit of rusty old plough — with a thick stick, and I was woken up from a very deep sleep. It was real agony trying to move my painful body and sit up. The pain in my fingers was terrible when I tried to move them after a night's rest and blood oozed out of the cuts. The cracks were wide with drops of blood here and there, and looked horrible.

Carrying a woven basket, together with twenty-odd women, I walked to the maize fields in the early morning. The basket was about one metre high and half a metre wide, heavy and awkward on my back; two pieces of rope were attached to it from both sides of my shoulders. Back bending, heads low, we stood at the end of the fields. The headman of the team gave his orders: 'Everyone is to work along one line of the maize. Don't try to be lazy. If you are slower than others, you will not only miss your lunch but might get a bite from a wild boar.'

Wild boars often came up to the fields in autumn. They trashed huge

63

sections of the crops. When the men from the team caught some in traps, we had the meat to eat for days. It was tough but tasted delicious, considering we had not eaten any meat for months.

The maize plants were tall and dry, their ears half a metre long. As a newcomer, I couldn't work fast and after a while I became very scared because everyone else was ahead of me. The only noise to be heard in the field was the wind whistling through the maize leaves. I looked around and could see nothing but row after row of dried maize plants. The basket on my back was deadly heavy and my fingers, slashed by the sharp edge of the leaves, were bleeding. My heart beat hard and sweat dripped into my eyes.

In panic, my arms and fingers became clumsy. I couldn't throw the ears into the basket accurately, and I had to bend over to pick up the ears I'd dropped on the ground, so other ears slipped out of the basket. I then had to take the basket off my shoulders and squat down to pick them up in a hurry. All the other workers were now far ahead of me. With tears in my eyes, I toiled on. I was very thirsty but I had missed the break when drinking water was supplied. I couldn't afford to miss lunch. Forgetting the pain in my fingers, I hurried to pick up one ear after another, throwing them over my shoulder into the basket while being careful not to let any more drop on the ground. How much I looked forward to reaching the piles of ears on the ground where I could empty my basket.

Lunch was at the end of the field. Learning from others, I picked up a piece of maize leaf to make a bowl, holding the cooked Chinese cabbage, using two pieces of the stem as chopsticks. The main food was a steamed wheat-flour bun as a treat for the hard work. For breakfast and supper there were only steamed cornflour buns.

In the grey dusk, we walked back to the camp. It took enormous effort just to get down to the cave along the eight earth steps. My legs were as stiff as an old man's and every movement caused pain as if my shin muscle was torn up. It was even worse when I touched the warm water to do some washing. My fingers were as if on fire and each touch of the water required huge willpower. However, a wash was absolutely necessary since my body was covered by an itchy film — dust from the air mixed with dust from the dried corn leaves. Squatting on the ground in the cave in front of an enamel basin, each girl washed: using a face cloth to scrub our faces, necks and arms before washing our feet. If the water was not too dirty yet, we would wash our underpants and socks. A shower or a bath was unthinkable. As for washing clothes, we had to wait till the weekend, and go to the only well, a hundred metres away in the open air. In the busy season, however, we didn't have any weekends until the job was done, which would be a few weeks or even a couple of months. The only chance for a day off was when it was raining, but that was very rare. When it did rain, the one who discovered the raindrops first would cheerfully shout out: 'It's raining!' and everybody would rush out of the caves and exclaim, 'Is that right? Really raining? Oh! We can stay for a rest to do some washing and mending.' Many times, however, the rain would stop halfway and then the headman would yell out, 'Go to work, at once!'

In the middle of October after the maize harvest, we gathered the cabbages. There were two hundred *mu* of cabbage field, and cabbage was one of our five staple foods all the year round. We had good food only three times a year: on the Moon Festival Day, New Year's Day and the Spring Festival Day (the Chinese New Year). On those days we had 'meat dishes': potatoes stewed with pork, cabbage cooked with mutton, stir-fried rice with eggs, and once a year dumpling filled with mince and cabbage. Weeks before those festivals everyone was chanting: *da mi fan chao ji dan, yi dun cha lang wan*, stir-fried rice, I eat two big bowls.

The weather in November in the Gobi Desert was freezing cold, and this was the time we harvested the Chinese cabbages. My thick cotton padded gloves soon became soaked and frozen, and my hands grew stiff and numb. Each time I touched a cabbage leaf, the ice on it stung like a burn to my cold fingers. The cabbages were picked up by hand, one by one, and stored underground for the whole winter. They would be our only vegetable from November to April, the winter season of the Gobi Desert.

When winter arrived, the temperature dropped dramatically and snow started in November and lasted till March.

One night in December, I woke up feeling frozen. The two quilts felt as thin as two sheets of paper and I had to get up to do something. I put on my cotton padded coat and stuffed some firewood into the mud stove and then lay down again. But I was still too cold to sleep even though the fire was roaring in the stove beside me. Later I was told that the temperature that night was minus forty-four degrees centigrade. The next morning the headman was yelling outside our cave: 'Everybody goes to Ten Thousand Mu to build tunnels.'

We ate breakfast at home as a special treat in bad weather in winter. It was a maize bun, a bowl of cornflour porridge and a little pickled cabbage root. At seven-thirty we set off through the snow. On such a day we would be a team of only about thirty men and women.

Everybody tried to avoid the heavy labour. Women tried to be pregnant as frequently as possible to get maternity leave; some slept with the head or the deputy heads of the team so they could get light work allocated. Others feigned being sick to get a day off. The remaining number of people had to do more jobs to make up for the ones who didn't come. The most common trick was to work very slowly to save tired muscles. The headman was annoyed by those slow movements. He would shout, 'Don't come to the workplace idle!' Apart from the shouting, there was not much else he could do to speed up the work. Everyone got the same fixed wages — forty-one *yuan* a month (about five US dollars), no matter how hard you worked. That was what I got for the next ten years.

It was snowing hard; big flakes were flowing in the air and covered the whole barren plains. On the ground the snow, reaching to our shins, was soft and crunchy, and every step was an effort. We walked in a single line following the footsteps of a strong tall man, our platoon head, who was wearing a pair of gumboots stuffed with wool and cotton.

There was no wind and I could hear the vibration of the air flowing. Winter in the Gobi Desert was quiet and serene. The branches of the poplar and tamarisk trees were covered by snow, looking like flowers in full bloom. It was actually a very beautiful world if we had not been too frozen to enjoy the natural beauty. Suddenly I felt my cheeks aching as if something was slashing them. I stretched out my fingers from the thick cotton mittens and touched my cheeks. There were blisters, caused by the cold, on both sides of my cheeks, as big as plums. My ears underneath the cotton scarf were swollen and became as thick as a piece of sliced bread. My breath, as soon as it emerged out of my mouth and my nose, was a bulk of white steam and in no time would turn into frost, clinging onto my fringe, my eyebrows and my lashes. I must have looked like a female Santa.

Forty minutes later we arrived at the Ten Thousand Mu. The spades we'd used the day before were covered by snow. We took them out, shook off the snow and started to dig the earth. Someone was setting up our fire beside the work site. He swept off the snow and then the soil we'd piled up on the half-burnt firewood the day before. The firewood was smoking blue, thin and drifting. He collected some dry grass and bits of sticks, heaped them onto the smoking pile and blew on it. The blue smoke became thicker and thicker, and at last the fire took hold. Some bigger branches were stacked on the fire and its flame was flapping like a red flag. The fire looked so lovely to us and everyone was looking forward to the break time so they could huddle around it. We were lucky that we still had bush as firewood to burn, since we were at the edge of the agricultural area and some of the ancient plantation was left. Other teams had used up all their firewood. The only way to warm themselves was to pour petrol on bulks of clay and set fire to it.

One spadeful after another, thousands of them, in a mechanical movement, we dug up the soil and threw it up onto the top of the bank beside the channel, high up above our heads. We were building a trench, the main irrigation system, to bring snowmelt down from the mountains to the crop fields. Time passed slowly. At last a woman appeared on the horizon and our lunch was delivered. This job was an envied one and was done by breastfeeding mothers.

The headman said: 'Time for lunch!' Everybody stopped and picked up a lump of clay mixed with snow and scratched their spade until it was shining. The spades were going to be our meal dishes to hold the cooked Chinese cabbage, and after lunch we would use them to dig up soil again. Two stems from the dried maize crop were our chopsticks: this was humorously described as *jin kuai zi yin wan, chi le jiu ban*, silver bowls and gold chopsticks, throw them away after meals. We all huddled around the fire, holding our 'silver bowls and gold chopsticks', waiting for our lunch. The woman placed the bamboo pole on the ground, untied the water bucket from one end of it and a bowel of cooked Chinese cabbage and a bundle of steamed buns from the other end. She used a scoop to dollop a small pile of cabbage onto each spade; then she accepted our tickets and distributed the buns. We all squatted down around the fire. The buns were frozen even though they had come from the steamer not

67

long before. We put them on the ash of the fire but they were soon burnt on the outside although they were still frozen in the centre. A stinky burning odour was always part of our lunch as someone's hair burnt when he or she tried to reach the fire too eagerly. I huddled myself close to the fire and my hair caught fire. My back was still frozen.

That evening we heard some horrible news: the man who stayed alone in the hut to mind the flock of sheep had woken up in the middle of the night and found his feet painfully frozen. He put his feet into a basin of warm water and felt a sharp pain. He touched his toes and saw the skin and the flesh peel off. Only white bones were left. I learned a lesson from that — in dealing with frozen flesh, never use warm or hot water but rub the skin with snow until it turns red and feels warm and then you could use warm water.

In spring of 1966, we received orders from the upper boss that some veterans and their wives were coming to our team. We were to built real houses for them, 'high houses', as they were called in the Gobi Desert. The veterans were from army, the high and glorious rank, and the high houses for them must be made as soon as possible. Spring started as early as March and the temperature rose suddenly. March and April was the snow-melting season and roads became muddy and sticky. No vehicle could run in the daytime, so for those two months all transportation had to be done at night when the road was frozen hard.

One night in early March, I was woken up by my group's head. Glory told me we had a job to do. I put on my clothes and followed her outside. It was dark, quiet and cold. A pale yellow moon gave out a hazy light above the horizon. I saw a few other city youths standing in front of the rubber-wheeled tractor. We got on the trailer of the tractor and moved on the rutted muddy path, which was frozen and rough. The bumpy tractor moved very slowly. We were to go to a brick factory forty miles away to get some bricks.

We were sitting on the bare top of the trailer and were attacked ruthlessly by the cold. It felt like a slice of ice cutting first my feet, then my hands, then my face and finally my whole body. It was so acute that I felt I was lying in a frozen field naked and a thousand knives were slashing me at the same time. Holding one of her feet with both hands, Bright started to cry. Following her, we all either cried or screamed loudly to protest the coldness. The tractor moved at the most five kilometres an hour, and the rough road made it bump all the time. We were thrown into the air with each bump, as high as a foot into the air and then dropped down onto the hard floor of the tractor with a crack that jarred our whole bodies.

The coldness became worse and worse every minute. Every bone in my body was aching but we had only completed one-third of the trip and nobody could bear any more. We called out to the driver to stop and got off the trailer. When my feet touched the ground, the pain was so excruciating that I almost collapsed. Others also got off the trailer, crying from the pain when they touched the ground. We then stumbled behind the tractor, which was going so slow that we had no difficulty keeping up with it. After a while we would get on the tractor when we were too tired to walk. Everybody was exhausted by the time we arrived at the brick factory, yet we had to immediately start work, shifting the bricks onto the trailer, for four hours.

May was a windy season and the air became extremely dry. The wind threw the dirt into the air, and the whole sky became so dark that you couldn't see another person even if they were only a couple of metres away. Everybody's skin became rough and dark. I looked like a forty-year-old woman even though I was only twenty-two. But the real killer was dehydration by the dry weather.

One day in June a little girl of four went missing and the whole team of the camp set out to look for her. On the third day we found her, only five hundred metres away from home. Surrounded by dry bushes, she was lying on her tummy in front of a little pond of salty water. Her mouth was touching the undrinkable water, dead.

One day in July we went to collect reeds. We were a group of four, a male driver and three working hands — one man and two women. We put a bucket of water on the trailer and set off to the deep desert. The rutted earth road was very rough and bumpy, and the water was thrown out of the bucket. When we realised that we would have no water to drink, everybody was in a panic. The shadow of death appeared in our minds. The sun was like a huge fireball; the dust around the tractor wheels was like yellowish whirling clouds; there was no chance of finding any water on the way. We saw empty land, dry bushes, dry weeds and white-coloured alkaline spots, nothing else. It would be easier to find a diamond in the Gobi Desert than a drop of drinkable water. I felt unbearably thirsty, with no saliva in my mouth and my lips cracked and bleeding. When we arrived at the work spot we saw dried reeds, white and tall, but no water. It must have had some water sometime if reeds could grow, but not at that time of the year. We saw no sign of a drop of water, only dead tall reeds, like the thin bones of a skeleton. We started to cut off the reeds and carried them on our shoulders and placed them on the trailer. The sun was deadly hot and the earth was like a big wok. Everybody was madly thirsty and our skin was giving out sweat like hot oil. The driver, Army, was a small man whose five-month-old baby suffered from cartilage disease, which was a common complaint amongst babies in the Gobi Desert. She was too ailing to sleep and cried a lot at night, so the driver was suffering from sleep deprivation. Suddenly on the way to the tractor, he fell down to the ground, and a big bunch of reeds, long and heavy, fell on his unconscious body. The rest of us threw away the reeds from our backs and ran towards him. We shook him, called his name and tried to wake him up, but in vain. In a while he opened his eyes, mumbled 'water' and fainted again. The rest of us, lying on the ground, could not move. The other man, Iron, said, 'Look! There is snow on top of the Sky Mountain. Let's go to the snow.' We were on all fours and frantically crawled towards the snow mountain. We were mad with thirst and forgot that the mountain was a hundred miles away. We soon lost consciousness.

The next thing I knew was a cool refreshing sensation. A young Kazakh lad was holding me in his arms, feeding me with water from his water jar. His dark bright eyes were watching me with mixture of anxiety and appreciation. I lifted up my head and saw two other Kazakh men and three horses around. The Kazakh lad cheerfully called out, 'She is alive!' The two men, squatting beside Satin, the other girl, and Iron, the working man, smiled at me. The driver's body was lying motionless on the ground, dead.

The Kazakhs had been hunting in the area when they saw us. They were in striped robes, high boots, wide-brimmed hats, with bows and arrows in long leather quivers on their shoulders. The young lad was in his early twenties, and handsome. He put me on his horse in front of him.

Satin was on the other Kazakh's horse and Iron, holding the driver's body in his arms, mounted the horse with the third Kazakh. The young Kazakh was holding my waist tightly. I felt romantic love for him, my rescuer. When he slowed down the horse and kissed me, I didn't refuse him.

Two months after the wheat harvest, Satin and I had three days off to see the Kazakhs to convey our gratitude. We arrived at the foot of Sky Mountain and saw a different world from our Gobi Desert area, a huge grassland dotted with yellow, white and blue wild flowers. Its beauty rendered us speechless. Horses and cows were grazing idly on the meadows. A gem-coloured stream was running briskly at the foot of the mountain and Kazakh yurts, like big black mushrooms, dotted at the side of the river. A short distance away we could see brick and mud houses belonged to Uighur, Kirghi and other minority groups.

Night fell on the prairie and under the moonlight Tajik, my young Kazakh friend, held my hand while Satin and another lad were dancing and singing underneath the grapevines. From the village came a team of singers, the leading singer playing an accordion, and the whole team was marching and singing along the river bank. No fixed lyric was needed. The leading man was singing from his heart and his mates were following him in rhythm and response. Little children, of whom the youngest was no more than three years old, with the innate ability to understand the music, were following this team and dancing with perfect rhythm. Joyful singing and dancing carried on till the early hours of the morning, stopping only at a long table where the dancers picked up a wine bottle and drank some of it straight from the bottle. At dawn we went to Tajik's family tent and his mother offered us horse-milk tea. We drank one cup after another until we had to put the cup upside down to show the hostess that we had enough, according to their custom.

Summer started in June. The days were very long and it didn't become dark until eleven in the evening. Our summer job was to harvest wheat. We got up at three-thirty in the morning for the fields. Every one had a *Little Red Book* in their pocket. To forget it would result in the person being mass criticised for 'not have proletarian class feelings to Chairman Mao', an accusation nobody wanted to face. A straw hat hanging around my neck, a cotton scarf around my waist like a belt with an enamel mug dangling on it, I set off in the grim dawn light. I had learned to be resourceful in the Gobi Desert. A square cotton scarf had multiple uses in the wild Gobi Desert life. It could cover my face from sandstorm attacks; it could work as a tissue to wipe sweat; it could protect my neck from the itching wheat dust; it protected me from mosquito bites; it could work as a seat or a mat on the bare ground . . . In the mean conditions of the Gobi Desert, I learned to put everything to multiple uses.

After climbing up several sand dunes on the way, we arrived at the wheat fields shortly after four in the morning. The first thing to do was to pay tribute to Chairman Mao. Twenty-odd women in dirty clothes, exhausted from lack of sleep and malnutrition, lined up at the side of the wheat field, holding copies of the Little Red Book in our right hands over our heads, chanting in unison, 'We wish our great leader, great general, great helmsman, the red sun in our hearts, a longevity of ten thousand years! We wish our dear Vice-chairman Lin good health forever, good health forever!' At that time, Lin Biao was Mao's favourite follower but later on, of course, when he lost favour and died when his plane crashed in Mongolia, we didn't mention him any longer. Instead, we had our 'Loyalty Dance to Chairman Mao' after the chanting. For ten minutes every day, we would shake our legs, move our arms, wave our hands, nod our heads and twist our torsos, dancing and singing, 'Dearest Chairman Mao, red sun in the bottom of our hearts, I miss you so much and I want to tell you, I have thousands of words to tell you how much I love you.' This ritual was a law in China for quite a few years. Failure to obey it could lead to being accused of being anti-revolutionary, and the punishment varied from mass criticism to prison, even death. A woman named Zhang Zhi-xin had her throat slashed open when she refused to pay tribute to Chairman Mao.

After the ritual, we started our labour, cutting off the wheat crops. Two hours later, at seven, breakfast was delivered, and we had a half-hour break and ate a corn bun and salted cabbage while sitting on the ground. After breakfast we started working again. At twelve-thirty, lunch (another steamed bun and a little boiled marrow) was delivered to the work site and we had a two-hour lunch break sitting on the bare dusty land in the hot sun. The water delivered to us was tainted with a disgusting smell of petrol since it was held in a used petrol tanker. The temperature was high, averaging around forty degrees centigrade. There wasn't a single tree around. We were exposed in the dry, unbearable heat. During the lunch break, the men would roll up their tobacco and have a smoke and the women would do some needlecraft: mending clothes, sewing cotton socks or making shoes. Sometimes we would try to have a nap. I would lie on my scarf as a little protection from the dirt, and lay my straw hat over my face. I would have no difficulty falling sleep since I was so exhausted. But a proper nap was impossible. A few minutes later, I would wake up panting; oily sweat was all over my skin.

After the lunch break we went back to the field and worked till eight in the evening.

Dragging our tired legs, we walked home, and by the time we arrived at the camp, it was nearly nine in the evening, although it was still light.

Being tired by the heavy and long hours of physical labour as I was, I did not complain. I didn't try tricks, pretending to be sick. I liked to think I was a good youth answering Chairman Mao's call to help develop Xinjiang. I wanted to work hard so that I might be chosen as a model worker with my picture appearing in newspapers. 'I will show my big smile in the picture. How glorious it would be!' I told myself. And there was Minister Young's promise to give me hope. I expected one day that good news would come from him, and I would shift to Ulumuqi to be a school teacher or a performer. These dreams inspired me and I clenched my teeth to bear the harsh labour and empty life in the Gobi Desert.

My hopes were suddenly smashed. In June 1966, the mass movement of the Great Proletarian Cultural Revolution broke up and soon I heard that Minister Young had lost his position and was denounced as a 'capitalist roader', an official who was going along the capitalist route, being the follower of the vice-chairman of China Liu Shaoqi, who was Mao's major rival. Before long Minister Young was sent far away to do heavy physical labour in custody.

The term 'Cultural Revolution' had nothing to do with culture but was a fancy word game of Mao's, indicating that he didn't want military force involved in it. And the word 'proletarian' had the precise meaning that the revolution was a fight between different classes, the working class fighting the upper class. However, since everyone was working in Mao's time and there was virtually no upper class after 1949, to suit his aim Mao created the theory that everyone's class was decided by what they did before 1949. As for young ones, their class was decided by what their parents did before 1949. This theory had been in use since the 1950s but it became much more powerful during the Cultural Revolution. *Chu shen*, family background, became the dominant power: it alone decided if you were good or bad. The rhyme that the Beijing Red Guards made at the time became the principle of society: 'Dragon produces dragon, phoenix produces phoenix, and mouse knows how to dig holes. Good parents produce good children, bad children from bad parents, and if your father is from the working class, you are red and good. You've got to be bad and black if your family is rich or learned.'

In every corner of China, the vicious and wild fire of Cultural Revolution raged wide and long. In No. 13 Team of the Gobi Desert, a handful of city youths and veterans from red families turned into Red Guards. They stopped working in the fields and conducted 'revolutionary acts'. Yelling revolutionary slogans and Mao's quotations fanatically, they pushed doors open like wild animals and rushed at their prey. They looted people's homes and dug into their belongings, which was called *pe si jiu*, smashing the four old things — old tradition, old culture, old customs and old philosophy. They took away all the books I had brought with me from home and put them in the fire. I felt a piercing pain in my heart when I saw my beloved books written by Lu Xun, Gogol, Tolstoy, Balzac and Dostoyevsky disappear in their crazy hands.

That night in darkness, I quietly got up and walked to the place where the Red Guards had been burning the books in the daytime. I squatted beside the ash and tried to see if any paper had survived. I turned the ash over from top to bottom slowly and carefully, and suddenly I felt something heavier than ash. It might be some paper or even a book. My heart leapt with excitement. I shook the ash off it and tried to feel what it was with my hands. My heart was jumping frantically. If I was caught at this moment, I would have a huge price to pay, maybe I'd be beaten up by the Red Guards or be sent to endless 'struggle meetings'. Still, the risk was worthwhile after I found out what it was. I looked around like a wary animal, eyes open wide, ears sharp, breath held. I turned on my little torch after I was sure nobody would see me. In the quiet motionless night of the Gobi Desert, with joy, sadness, fear and excitement, I saw that it was my high-school English textbook.

The book had been roughly and poorly made during the starvation years. Since even straw was food and there was a great lack of material for making books, they were made of rotten waste. It was no wonder that the Red Guards did not bother to make sure it was burnt.

As if I had found a pile of treasure after great endeavour, I held my English textbook and wept. This little book was the only reading material left to me now.

One day in autumn 1966, I received a letter. The handwriting was my mother's, but the return address was a strange place — Sunge Village, Changle County. My heart pounded and my hands were trembling as I held it. What had happened to my mother? Why did she write from Changle? My heart sank when I read it:

> Dear Daughter Weijun,
>   Your brother and I are living in Sunge Village now. We were exiled here by the Red Guards of the Teachers' College. We are luckier than some as we are still alive. Don't worry about us. Take care of yourself and write to me at the new address . . .

I realised, with pain, that my family, as one of the black families, was exiled by the Red Guards to the poor countryside, our home village, where we came from just before 'liberation' in 1949. I worried about my mother and brother so much that I could not manage any sleep. I drafted a long letter to my mother, trying to console her and my brother. The next day happened to be the National Day and a day off. I climbed onto an ox-cart alongside several other people. I wanted to go to Caijiahu, the headquarters of our regiment, to post the letter at the post office, the only one for all the regiment. Just before the cart was ready to move, however, the head of the Red Guard, a severe-looking girl from Tienjin, rampaged to the cart and shouted: 'Liu Weijun, get off the cart!'

'Why?' I asked, flinching.

'You are not a revolutionary member. We Red Guards confine your actions.'

'I just wanted to send my family a letter, please.'

'I say get off, otherwise I will command a revolutionary act on you!' she yelled.

'I have not done anything . . .'

Strong male hands pulled me out by my arms and I dropped on the ground in pain. My hair was loose, my clothes torn, and smirking faces were watching me. I was so ashamed and wished the earth would crack open and swallow me up.

My social standing deteriorated during the Cultural Revolution. I was scorned and rejected by those who were from red families and shunned by those who were black as they feared being accused of 'organising reactionary behaviours with the same kind'. People who used to be nice to me now turned their backs on me. Public criticism was as common as meal times. Hardly anybody would talk to me, and if I tried to talk to anyone they would turn their head away from me. My dormitory mates would whisper in a tight group. Every now and then my name was spoken of in a contemptuous way in public. The Red Guards wrote big character posters about me and posted them on the wall of the public kitchen. They ridiculed me as 'a bad element and a stinky intellectual'. Anyone who could read and write was an intellectual in the Gobi Desert society, where most people were illiterate. How much I regretted telling the truth, that I was a high-school graduate, and how much humiliation I suffered because of it. I decided I would pretend to be illiterate in the future.

The sadness caused by isolation and humiliation was terrible. I worked in the fields in silence and spent the evening by myself in silence. I was bordering on suicidal until one day I found a letter underneath my bed:

Dear Comrade Weijun,

Even though they humiliate you and curse you, I have a strong belief in you and I know you are a good person. Please be strong and the ugly clouds will be gone.

Yours sincerely,
Shao-li

I could hardly conceal my tears. There was kindness in life after all.

CHAPTER FIVE

Chi-huan Gong, the Emperor of China in 499 AD, had several concubines and one of them, Pearl, was his favourite. His queen, jealous of Pearl, tried a trick. First she pretended that she was nice and kind towards Pearl and after she won trust from her, she told her: 'Our master likes to see a pretty woman smile with her hand clutching her mouth and covering her teeth.'

Pearl smiled in front of the Emperor with her hand in front of her mouth; and the queen said to him: 'Do you know why Pearl puts her hand in front of her mouth? She loathes your bad breath.'

The Emperor was outraged and had Pearl's head cut off.

FROM *TRUE RECORD OF HISTORY* BY SHI MAQIAN.

Now I was an inferior even in the Gobi Desert. With hope gone, my spirits were low. The meagre life became ugly, the labour unbearable. I began slacking in the fields, which made me even more unpopular. The only thing I could enjoy was sleep, when I could escape into my dreams. In my dreams I saw myself walking in strange city streets. I would dream about places I had never been to, exotic cities and beautiful country scenery.

My daytime became a nightmare and nights were my real life, and helped me to survive.

I wrote letters whenever I was tormented by loneliness. It was the only way to soothe my soul, to forget the harsh reality and to keep in touch with the outside world. I wrote to my mother and brother, to Pine and Bliss.

Bliss was a man in his early thirties I'd met on the train, an agricultural technician from Guangzhou, who now worked in Shihezi, a town further north of Ulumuqi. He liked to write to me frequently but I regarded him as an ordinary friend. Pine, on the other hand, was where my heart lay. His letters, though rare, became the main source of my romantic fantasy life. I read them repeatedly, trying to interpret them in a positive and inspiring way. His handwriting was beautiful, and my imagination helped me create an ideal young man — one I wanted to love. Occasionally he would write me enthusiastic letters, which would give me hope. I had great expectations of love. I believed love could change everything. If I married Pine, I thought, he would take me away from the Gobi Desert and I would have a happy life somewhere with him and would never come back to | the desert.

In November 1967, twenty-six months after I was exiled to the Gobi Desert, I eventually obtained a permit for a holiday to visit my family in Qingdao.

After nine months of exile in Sunge Village, my mother and my brother were allowed to live in Qingdao again. This resulted from a new policy initiated by the moderate members of the central Party committee in Beijing, and many who had been exiled by the Red Guards during the previous chaotic time were allowed to go back to their city homes. This good news brightened my mood tremendously. I was happy not only because my mother and brother didn't have to suffer the hard village life, but also because I could visit my family in Qingdao. How I longed to see my dear home city again.

The train was extremely crowded, much more so than the last time I took it in 1965. The Cultural Revolution was in the fervent stage. Schools were closed, factories didn't operate to a normal routine, and local governments were collapsing. There was chaos all over China. In the train I didn't have a seat and had to stand in the aisle in the daytime and sleep under the seats at night, which I called the under-seat sleeper. The train seats were low and I needed to fold my body double, as low as a lying dog, and flatten my belly to crawl underneath the seat. Once I was there, it wasn't too bad. After more than two years of hardship in the Gobi Desert, I could easily cope with these tough conditions. For the four days and five nights of the journey, I managed all right by crawling through others' legs into the space beneath their seats, and even had some fairly good sleep, although I was constantly dirty with fruit peelings, waste papers, shells of nuts and other rubbish. The people sitting on the seats above me were quite nice and tried not to spit on my legs. Only once did I have a conflict, and that was with somebody who was also an under-seat sleeper. We both tried to protect our own territory and initiated a good fight, kicking each other severely each time our feet touched. My rival must have been a man since his kicking was so strong and I could feel his big leather boots. I couldn't help laughing afterwards and tried to imagine who he was and what he would think if he found out that his enemy had been a girl. Would he still have kicked me so hard?

I got off the train at the railway station of Cangkou, a suburb of Qingdao. In the gloomy twilight, I found myself walking along a pathetic muddy path towards the village my family were living in now — Crab Village.

My heart pounded as I pushed the door open. My mother, although it was only twenty-six months since I last saw her, looked at least ten years older. She smiled at first, and then tears began running down her face while she hugged me. 'I thought I wouldn't be able to see you again,' she sobbed. I cried out: 'Niang!', an intimate term used in some of the northern parts of China for 'mum'. My dear mother told me how she had coped with the crisis.

Early one morning in July 1966, soon after the Cultural Revolution broke out, my mother was in bed after Main had gone to work. Suddenly she heard a deafening noise and within moments dozens of Red Guards rushed into our home. Shouting revolutionary slogans, they pulled my mother out of her bed. Two boys twisted her arms behind her back and pulled her outside while she was still in her pyjamas. The others started to loot the entire contents of the single-room flat and the attached kitchen. They pulled down the photos from the walls, shoved them into the stove and set fire to them. All the old photos, including the precious only photo of my father, were in flames. A boy was teaching my mother a lesson while she painfully watched the beloved faces in the pictures turn to ash. 'Photos are bourgeois stuff. They have no use. Never try to take photos again!' the Red Guard leader lectured my mother. One girl saw a biscuit tin with a picture of a golden-coloured rooster on it and she took a fruit knife from the desk drawer and scratched it sharply, while yelling at my mother, 'You

79

bloody worm of a black class. Don't you know gold is not our proletarian colour? If we find this stinky capitalist colour in your place again we'll take your rotten life!' Everything pretty was considered bourgeois and was smashed, destroyed or burnt.

In the afternoon they came again and put a tall hat made of white paper on my mother's head. On it they wrote her name and put three red crosses over it, as would be done to a criminal sentenced to death. Three Red Guards dragged my mother to the public courtyard outside, where the wives of teachers in the college, wearing red sleeve-bands with murderous faces, threw themselves on my mother, kicking and cursing. My mother couldn't understand why her neighbours, so nice to her previously, had turned into devils overnight. She was kicked from behind at the back of her knees and collapsed on the ground, but before she could manage a breath she was caught by her collar and pulled along the road to the college playground, where a team of teachers were kneeling down with denouncing paper hats on their heads. Seeing my mother approaching, thousands of students in the audience yelled, 'Denounce the Party's traitor! Down with the stinky wife of the historical reactionary! Damn you, the daughter of a rich mandarin! Curse you, the stinky intellectual! Ten thousand years of life to Chairman Mao!'

Some were yelling at my mother, 'Write to your daughter and let her come back from Xinjiang. We want to take revolutionary actions against her. We'll condemn her and turn her pretty bourgeois face inside out!'

The Red Guards of Cangkou Community School were also extraordinarily cruel and brutal to the teachers. My ex-boyfriend Mainspring was badly tortured only because he had been friendly with me for a short while, and he was capped as 'a traitor of the working class talking love with the capitalist girl Liu Weijun'. Miss Han, a young English teacher, was tortured because she taught English, the imperialist's language. The students had never liked her since she was considered snooty and arrogant: they had nicknamed her White-Bone Witch. As soon as the Cultural Revolution started, the Red Guards denounced her and beat her up mercilessly. She lost control of her bladder and wet her trousers with hundreds watching her. Another time she became so fearful that she lost control of her bowels but she had to wear her smelly soiled trousers for days in detention. Her hair was cut into an insulting style called 'hair style of yin and yang' — half bald, half with hair. It looked ridiculous and she cried her heart out as she was a woman who had been obsessed with her own beauty. She tried to commit suicide but was found out, and this invited even more torture as anyone who committed suicide was regarded as a devil who betrayed the people and the Party. She was crippled, with one eye blind and one leg lame for the rest of her life.

The death of thirty million people in the Three Years' Starvation had taught Mao the lesson that the people who produced food must continue to do so in order to support the revolution. Consequently the revolutionary actions in the Gobi Desert were on a much smaller scale, and over a shorter period compared with the cities. Staying in the Gobi Desert might have saved my life.

The denouncing meetings on my mother were held every day. She was forced to stand on a narrow bench, her arms tied by a rope behind her back. Two male Red Guards stood on either side of her, using their fists to push her head down again and again until the tip of her nose almost touched her chest. Meanwhile the crowd was roaring at her: 'Confess, why do you let your son listen to the enemy's broadcast, the *Voice of America*?' My mother tried to answer, but her voice couldn't be heard. Once a man with a whip in his hand jumped onto the stage and ran behind the bench she was standing on. He hit her with the whip, and she was so startled that she fell off the platform onto the ground, groaning and bleeding.

One week later my mother and my brother Main were sent to Sunge Village, three hundred miles away, escorted by a group of Red Guards. With the few possessions they were allowed to bring, my mother and brother settled in a peasant's house, doing harsh labour in the custody of the revolutionary peasants.

When they returned, my brother got his job back as a schoolteacher and my mother's pension was restored. However they had lost most of their belongings as well as their place to live. They managed to rent the small peasant house in Crab Village.

Our new home was a small brick house divided by a mud wall into two rooms. To the south of the house was the owner's bigger house with three rooms in a row. My mother's was called 'a southern house', which meant it was on the southern side of the courtyard and its only door faced north. A southern house was not good to live in as it was cold in winter, since the cold northwest wind could rush in through the door, and it was hot in summer as the strong sunshine during the day came through the door. But it was almost like a palace to me after living in caves for more than two years.

Crab Village was very close to the city, only one mile away, but the villagers were countryside *hu kou* holders. They didn't have any of the benefits from the government that the city residents enjoyed. They ate what they produced in their tiny plots of land; the government never offered them anything but asked them to support the city people if necessary. They had no reliable income since they were not allowed to work in the city; they did not have housing benefits and medical subsidies. Worst of all, they didn't have pensions. Worries about old age were a constant concern. Their children were also trapped in this poverty cycle, since they were compelled to hold the same status as their parents unless they could manage to pass the state examination to be able to go to university, which of course was very hard — fewer than four percent of all those who sat the exam would pass.

They were thoroughly second-class citizens, so it was no wonder that they were rough creatures full of self-pity, jealousy and hatred. Their inferior life had trained them to be vicious, wicked and sharp. It was a terrible misfortune that my family had become involved with Crab Village.

While I was staying in my mother's place at Crab Village for the holiday, we had a visitor who was new to me. She was a girl in her late twenties named Superb. She had a small frame and bow legs. Wearing a grey blouse, buttoned up on the right with complicated cotton tassels and a stiff high collar circled tightly around the neck, she walked in with arched steps. She had a tile-shaped face, thin in the middle and sticking out at both ends: her cheeks were unbalanced, one side bigger than the other, a symptom of popping-out veins. Her eyes were small with swollen lids; her mouth was tight with her lower jaw protruded, giving her a look of a toothless old woman. Her expression was sad and sore, as if she was going to cry at any time. Humble as she looked, she had very nice manners. She moved her head elegantly; her neck was flexible. She was calm and quiet and she knew when and how to talk. When she talked, her language was impressive.

She was introduced to my brother by a neighbour in Crab Village. My poor mother had been sad for Main. 'Poor Main, he's already twenty-eight but he has never even smelled a woman!' sighed my mother. She talked to the neighbours and begged them to introduce a girl for him.

'Ugly!' Main said after he met Superb for the first time. My mother sighed again and said, 'Main, you are already twenty-eight and we are a black family. Try not to be too fussy.'

Main was tall and handsome, with a gentle intelligent look. The square corners of his mouth were his only flaw, betraying his weak nature. He had no girlfriend partly because our family was politically inferior, partly because of his weak character. Main was not happy with Superb, but he was not firm enough to say no to her either. So he maintained a polite but unenthusiastic attitude towards her.

Superb was born into a poor peasant's family and was given away by her parents soon after she was born because she was a girl. She was brought up by a relative, and the stepmother was a bitter-hearted woman since she was infertile. 'Of all the bad things you could do for your ancestors, the worst was to bear no children' — this statement of Confucius more than two thousand years ago had dominated Chinese women generation after generation and condemned those who had no children. Some accepted the misfortune submissively; some became wicked and vicious and alienated others' relationships to balance their own bitter feelings. These women could be very cruel to other women, even more so than their male masters. Their female relatives were their deadly rivals and they would ruthlessly destroy them if chance allowed. As for their husbands, since they were in perpetual fear of being abandoned for the 'sin' of childlessness, they tried all sorts of insidious tricks to keep their status as wives. Pleasing, flattering and fawning were the usual tricks, but these were not enough: manipulating, threatening and intimidating were more efficient. Last but not least, they were great artists of the tragedy show: as a saying puts it, 'Pathos is always the winning tool.'

Superb was aware that Main was not interested in her. Instead of approaching him directly, she made friends with me and her way of flattery was as fawning as if I was her life-long friend. To start with, her obsequiousness made me embarrassed, but I was grateful to her since I was lonely and hardly anybody was friendly to me, a black element from a bad family. Even a feeble smile would easily buy my gullible heart.

83

Superb was a very clever and sophisticated talker. With well-chosen words she convinced me that she was a virtuous person with great integrity. But I did feel puzzled by something: Superb frequently contacted her girlfriends in the village, and meanwhile she told me they were wicked and vicious. She talked in such a vivid and convincing way. She expressed her hatred for those women deeply and sincerely, so it was difficult for the listener not to be infected. I believed in her and believed those women were villains, so, I never dared to make contact with any of them. Nevertheless, Superb kept up a close relationship with them: visiting them, entertaining them at her place, going out with them and having long talks with them. Only later did I realise this was her way of alienating people from each other, so that she could manipulate both sides.

The day when Main met Superb, he saw a snake stopping his way on the road. 'It was dark-coloured, thin and ugly. It was boldly lying in the middle of the road, refusing to allow me to pass. Its small eyes gave off a green light, sending a chill to my spine,' he told me.

Pine was in his last year of university, ready to graduate and get a job. I was waiting for it eagerly. As soon as he started to earn money, I thought, he could support me and we'd get married and live together happily ever after.

One day a letter from Pine arrived at Crab Village. I was very excited as always, and couldn't wait one more second to tear the envelope open. To my dismay, it brought shocking news — Pine had changed his mind and he wanted to break up with me:

> I am sorry but as our family backgrounds were, our future has already been decided and of course you understand I need to look after my future. I would be very sad if I became a victim of something your family did in the past . . .

My mind became blank and everything went dark. No words can describe my pain after I had finished reading the letter. I felt as though my heart was torn up and all my veins became bitter rivers pouring acid into my eyes. I wept in despair and torment.

At dinner-time my mother noticed me behaving differently and asked why.

'Pine doesn't love me any more,' said I, trying hard to conceal my agony.

My mother sighed. 'Our family political background is humble. He comes from a peasant family and he could find himself a girl from a red family and secure his future. I suppose we can't blame him. This is the trend nowadays. Everybody tries to choose someone from a better political class as a future spouse.'

I was enraged by the unfairness of life and was haunted by lost love. I couldn't say anything to express my anguish. My brother Main said: 'Why not marry Bliss? He has a good job and he will give you a good life.'

I said nothing. I didn't want to say anything. I didn't care about anything any more.

Bliss had come to Qingdao and visited my family for three days after I arrived. Seeing that neither I nor my mother was interested in him, he took the train to Guangzhou, where his parents lived.

Main said, 'I will go to the railway station and try to buy a train ticket to Guangzhou for you. Tickets are difficult to buy nowadays. If I can get one, it is your fate to marry him.'

My mother didn't say anything. She was used to listening to the male members of the family from her early life. As Confucius taught: 'Be obedient to your father as a maid and to your husband after you are married, then to your son after your husband dies.'

I was too anguished to think clearly and I didn't care who I'd marry. Like a kite with a broken string floating in the air without clear direction, I didn't have any idea of what my future held. Thus I escaped from one pit of pain only to fall into another.

Half an hour later, Main came back with a ticket in his hand: 'Go on, you are destined to marry Bliss.' In numbness and pain, I had neither the interest to argue nor any real intention of doing so. I arrived in Guangzhou a couple of days later.

Bliss welcomed me with geat excitement: 'I knew you would come to me. You are just a labourer in the Gobi Desert and my working place is much better than yours. You'll have better food to eat. I will be able to shift your job after we get married.'

The next day he said: 'The situation in Guangzhou is in chaos and nobody can register our marriage certificate. But I can shift your work as long as you offer yourself fully to me.' So I did what I was told.

I was twenty-four but knew nothing about sex. When I saw his aroused penis, I was astonished! It looked like nothing that I knew. I had seen little baby boys' penises and they looked quite different. I couldn't understand how the cute little thing with the elegant pointed shape could become a thick hard pillar. Was he abnormal? Did he have a disease? What was going to happen to him and to me?

The next morning when I made the bed, I saw my blood on the sheet, a dark broken chrysanthemum, like a freshly cut wound. And I felt the stinging down there and it triggered a piercing pain in my heart. I thought of Pine. Where is he now? Has he already forgotten me or does he still remember me? Does he miss me? What is the use even if he still misses me? I am lost and broken. I am not worthy of love now. Happiness is out of my reach. I am inconsolable.

Bliss was strutting around like a prize rooster. His bow legs arched, his feet hit the ground noisily. He chanted, 'I told my friends, you had blood!' He laughed, showing his uneven yellow teeth. Bliss liked to call me *lao po*, a vulgar term for wife. Whenever we came back home from a shopping or sightseeing trip, despite the fact that I was just as exhausted as he, he would howl at me, 'Come on, *lao po*, I want you to boil some water for me and cook a Guangzhou-style soup.' His manners were abominable and difficult for me to bear.

After staying a week in Guangzhou we set off to Xinjiang; Bliss went to Shihezi where he worked, and I went back to the Gobi Desert, waiting for him to shift my job.

At first I was longing every day for the good news to come from Bliss that he had transferred my job to Shihezi. Many weeks passed without the good news, but only his letters, in careless, crude and rustic handwriting. I eventually realised that shifting my job to any better place was beyond Bliss's reach. I became more and more irritated and I missed Pine even more — in fact I was even more lovelorn now that I'd realised nobody could take his place in my heart. I was even more remorseful after I realised that he had regretted his decision. According to my mother, the day after I left for Guangzhou, a letter had arrived from him claiming he was still in love with me, apologising and asking me to join him in Beijing. My mother wrote to him that I had gone to Guangzhou to marry Bliss. Imagine how regretful I was! I could have had a happy time with Pine if only I'd postponed the trip to Guangzhou for one day. It was so painful to think I'd been only one narrow step away from happiness.

Days, weeks and months passed with hard work, my miserable mood and monochromatic everyday life in the Gobi Desert. Suddenly I felt surges of emotion, and in a flush of boldness I wrote a letter to Pine, the first since I had received his letter breaking it off with me months ago. I told him that I did go to Guangzhou to meet Bliss but that I hadn't lawfully married him. His letter came soon:

> The day I received your letter was the happiest day in my life. Come to me as soon as you can, my pretty white dove. We will never separate again and I will offer you inexhaustible love.

The year 1968 saw my life descend into another layer of hell in the Gobi Desert. The authorities had decided to develop another camp, No. 14 Team, which was further into the deeper bare land fifteen miles away from No. 13 Team, where there was no road to the outside world apart from barren paths amongst sand dunes and ancient bushes. We grew more maize in this area, much more, and we had to work even harder. The harshest job of all was thinning the young maize plants for two months. The maize seeds were sown by the tractors and our job was thinning the young plants when they were two inches high. Every day, with small steel spades in our hands, we arrived in the maize fields in the early morning. Backs bent, legs bowed, faces against the soil, stooping and unstooping uncountable times. We toiled and drudged on the ground for ten hours a day, digging out the extra maize plants. The young plants had long straight roots that stretched deep into the arid soil. It was a hellish job, even for tough Gobi Desert people. It stressed our legs to breaking point; it hurt our backs to the bone; and the metal handles of the tools cut into our calloused palms, causing blisters and bleeding.

We also grew opium in No. 14 Team. It was called 'No. 100', a secret code for it, and we were told it was for the war with Russia. We were watched closley by gunmen when we worked in the opium field and when we walked back home with the poppy sap held carefully in hands, they walked close beside us.

No. 14 Team was as safe as a prison since it was so remote — an ideal place to grow this secret plant. The field of opium, about five hundred *mu*, was in an area close to our camp surrounded by maize plants. Plenty of water was allowed for opium plants, which made the area a heavenly place in that boring dry land. Around the opium field the land was lush from the water, with the subtle aroma of the opium poppies wafting in the air. Jumping field mice, which lived in holes in the ground, would come out for drink and food; the white ends of their long fluffy tails blew lively in the air as they jumped about. Mongolian gazelles would run up to our opium field, quickly take some water from the ditch and shoot away like golden lightning.

The opium poppies with their greyish-green stems and leaves blossomed in early summer in pink, mauve and white. Later it was decided that the white-flowered plants produced more opium, so in later years only the white ones remained. The green globes of opium formed soon after the flowers finished and became bigger and bigger until they were the size of apricots. September was the harvest season, and the best time to collect opium was in the dawn before the sun came out. We went to the field at five in the morning, worked for two hours, went back to the camp, had breakfast and then went to do other labour.

Harvesting opium was like collecting sap from rubber trees. We slashed each globe once every day in a different place, not too deep, not too shallow, as the sap was on the surface of the globes. We procured the opium sap by puncturing the globe, which was still green, with the thin edge of a sharp knife. The sap poured like thick milk, and we wiped it with our fingers into a little enamel mug. Each person could collect about five grams of sap every morning. Then we carried the enamel mugs under the close watch of the military men as we walked back to the camp. One by one we poured them onto a big piece of plastic sheet, spread out in the sun; and the sauce would become darker and darker until at last it became brownish clay-like ointment. The military men would deliver it to the upper authority in the regiment.

A short, square-figured, pockmark-faced woman was chosen to take care of the opium sap before it turned into ointment. She was trusted and chosen because she was from a 'revolutionary family'; five generations of her family were all poor peasants. How much I envied her! I would have paid any price to have become her.

Anything about opium growing was secret. One day the members of the Communist Youth League had a meeting to discuss something about it in my cave. They threw me out when I was just about to enjoy a rest after a hard working day. I had to go to the open land, and I hid myself behind the sand dune and sobbed to the wind. After a while I stopped crying and started to plan my future.

It was soothing to think about Pine. He was writing to me much more frequently now. It normally took ten to twelve days for mail to arrive from the inner land to Xinjiang and he would write me three letters a month, which was enough to keep me happy. In one of his letters he even told me: 'Don't worry about money. I can give you several hundred *yuan*.' He must love me deeply to be so generous, I thought, and how much I was moved by his love!

I felt guilty about Bliss, though. I didn't know how to tell him about Pine without hurting his feelings, so I just didn't write to him. Only once I tried to tell him the truth but I wanted to be very polite and the words I used were very vague. I knew this wasn't a good way to finish a relationship but it was many years before I learned to communicate properly when dealing with difficult situations. When I was in my twenties the only way I knew was to listen to my natural passion. I had no idea that Confucius's thinking still dominated the society, nor did I appreciate that women weren't accepted as full human beings in Chinese society. Worst of all, I didn't know sex was considered so important that if a woman slept with more than one man, her life was ruined.

Sitting on the bare ground, letting the wild wind pass through my hair, I fell into daydreaming. I decided to go for a love run, to elope, like the ladies and gentlemen in Western novels. How romantic!

The sky was aqua and huge, the moon orange and pretty. My heart was excited by my imagination. I would leave No. 14 Team and join my sweetheart and never come back to the Gobi Desert. I would never come back, not even for a glimpse! Never!

CHAPTER SIX

The three weeks of opium harvest were followed by the maize harvest for nearly two months, and then three weeks cabbage collecting. At last, in November 1968, the busy seasons were behind and I started to deal with my plan of eloping.

To save a little money, I sold almost all of my belongings except one quilt. I sold my imitation-leather luggage for twenty *yuan*, two of my quilts for eight *yuan* each, a cotton-padded mat for five *yuan* and a padded jacket for ten. As for the bed board, which was such a great asset in the Gobi Desert, I gave it free to a woman named One-eye out of sympathy because her younger sister had slept on the ground for weeks ever since she came from Sichuan province to look after her sister's new-born baby. My wooden low stool, which I'd been given by a tractor driver when I was popular, was presented to Blossom, my Shandong folk friend. As the dwellers of the Gobi Desert were from all over the country, there was a tendency for people to stay close to their own provincial folks, to enjoy the same accent and the same customs. Blossom and I were close friends, so, apart from my stool, I gave her my eating bowl and spoon, and received sincere thanks.

Every year in autumn for a few weeks, trucks would come from Caijiahu, the regiment centre, and Wujiaqu, the division centre, to carry the maize for processing and then to be distributed as food rations. One Sunday afternoon, I quietly packed my travel gear — a handbag, my old green travel bag and a quilt — climbed up on a truck and left the No. 14 Team. I didn't even try to get a holiday permit from the head as I knew I couldn't get one.

Once on the train, I sighed and relaxed a bit. Subconsciously, I knew I was doing a dangerous thing and would face unpredictable consequences, but my heart argued that love would support me. I did, sometimes, ask myself questions in doubt. Did Pine really love me enough to support me? I dared not think too deeply since I was taking such a huge risk. I was away from the only place I had the right to stay in. The place I had a job, income, food rations and a registered residence. Could I survive without these essentials? Would Pine's income be enough to support me? 'I will think further after I cross the bridge,' I consoled myself. How much I missed Pine. I loved him so. Recalling the loving words in his letters, I felt ecstatic and intoxicated, but then at the next second I thought about my mother and brother, I worried what they would say about my eloping. I didn't know how they were getting on now and, apart from a short note a long while ago, I hadn't received any letters from them. The political and social situation at the time was even more tense, it was into the deep turbulence of the Cultural Revolution. Red Guards were travelling all over China to 'sow revolutionary seeds' — to smash the government administration, to denounce the officials as capitalist roaders and arrest them. The whole country was in anarchy. Gangs from revolutionary families had formed 'rebellion teams' and tried to grasp power over town, city and provincial governments. Many gangs were fighting violently with each other for power. The previous government function had collapsed and the rebellion teams were the only authorities. They were doing whatever they could to keep power in their hands. Gang fighting, armed battles and killings were commonplace. To maintain legitimacy, each rebellion team tried to become more Maoist and carried his class-struggle theory to the extreme. People from the black elements were more vulnerable than ever. The rebellion teams, competing with each other, tried to catch more class enemies in order to show they were legitimate. I was worrying about my mother and brother, but then I was in love, with an optimistic vision of life. My mind did not linger too long on the grim and gloomy side of the possible ill fate of my family.

I had a bit of money in my pocket, about three hundred *yuan* or so. Apart from the money I'd got from selling the luggage, the quilts and bits, I had also saved hard. I had worked as a seamstress in my spare time, sewing shirts, trousers and jackets for others and for each piece of garment

I earned a free meal. I was going to use this money to support Pine until he graduated. Once he graduated he would have a job with an income and we would be all right. Life in the future seemed rosy.

I burst into tears as soon as I saw my mother. Her face was pale and strained and there was a cloud of bitterness on her kind, wrinkled face. She was very astonished to see me home, since I had never mentioned my escape plan to her in my letters. But she didn't object when I told her that I was in love with Pine, that I couldn't live with Bliss or anybody else but Pine. She listened to me in silence and instinctively understood my trauma. She didn't say much afterwards either but cooked a nice meal for me: frozen fish, steamed buns, millet porridge and sweet potatoes. Food was the symbol of mother's love. I almost forgot the blood wind and flesh rain in the outside world when I enjoyed *niang*'s nice food.

My brother Main went to work every day. His workplace, a secondary school in Qingdao, like all the schools in China at the time, was having fervent revolution actions. There were no classes in the schools. All authority had collapsed. The teachers were asked not to get in the way but to follow orders from the students. The students and young staff from red families had formed rebellion teams and became the authority of the school, deciding what to do for everyday activities — mainly studying Chairman Mao's works, writing criticism big-character posters and holding meetings to condemn the staff who were not revolutionaries. Already nine out of thirty-odd staff in the school were condemned as 'reactionary elements' and were badly tortured. Main was nervous all the time as he was afraid he would be condemned sooner or later. Every evening my mother and I would anxiously wait for him to return home. However, a few weeks passed and Main was still one of the members of the revolutionaries, which was absurd and we couldn't really relax as we knew he could hardly escape ill fate as one of the black elements.

One day in December 1968, Main came home in the evening with black eyes and swollen cheeks. He had been condemned as an 'active reactionary' by the Red East Rebellion Teams, most of whose members came from Crab Village. They pulled him up to the 'great revolutionary platform' while hundreds of people shouted out, denouncing him and calling him names. After that he came home every day bearing bruises and scars.

Superb became an activist once she found out it was a perfect chance to ease her personal hatred. She went to the primary school where she had once been a relief teacher and organised a rebellion team. Using her sharp and elaborate verbal talent, she persuaded Aroma, a woman teacher of whom she was jealous, to be the leader of their rebellion team, and fought violently with their opponents. After many fights, she abruptly retreated and hid herself away, leaving Aroma alone to face the opposition. They tortured Aroma terribly, eventually driving her insane. Not long after this, Aroma slipped into a pond and drowned one rainy night, as she ran naked and yelling through the streets.

At his school the torture for Main was going on and on. Nobody knew where it would end and what would happen next in his life. The atmosphere in our place was devastating.

One day, Main was ordered by the revolutionaries to paint the walls of the school building. When he was walking down the stairs with a bucket full of whitewash on his shoulder, two students kicked him from the top of the stairs, laughing hysterically. He fell down the stairs, whitewash all over him. His skin was bruised and his face black and blue. With wet clothes, he did the brush job in the morning and took the condemn meeting in the afternoon. In the meeting he was smashed hard by the Red Guards. By the time he finished the day he was in an terrible state and he dared not go home to sadden Mother's heart. Instead, he went to Superb's house. She was not surprised to see him — she knew he would come to her one day. With great enthusiasm she offered him new clothes that she had prepared for him, and warm food and comforting words.

A couple of months later, Superb came to our house and told us that she was pregnant. She looked so pitiable and remorseful that both my mother and I were deeply moved. We immediately took her side, comforted her and supported her. But it was a crime at the time for a black element to make a girl from a red family pregnant outside marriage. Main could be tortured to death by the revolutionaries. He was cornered, since Superb wouldn't let him go. He had no other option but to marry her. Superb had achieved her aim. She chose to have an abortion first, and afterwards they got married.

Superb didn't show her satisfaction even though she had finally caught Main, a good-looking educated man from the city. After she became a member of our family, it soon became apparent that Superb was from a different world and we were a vast distance away in our understanding of life. She did not like books. 'Books,' she scoffed, 'are the worst stuff in the world. Writers are often wrong.' She didn't allow anybody in the family to buy any books or to do any reading. She decided that the Liu family (my mother, Main and I) was silly and bad while she was *lihai*, fierce and ruthless (a positive term in Chinese — surprise!). She acted haughty and self-important since she was from the leading class, a peasant family. She would say to us: 'I am the red umbrella over you, the black elements, so you must listen to me.' Her favourite motto was: 'The one who doesn't let me live, I will kill their whole family.'

She was actually terrified of being abandoned by Main, which was a trait inherited from her stepmother. Main was not only much more handsome than her, he also held a higher social status as a city resident. Although he was low during the Cultural Revolution, everyone knew it couldn't last forever. She took domestic life as a stage of battle and was determined to win. She controlled Main by pleasing and intimidating, using a tragic performance when other tricks failed. A tragic show was very powerful to soften hearts and she was a talented tragic actress, able to cry bitterly or smile sweetly anytime she liked. If necessary she would give a wonderful performance as a pitiable woman. Head hanging, forehead frowning, eyes half-closing, back curved, arms dropping limply, her whole figure looked weak and feeble. She uttered her laments with a moving and wailing sound, powerful enough to make anyone soften and melt.

She frightened my mother with her malevolence. But she liked my mother's money very much and, as soon as she took control of Mother's pension, she treated her as a house char and a babysitter. As for me, I was a grain of sand in her eyes, a target of deadly jealousy. There might be a smile on the face, but her fists and feet were never relaxed. Unfortunately I was too naïve to realise it. I regarded her as a family member and loved her as my clever and capable sister-in-law.

I began to realise her true nature when she took me to see her mother (after she was seventeen, she had no longer lived with her stepmother but came to live with her real parents at Crab Village). Her mother said, 'What a pretty girl. I've never seen anyone prettier than Weijun.'

'Don't talk like that, Mum. You'll make Weijun embarrassed,' said Superb, and at the same time her eyes glinted with jealousy. I felt a chill of apprehension down my spine although I didn't know exactly what it meant.

In feudalist Chinese society, women were considered inferior so they were trained to be humble, if only superficially. When these women confronted their enemies, they did not fight openly. Instead, they used deceiving ways. After Mao's superb example, to ruin your enemy was a common strategy.

The traditional ideas from Chinese culture encouraged family members of different generations to live in the same house. Fighting between in-laws, especially female in-laws, was commonplace and it could be very cruel and poisonous since the females had little chance to go out to the greater world but had to stay within the four high walls of the house. It was not surprising that they were depressed, upset and unhappy, which caused them to be unkind to others. To fight for their position — not to be abandoned by their husbands — was the main meaning of a female's life; and to achieve this, ruining others' lives was their priority.

A letter from Pine arrived informing me that his university time had finished and he was waiting for his job allocation. He invited me to Beijing and I happily accepted his invitation. What a happy time I had there with Pine. Every second was a honey-filled moment sweetening the thirsty field of my love-deprived heart. We dined at restaurants, visited the Forbidden City and walked around the Summer Palace. I sang romantic songs and he sobbed while he hugged me with tears in his eyes. I felt I was the happiest woman in the world. The third day when Pine and I were walking around his university campus, we met a group of his classmates and they cried out, 'How nice!' That evening they left the room for us and we stayed there alone and had an intimate time. We didn't make love but cuddled each other passionately.

On the fourth day, unfortunately, I had to leave because the money left in my pocket was only just enough for the train ticket back to Qingdao. We kissed sweetly and parted reluctantly. On the train journey to Qingdao, I was recalling every minute of the three happy days in Beijing with intoxication.

As I walked along the earth path to Crab Village, somehow my mood grew uneasy. A cold wind from Siberia was attacking Qingdao and the temperature dropped tremendously. Crows were crying miserably on the bare branches and the trees were shivering in the violent storm. The wind howled as violently as a wild animal. A few snowflakes were rolling in the cloudy sky and the frozen land was barren. There was nobody in sight: I was the only person on the road. The happy time with Pine seemed like a vague dream, while the dangerous situation of my family took an iron grip of my heart. I felt a terrible anticipation that something was wrong. I strode quickly and frantically, keen to see my mother and brother so that I could be sure they were safe.

Their small house at the edge of the village was getting nearer and nearer. I passed through the gate of the courtyard and turned to the left to the door of our southern house. To my surprise I saw a huge black lock on the door. Why this lock? Sometimes my mother would go shopping, leaving the door locked with a blue lock, but I had never seen this black lock. Dismayed, I went up to the window, which was at the roadside. Some children in the distance were looking at me strangely as if they were waiting to see something unusual happen. I pressed my face against the window and tried to see through. It was dark inside and for a while I could see nothing. Gradually my eyes got used to the dark, then I saw bare walls and bare ground. My eyes must be wrong, I was thinking. I stared harder, but still I couldn't see anything familiar. I shifted to the window of the bedroom but it was the same — all I could see were the bare walls and the bare ground, dusty and dirty. I stood there frozen, not knowing what to think or what to do. It was unbelievable that I had only left for four days and now my family had disappeared, evaporated. Where were they? Were they still alive?

I don't know how long I was standing there. Eventually I heard a child calling my name, saying, 'Superb wants to see you.'

In her parents' house, Superb was sitting on her *kang* (a kind of bed made of muddy bricks, commonly used in northern China). She smiled sweetly and said, 'I'll tell you what's happened to your family, but first of all let's get you warmed.' She helped me to take off my shoes, pulled me onto her *kang* and spread a quilt to cover my feet and legs. The *kang* was warm, as the stove attached to it had a roaring fire. With a honey voice she said: 'Your mother and brother were exiled by the Red Guards to Sunge Village two days ago.' Then she cried, 'Poor Main!' I burst out weeping and Superb caressed my hand gently. It made me feel better that I had someone sharing my ordeal.

The day became dark. Superb's parents were having supper in the kitchen. She fetched some food for me and urged me to eat some. After supper I felt a lot better. With the quilt covering our feet and legs, I felt very close to her and we chatted and chatted. I can't remember how it started but we ended up talking about sex. She vividly described the sex between her and Main, and she sounded so naïvely keen for knowledge which increased my eagerness to share with her what I knew about it. I answered all the questions she asked. She showed great interest in how Bliss and I had sex. At the time I didn't pay enough attention to the excited expression in her eyes: the excitement that was like a snake that had caught its game.

CHAPTER SEVEN

News came from Pine that he was allocated to a farm as a working hand in Jimo County, one hundred miles away from Qingdao. This was the kind of job for people who were not politically trusted by the government or the Party. The reason Pine got such a poor job was because his older brother had committed suicide shortly before Pine graduated, when his brother's relationship with his wife had deteriorated. I didn't mind that Pine had a humble physical job. Instead, I felt it lucky that his social status as a farm hand wouldn't be higher up than mine as a labourer in the Gobi Desert, and I rejoiced that we were equal on the social ladder, which meant that it might be easy to transfer my job to his farm after we got married and lived together. So I went together with him to his home village, Yuan Village in Ye County, four hundred miles away from Qingdao and there we went to the marriage registry office and got our marriage certificate. We didn't have any ceremony but I didn't mind. I loved him and that was all that mattered. We were staying with his parents in their house and spent the Chinese New Year of 1969 together. His parents' house was a greyish brick house with a spacious courtyard and patches of vegetable garden attached to it. I was one of the new wives in his village for the year. According to the local custom, all the new wives of the year were the stars of the village and they were visited by villagers during the time of Chinese New Year. The new wedding room, the bedding, the furniture and other bits of this and that were attentively observed, and of course the bride was closely scrutinized. Comments and gossip would be the major topic for the whole lunar January in all the households of the village about which woman was the prettiest, whose clothes cabinet was the most fashionable, and whose dowry was the best.

When the villagers came to visit me, they were surprised that I didn't have any new stuff. They asked me: 'How much money did your parents-in-law give you when you were engaged? How many suits of clothes did your husband offer you when you said yes to him?' The answer was none. Pine didn't have any money to give me and I didn't ask for any stuff or money from his parents. The villagers were very surprised when they heard my answer.

The old custom in China was that the woman's parents had to prepare a dowry, but the direction of the wind had changed since the 1960s. There were more unmarried men than women, especially in rural areas, and to get married could be very expensive for the men and their parents. The man's parents had to offer a house for their son to start with, and then there were other expenses, which was always a big burden for the old couple as well as the single man. It was still considered good luck to have a son but it brought worries for the family. It was the custom, especially in rural areas, that the man's parents should offer a considerable amount of money to their future daughter-in-law, as well as some assets according to the prevailing fashion. In the 1960s when I married Pine, the amount of money was at least two thousand *yuan*. The bride would use part of the money to provide new bedding and clothes, while the man and his family had to offer the house, the furniture and the fashionable assets which were at the time 'three wheels and one sound'. The three 'wheels' were a bicycle, a sewing machine (which had to be made in Shanghai) and a watch. The one 'sound' was a radio. And if the money and assets the woman asked for were not agreed to by the man and his parents, the woman would refuse to marry him. It was not unusual in rural China for men to be bachelors all their lives because their families could not afford the expense of marriage.

I was sure I had done the right thing when I knew more about the old couple's life. In their late sixties and late fifites respectively, Pine's father and mother went to the fields to work all year round. The pay for a man per day was twenty *fen* (two US cents) and for a woman ten *fen*. They must have used up their last drop of sweat in order to offer their son a tertiary education. To save lighting a match, the old woman would hold a bunch of dried grass to the neighbours' fire when she wanted to ignite her own. As sometimes the wind blew out the fire, she would wobble on her little bound feet, keeping on going to the neighbour's again and again, until her fire was set up. The quilt and cotton mats on their *kang* had been part of her dowry forty-four years ago. She offered some sugar to me which had been bought by her husband when she had her first baby forty-three years ago. She had given birth to nine children: only three survived. When she fell pregnant for the tenth time, she had given herself a barbaric abortion by prodding several bamboo sticks into her womb and scratched the foetus into bloody pieces. The murderous sticks were still in use for knitting socks.

Pine and I stayed in his parents' house for one week. How happy and peaceful I was. It was the life I wanted, simple but surrounded by my husband and family members. But the happy time was too short and one week later it was time for Pine to go to work on the farm and for me to visit my mother and brother in Changle. We set off together for a bus trip to Qingdao and decided to stay with Superb for a night, as we didn't have money to pay for a hotel or even a humble traveller's inn.

The sea was roaring fiercely in front of me, and so was Pine's voice. He had taken me to the rocks on Qingdao Beach near the pier. The red rocks at my feet looked as if they were bleeding and the pier was no longer elegantly pretty in Western style, more like a scary mysterious figure shaking in the violent wind in horror. A sole seagull was shivering in the wind on a cliff, as pathetic as I was. My soul was screaming and protesting at the same time and my body was trembling. I was too shocked to speak a word while Pine was outraged. Superb had told him what I'd told her about what had happened between Bliss and me. Pine was shouting angrily in my face: 'Bloody Bliss took your virginity instead of me! You're a damned fool to tell your sister-in-law about it, and you have made me lose face! My whole life has been ruined!' He hurt me: 'Superb calls you a *liumong*. You are a deadly true *liumong!*' (The Chinese term *liumong*, a very vicious and strong word, refers to morally bad people.)

It seemed I had dropped into a deep and complicated trap but didn't know why and how.

Virginity-taking was very important for a man in Chinese tradition. For many years it was the custom that a piece of white cloth would be put on the bed of the newly wedded. The next morning the cloth would be hung at the door high up to show the virginal blood on it and villagers would come to look at it. If there was no virginal blood on it, the family would be degraded and the woman in disgrace. Sometimes she might be thrown out of the house and, if her parents didn't tolerate her, death would be the only option for the poor young woman.

Pine abandoned me in a huff, and I was left penniless to face my future life. After lots of struggling I managed to borrow a few *yuan* from a friend and took the train to Changle.

I hadn't been back to Changle since I left the place when I was a little girl. Walking along the country road, I found the place poor and backward. The villagers were standing in the narrow paths of their villages, wearing black square jackets and absurd white trousers, which were dirty and had become grey-coloured. Their clothes were made of hand-woven fabric; thick, stiff and coarse. Their dirty faces and hair showed that they hadn't had a good wash for ages. The road was rough and primitive, without any form of public transport, and it took me many minutes to walk after I got off the train at Changle railway station.

At the end of Sunge Village I stopped a man and asked him to show me my mother's place. When he did, I couldn't believe my eyes. In the bare field, far from other houses, was a tiny broken shack. It was so small that you could mistake it for a privy. The thatched roof was old and broken, the reeds on the roof were flipping in the wind, and the mud walls were covered with holes. The door, woven from tree branches, was only half a person's height. The whole thing was like a wrecked boat in a fierce sea, skaking and rocking as if the storm was going to blow it away at any moment.

I touched the shabby door open and stepped in. I was wobbling since the ground was a foot lower than the door frame. The earth floor inside was wet and icy from snow coming through the hole in the roof and the paper covering the window-hole was torn. There was barely any furniture apart from a makeshift bed and a mud stove. On the edge of the stove were a couple of cooking and eating utensils. That was all there was in the house. My mother's pension had been confiscated and my brother's job lost, so they were in dire poverty. The villagers had lent them a few kilograms of dried sweet potatoes, but that was all they had.

I took out the wheat-flour buns my mother-in-law had given me and put them on the bed. My mother hurriedly covered them with an old face cloth. 'Villagers could pay a visit at any time and there aren't enough for them,' she warned me. No sooner had she spoken than a visitor came, a teenage girl, thin-faced, wearing a black baggy garment. Her hair was thin and grassy from malnutrition. She touched the old cloth and saw the buns and her eyes widened. 'Well, white buns! Mum has promised to make white buns for me for my wedding,' she exclaimed in hopeful tones.

From his pocket my brother took out an envelope, and from it he removed a small pile of banknotes plus a letter and handed them to me. 'These came from Bliss a few days ago,' he said. I read the letter:

> Weijun, I wrote to No. 14 Team and the head of your camp answered that you had left without a permit. You must come back as soon as possible otherwise I will go to Shandong until I find you . . . I am sending you one hundred and fifty *yuan* to help you. Come back for me soon. You must learn to be an obedient and good woman . . .

My mother's shed was too small to hold three people. I knew I had to go back to the Gobi Desert, which was the only place for me to survive if I wanted to support my mother and brother as well as myself. With great pain, I realised I could not rely on Pine, even though he was my husband and I was still in love with him. I was grateful to Bliss for sending me the money. It would have been impossible for me to find money for the train ticket to Ulumugi otherwise.

Heartbroken, I said goodbye to my poor mother and brother and put eighty *yuan* into his palm. Main and Mother tried not to accept the money. 'You will take a long-distance trip and you will need money on the way. Please take it with you,' they said.

'Seventy *yuan* is enough for me. The train ticket is only fifty-odd *yuan* and I still have more than ten *yuan* to spend on the way, and when I arrive in the Gobi Desert I will receive my wages.' I urged them to accept the money and stepped out of the shack and quickly walked away. When I had walked a few yards, I looked back and saw my mother and my brother, standing in front of the shack in the high wind, waving to me. Their thin figures were shivering like dried leaves in the wind. Tears poured from my eyes. I dried them with my hands and turned to the unknown future.

In the town of Changle, I saw a long queue of people who were waiting to buy something. In those days queues were common and for virtually anything you wanted to buy you had to wait in a queue. Everybody would automatically join in a queue whenever there was one. There was a joke that someone saw a queue and joined it only to find it was a coffin for sale. Anyway I joined the queue, standing for half an hour, and bought my ration, twenty pieces of fruit sweet. I was very happy, and I thought of Pine. Yes, I should visit him and give him the precious sweets. Despite what he'd done to me, I was still in love with him and I wanted to see him before I left for the far northwest. So I took the bus as far as I could, and then excitedly walked the rest of the way to his farm.

Pine and his colleagues were digging up the land when I waved to him. When he saw me, his face turned dark. He threw down his tool and walked hastily to me. 'Why do you come here without telling me?' he said angrily. 'I haven't told anybody I'm married. What a silly woman you are!' He tilted his head to one side, indicating that I should follow him and we came into his dormitory where there were two rows of long boards serving as beds. As soon as we were inside, he asked: 'What the hell did you come for?' I took out the sweets I'd wrapped in a handkerchief and said pensively: 'I am leaving for Xinjiang. I've brought these for you.' He fiddled the sweets in his fingers and grunted, 'How could I dare to eat your things? They might be poisoned. Bliss and you might try to murder me.'

I wanted to shout back to him, 'How mean you are!' but I didn't. We were to be separated by a long distance and I had no idea what would happen in my life ahead, nor did I know if I would ever see him again. I didn't want to ruin the last moment with my only love. I managed a smile at him.

He looked at me, thought for a while, and then he said: 'Stay for the night. I will go to the boss and ask for a half-day off.'

We went to a small village nearby a few minutes later, where we stayed for the night in a holiday inn. In the morning after seeing him walk back towards his farm, I set off to the railway station.

The train ticket to Xinjing was fifty-three *yuan*, a huge amount for me since all I had in the world was less than seventy *yuan* to support me for the food on the five-day trip in the train and my everyday expenses in the

Gobi Desert before the monthly payday was due. In order to save a bit of money I decided to take a risk — to not buy a ticket, but to get on the train with a platform ticket, which was only five *fen*.

A day later I was wobbling along the railway with the quilt on my back and the travelling bag in my hand; on my shoulder I carried my handbag. I had hidden in the toilet and waited until the train halted at a deserted small stop. I came out of the toilet window while the conductor was checking tickets. If he had caught me I would have been taken away for punishment and I would also have had to buy a full-price ticket.

My legs and back were aching from the bump when I landed on the ground, but I had to walk fast to avoid the railway police and try to find the exit from the station. In the darkness of the night I walked and walked; the parcels and the bags became so heavy and I was exhausted. To save a little energy, I walked along the tracks with slow steps. Then I heard the siren of a train coming towards me, its bright headlight blinding me. I had no time to hesitate. I threw the parcel and bags with all my might to the side and I jumped. I was just off the tracks when the train thundered past, death beneath the wheels only a few seconds away.

With a thumping heart and exhausted body, I continued to walk for another two hundred metres or so until the station fence ran out and at last I was outside the fence. Then I tumbled back along the fence and reached the station again. Here I bought another platform ticket for five *fen* and had another try. After much danger and risk, eight days later I managed to arrive in Ulumuqi.

With a broken heart and terrible embarrassment I returned to No. 14 Team in the Gobi Desert in March 1969. The angry team head let me stay in a newly built cave which was still wet. I tried not to think about my humiliating elopement, but the smell of the damp cave made me nauseous. I realised I was pregnant.

I was in desperate poverty. I didn't have a bed. I didn't have a mat to sleep on. I didn't have a pillow. All I had was a thin quilt, the winter clothes I wore, and an old padded coat covered with numerous mending patches that I had got from Pine's parents. I did have a toothbrush and a face cloth, but that was all. For several nights I had to lie on the ground in the cave. The quilt was too thin to keep me warm; I kept waking up, sighing and sobbing.

Fortunately my friend Blossom saw my desperate situation and she returned the quilts that I had sold to her, free. She also gave me back the wooden stool, the bowl and the spoon I'd left with her family. Before that I'd had to use my fingers to hold the bun, and without a bowl I hadn't been able to have any dishes for days.

Not everybody was as kind as Blossom. When I failed to get my bed-board back from One-eye I begged the head of the team and his five assistants again and again for a bed-board but the answer was always 'no', and I was laughed at as 'the beggar of the bed-board'. After days of sleeping on straw on the bare damp ground my back was just about to break, but a good surprise came. A young man came up to my cave, stood on top of my cave door and held a whole piece of bed-board. I was bewildered. Of course he couldn't give me such a precious asset. Any wooden material was invaluable in the Gobi Desert — many families didn't even have a table. He said, 'I'm leaving for another team and I know you don't have a bed. I leave this to you.' He handed the bed-board to me and left, not even waiting for me to say thanks. I said many, many thanks to him in my heart. My eyes brimmed with tears and deep gratitude filled my heart. A piece of bed-board was worth much more than any appliance in today's modern life. It was simply a basic living necessity. I was sorry I had nothing to show my gratitude to him, but he probably already knew that. Life was beautiful after all.

I had sweet sleep after that.

Soon after I returned to the Gobi Desert, I was lucky to receive seven months' wages piled up from the past. Our wages were often postponed due to the low productive income of the Corps. It was common in those days that we didn't get paid in time. This time we got paid seven months' wages from the last two years, which came to 288.75 *yuan* altogether. I immediately went to the post office in Caijiahu, the headquarters of No. 103 Regiment, and posted two hundred and sixty *yuan* to my mother and brother and then bought myself a padded cotton mat and a small cane chest, the most needed things in my life. I was happy I could manage to live now. I was even happier that I could have money to send to my mother and brother. I wanted to relieve their hard lives. No matter how difficult it was, I would bear it.

Time was dragging along with my belly growing bigger and bigger. I went to the fields to work for my future baby and myself. I could feel my baby kicking inside me, although it brought only sadness to my heart. I had written to Pine about the pregnancy but he was annoyed and replied that he couldn't provide any support.

I wrote to Bliss informing him I had officially married another man and was going to have his baby. This enraged him. He wrote heaps of letters, putting the address as 'No. 14 Team'. You can imagine how these letters became malicious advertisements of me and everyone was talking about them behind my back. I became the condemned 'broken shoe', a woman of depravity. I could feel I was treated badly by my colleagues but didn't know why until one day a small loud-mouthed woman came up to me and told me. I had just made her a shirt and a pair of trousers for free. Seeing me wobbling along the cave on the bare ground with my big belly, she took my arm and whispered in my ear, 'I want to tell you something secret but you must promise not to tell anybody that I told it to you.' Seeing her serious face, I realised it was bad news. My heart pounded. Still, I said, 'I promise.'

'Your man in Shihezi has written to our team and curses you — a lot of letters! The women's group is organising a denouncing meeting for you.'

I was shocked into a zombie-like state. For days and nights I was extremely anxious while I waited for the meeting. It seemed my nerves were going to snap any time. Lying in the dark at night, I tossed over and again while my baby kicked restlessly inside my body. I didn't know whether or not my baby and I could survive the ordeal.

The next Sunday was a rainy day and we didn't go to the field. Instead, everyone came to the cave I was staying in, one by one, until more than thirty women filled the whole room, making it difficult to breathe. I was made to stand in the middle of the crowd with the others sitting tightly around me. The woman head announced it was going to be a denouncing meeting to condemn me, a black element from a black family who did bad things when running away from the Gobi Desert. Malicious words as sharp as knives were thrown by the women around me; fingers pointed on my forehead, saliva shot onto my face, and I was like a trapped mouse, frightened and flustered. Only ten minutes after the meeting started, I was already feeling unwell. My breath was short, my heart was thumping.

My baby was jumping inside me. I could no longer hear what they were shouting. I felt I was pushed into a deep well, stifled. Darkness was all around me . . . Suddenly a man's voice came quietly from seemingly a distance away, startling me. It was Loyal Su, the deputy head of our team. In a kind and soft voice, he said, 'Comrade Weijun's personal problem is not the main business of our revolutionary goal. Let's follow Chairman Mao's teaching and focus on the big direction.' The iron mouths shut up. I was rescued from the drowning water. The atmosphere in the room lightened and the feverish women sighed disappointedly.

Loyal Su was from a revolutionary family. His brother was the Political Director of No. 103 Regiment, a powerful position in those class-ridden years. Mr Su used his privileged background to protect me and nobody dared to challenge him. I will never forget the relief he brought me.

Of the 41.25 *yuan* I got every month, I posted twenty *yuan* to my mother and brother straight away; ten *yuan* was for my monthly food, and the last ten *yuan* I saved for the trip to my mother's when I gave birth to the baby.

Summer came without summer clothes for me. I took the padded cotton out of the winter clothes and altered them into a summer blouse and a pair of trousers. In the daytime I wore them; during the evening I washed them while wearing underpants. The brown-coloured opium sap was difficult to wash off and I would wear my trousers inside out, with the two pockets dangling up and the seam of fabric edge showing.

The growing baby in my belly made me perpetually hungry. I missed food, especially fruit. Fragrant crunchy apples and sweet juicy water-melons appeared in my dreams. I was eating watermelon, concentrating my entire heart and soul on the pleasure of it. The watermelon was so delicious that I murmured happily, and the sound woke me up, leaving me to face the reality that there was no watermelon at all. The feeling of craving and hunger was so strong that I was almost driven crazy.

However, there was one meal during my pregnancy that was unforgettable.

In order to earn some free food, I did odd jobs for others in my spare time. One day I knitted a fishing net for a colleague named Three-fire. I was good at handcraft; still, it took me several evenings to finish it. Three-fire used the net and caught a couple of carp in the channel. To thank me, he invited me to his place for supper but I hesitated. A few days before, I had had an unpleasant confrontation with his wife when many women were in a queue waiting for the shop assistant to throw us some spare cardboard boxes. When the last one came, the shop assistant threw it to me although it was the turn for Three-fire's wife in the queue. The shop assistant gave the box to me because I had spent lots of time and knitted jumpers for her daughter, and the cardboard box was a handy way for her to thank me. Of course it was unfair to Three-fire's wife, so she was furious. She cursed both the shop assistant and me severely. 'I fuck your mother! You are a bastard! I have waited half an hour for the box — it should be mine!'

I understood her. A cardboard box was very useful — you could use it to hold your cornflour; you could use it to store your off-season clothes; you could make it a dining-table with some mud-bricks for supports.

Still, I couldn't resist the temptation of food. Although I had already eaten a quarter-kilo bun and some cooked marrows I was still terribly hungry. Afraid of seeing his sharp-tongued wife, I might have said no if my tummy hadn't been as empty as a hollow bag and the craving for food hadn't been a restless hot desire. I didn't hesitate for long before I eagerly followed Three-fire to his cave.

The smell that was wafting out was the most delicious in the world. Three-fire's sulky wife was putting a big bowl of noodles and a steamed bun onto the makeshift table as well as the fish. I sat down and forgot all the unpleasant things in the world and ate like a hungry wolf: two big buns, one big bowl of noodles and some fish, about one and a quarter kilograms of food altogether. It was months since I'd felt so contently full and I didn't feel hungry for days after the hearty meal.

The only time we had apples when I was in No. 14 Team was when I was about five-and-a-half-months pregnant. Almost everyone bought some. The apples were frozen hard when they were transported from the town to our camp, but the Gobi people knew how to deal with frozen apples. They put them into a bucket of cold water and soon a layer of ice mould formed around them. They broke up the ice mould and the apple skin was revealed. They peeled off the saggy skin, exposing the flesh of the apple which was mushy and yellowish, like cooked apples. Almost everyone in the team was happily eating the delicious apples but me. I could not spend my precious money on them and I preferred to help my mother and brother out of the shack.

The opium field was silver in the moonlight. The ripe opium poppies were standing in the dark, nodding and shaking in the wind like naughty goblins. I crept into the fields and broken the poppies from the stem, crashed them open one by one and poured the seeds into my palm. When they had made a small pile in my palm I threw my head back and swallowed them in satisfaction. I came to do this stealing whenever I was driven manic by hunger. The opium seeds were, like any seeds, full of nutrition and my baby was growing rapidly in my womb.

After the sixth month of my pregnancy, with other pregnant women, I was allowed to work at light physical jobs. In the small patches of vegetable garden, we picked up tomatoes, peppers, carrots and beans, so I had a chance to steal some to eat. These were the precious vegetables we were allowed only to grow in small quantities as water was scarce and expensive. In the open square, we scratched seeds from the sunflowers. Sunflowers seeds were the main resource of oil in northwest China, and we grew them in bulk. For the entire time when I peeled the seeds, I would take any chance I could to put handfuls of them into my pockets. They would be the only present I could afford for my mother and my brother as thanks for them letting me stay while I gave birth.

My plan was ruined just before I was going to take the trip for the birth when I was seven and a half months pregnant. Bad news came and I was not allowed to leave. The authority of Xinjiang province gave orders to all: there was going to be a war against Russia and nobody was allowed to leave Xinjiang. I was devastated by the news. To give birth in the Gobi Desert without a family, without any equipment, without even a cot for my baby, was an extremely frightening prospect.

I waited for days in anxiety until an ox-cart was available. Climbing up onto it with difficulty, I sat on the hard surface of the cart awkwardly with my big belly and rode three and half hours along the bumpy earth path. Finally I arrived at Caijiahu, the headquarters of No. 103 Regiment.

After asking several people amongst the mud houses, I finally arrived at the door of the head of No. 103 Regiment, Mr Chang, the Secretariat of the Regiment Committee of the Party. I pushed his door open and found that he and his family were having lunch. He was not happy to see me in his lunch time at home but I didn't mind. I had to save myself with my baby. I waited in silence for him to finish lunch. Finally his family disappeared to another room and Mr Chang was ready to talk to me. Carefully arranging my language and tone, I begged him to give me permission to go back to my home town for my labour.

'No, nobody should leave Xinjiang. Everybody must stay where they are,' he spoke in a perfect Mandarin accent. 'It is the supreme command from our Deputy Chairman Lin Biao. You'd better go back to your team and be ready for both of the tasks: take part in the war activities and give birth to a child. Both are glorious.'

'I have nothing prepared to give birth here. Where will the baby sleep? I don't have a cot or a blanket for my baby. What will I eat? I have no nutritious food saved. I don't even have one piece of napkin!' From this point, I was no long able to control myself. Suddenly, I burst into tears and for a moment I was embarrassed and frightened. How dare I cry in front of Mr Chang, a high-ranked and powerful man? I held up for a second or so, then, realising I shouldn't be ashamed, I let my tears flow down, down, like blood running out from a wound.

For weeks after the failed plea, I was devastated. Worry, stress and anxiety attacked me ruthlessly. During sleepless nights, I got up and in the dim light of the oil lamp, I tried to sew a few items for my baby. I made a little quilt, a suit of padded clothes and a little pillow filled with fine sand. I was told that this kind of fine sand from the Gobi Desert was unique and was good to help a baby sleep; but this was all I could afford. I still didn't know how I could get a cot to put my baby in. Even if I had a cot, where the hell could I find enough bedding to keep my baby warm in the frozen Xinjiang winter? More frightening was to give birth without any family with me. I did not know how I could manage it. For many days, I could do nothing but wait for terrible death. A frightening story often came into my mind, a true story that had happened in our camp not long before.

A woman started her labour on a cold day in April. The only nurse for the camp found that the baby was in the wrong position: his little penis was appearing first! The nurse managed to ring the hospital in Caijiahu after much effort as we only had an old wired telephone in the camp. However, the doctors in the hospital couldn't come over as it was snow-melt season and no vehicle could cope with the slippery and muddy road. The woman was crying in great agony; the husband was worrying to death. At last, the husband and one of the strong men in our team took action: each pulled up one of the woman's legs with all their strength, even though the mother screamed horribly. The nurse put both of her hands into the mother and dragged the baby out. The tiny ruined boy died two days later.

War didn't break out and my crying worked. Three weeks before my due time, I was allowed to leave. I waited in anxiety for a possible way to travel from the camp to the railway station in Ulumuqi. I even considered walking if I had to. At last a truck came to No. 14 Team to pick up the wife of the head of our team's Party branch, and I begged them to let me have a ride. She was going to her home town in Hebei province to visit her parents. The truck was driven by a previous army comrade of her husband, who came to our camp the night before for the purpose. I wondered maybe if it was her case that had helped me to get the leaving permission. Anyway, I felt extremely lucky that I had the ride in the truck. Normally, there were hardly any trucks or any other vehicles coming in winter since there was nothing to carry back.

On a cold day in November 1969, carrying my travel bag, I climbed onto the open back of the truck. On the journey I was sitting on the top of the truck, frozen to the point of fainting. The worse thing was the bumps. The truck was running so fast that it would throw me high up to the air and I felt as if my belly was going to separate from me.

I know now that when you are in the late stages of pregnancy, you can carry only light weights without risk of miscarriage. But nobody told me this when I was pregnant. I carried a big bag full of heavy things. Apart from the baby's quilt, padded suit and sandy pillow, there were a kilo of dried chillies that my brother had posted to me and at least five kilos of sunflower seeds. Carrying this heavy bag, I got on and off the truck for meals before we arrived in Ulumuqi. After I arrived at the railway station, I carried the heavy bag, waiting in the long queue to buy my train ticket; then I shoved in to get on the train, got off the train and got on another train; after the train journey of four nights and five days, I suffered through a long-distance bus trip; after the bus I walked for more than two hours before finally I arrived at my mother's place.

My mother and brother had bought a small peasant house with the money I had sent to them. It was a narrow mud hut divided into three cabinets by mud bricks. A small courtyard in front of the house contained a pigsty and a pair of millstones. Poor as it sounds, it was a proper house and was much better than their previous shack. Superb was five months pregnant at the time but she was still staying at Crab Village, and Main would visit Crab Village every now and then.

I helped my mother to push the millstones round and round to mill the dried sweet potatoes into flour. Dried sweet potatoes were the only food they had all year round. Dried grass, sweet-potato stems and the poorest coal thrown away by a nearby coal mine as rubbish was all the fuel they had. We had two cold meals a day to save the fuel. During the winter I was there, Main got up early in the morning every day; pushing the wheelbarrow, he went to Changle railway station thirty miles away. He waited patiently with his village friends at the side of the railway to collect coal dust from the chimney smoke of passing trains. Every time a train passed, groups of young men and women would run to where the earth was covered by dark dust. They swept the dust in piles and then they would wait another one hour or so for the next train. The coal dust could barely burn but produced a tiny little flame. When I was in labour, Main stood at the mud stove for hours to make sure there would be a kettle of boiling water to bathe the baby.

One day I went to the end of the village to visit my relatives: my older stepbrother's wife Cloud, their two daughters and his aged mother. The three generations of four women lived in a shed no larger than the space of three single beds. The door of their shed was made of dried grass and old newspapers, flapping and flipping in the wind. Apart from the mud *kang* and the mud stove, the space for them to move around was as small as half a square metre. The old lady, in her late seventies, back bent, thin grey hair unkempt, curled herself at the corner of the shed, using a pestle and a mortar to grind a few sesame seeds. Her old and fragile body moved up and down strenuously, she tried to express a few drops of sesame oil to add a bit of flavour to her dried potato soup. Seeing me, she looked up from the corner and smiled shyly and pitifully as if she was embarrassed for being greedy to desire for a few drops of sesame oil. It was heartbreaking.

A couple of weeks before I went into labour, Pine arrived from his farm. He talked rudely to me. One day he said, 'Who knows if this child is mine? It could be anybody's.' Hearing this, I was hurt, and in a terrible fit I threw myself on the ground, crying, 'Please, don't be so cruel to me! It is your baby!'

My midwife was an old woman in her late seventies. She had a pair of rubber gloves, a pair of scissors and a piece of plastic sheet. That was all. She sat on the edge of the *kang*, gloved hands held up, legs crossed, waiting for the baby to come. Lunch time came and my mother cooked some *jiaozi* (minced pork and vegetable filled dumplings, a festival meal). The aged midwife took the gloves off and heartily ate two big bowls of them and then put the gloves on again, and waited. Dinner time came and she took off the gloves, eating more *jiaozi*, and putting on the gloves again.

The whole process of my labour was tedious and horrendous. Knowing how dangerous it could be, my mother was walking to and fro inside and outside, crying to the stormy snowing sky in despair when I screamed with pain on the mud *kang* in the gloomy impoverished room. She bought two pieces of incense from a small shop in the village, which was extravagant considering she didn't have any income. Burning the incense on the ground, she knelt down and prayed. Never a religious person in her life, now she was calling God desperately.

There were no qualified doctors nearby. The nearest hospital was twenty-five miles away and the road from the village was only a little path just wide enough for a wheelbarrow to pass. If anything went wrong it could be fatal. In this area, for years, one out three babies died during childbirth and one out of ten mothers died during labour.

My waters broke in the late evening, nearly twenty-four hours after the contractions had started. My mother asked Pine to get onto the *kang* and hold me from behind. I felt a rare feeling of warmth and it made me happy and relaxed. I pushed hard and I could hear Pine was unconsciously making the pushing sound, too. 'What's the use of *your* push? The baby is in my belly.' I was laughing to myself between contractions.

Luckily, I had no knowledge about childbirth. I was absolutely naïve — ignorance is bliss and it made me bold, with no fear. I was in pain but not scared; I was suffering but not stressed. The labour was slow but I thought that was natural and normal. My bold and innocent spirit was my blessing and helped me come through the ordeal. My baby daughter Enya arrived safely.

There were many strange customs for post-natal mothers in the rural areas of China. You were not allowed to have fish, chicken, pork or beef because the meat was cross-lined and it would stop the breast milk flow. You were not allowed to have fruit or vegetables because they were cold and would upset your stomach. You were not allowed to have any salty food because you would have brown marks left on your face. You had to stay in bed for a whole month for a thorough rest, which is called 'sitting away the month'. It was a hellish time, really. I felt my bones go all soggy and painful and I could hardly walk after the month confined in bed, eating only bland noodles and eggs.

You might wonder how I could have noodles and eggs, the really luxury foods, to eat. It is another heartbreaking story, which is so sad that I am reluctant to tell it.

Living in the area during the Japanese war, to provide the family clothes, my mother, a highly-educated academic, had to learn to make cotton into thread on a primitive machine. She made cotton into thread, and sold it to buy fabric. Nobody ever thought the skill my mother learned in the wartime could be useful again. No wonder we have the sayings 'Think about the umbrella when the weather is dry', and 'Master as many skills as you can and they will never burden you.' To earn a few *yuan* for my post-natal nutrition, my mother, who was doing manual work under the watch of the peasants in the daytime, did the weaving at night, and ten days' labour could get her two *yuan* (fifty US cents). To save oil, she did the weaving in the doorway where there was moonlight. Often I was awake at midnight and heard mother's machine humming away. In those days my old mother's eyes were perpetually red for lack of sleep.

Pine left me the day after our baby was born. It was nearly the New Year time and his workplace would provide festival meals, so he said he had to go for the good food. I experienced terrible baby blues after he left me with nothing except two rolls of toilet paper and two cabbages.

Enya was a beautiful healthy baby but I was too poor to feed her. I didn't have enough breast milk and I didn't have money to buy milk or milk powder. When I woke up at night and found there were only a few matches in the box, tears flowed uncontrollably. Matches were rationed and one household could get only one box of matches every month. It was hardly enough for lighting the cooking fire and the oil lamp. I learned to feed my baby and change her in blind darkness. Without milk or milk powder, I fed her flour starch. For every feeding time, I set up a fire burning dried grass, between two bricks on the ground beside the *kang*, to warm her food. The whole process would last one hour and by the time the baby was fed and sleep, I looked at her lovely tiny face and wept.

When Enya was one month old, I took her to her paternal grand-parents' place. Thank God they were comparatively better off and they gave me some money to help me buy a nanny-goat to supply Enya with milk.

I dared not bring Enya to the Gobi Desert. The harsh conditions, the lack of nutrition and the long winter without sufficient sunshine were a mighty killer for babies, young children and old people. There were some babies born blind. Many developed leukemia and died. Some got lost in the huge empty desert and died; almost all the babies got cartilage disease — their bones were weak and they could not stand up even when they were three years old. Most of the parents tried their best to leave their babies in the care of their grandparents in inland China. I pleaded with my in-laws to look after Enya and was thrilled that they were happy to do it, with me sending them twenty *yuan* every month to help them manage.

CHAPTER EIGHT

At Chinese New Year of 1970, Pine came to spend the holiday time with the family at his parents' place. Excitedly he told us he'd got a new job in a factory in Beijing. 'I will work in the big city, live in high buildings, go up and down stairs!' he announced to his parents and me. 'You are earthy commoners, I am higher up than you all!' He showed his haughty side when his father held a milk pot above the meal table: 'Don't you know hygiene?' He then told us, 'I have a stupid classmate who exchanged his job in Beijing with a classmate in Jiangxi only because his wife works in the poor place.' I felt bitterly sad. How much I wished he would be like his 'stupid classmate' and be willing to have a job in Xinjiang.

Festival fireworks were cracking in the air but the sound was like hundreds of pieces of debris striking my heart. I had become ever more inferior than Pine now that he had a job in Beijing. It would be impossible for me to shift my work to Beijing, and he would never think about working in Xinjiang. We were to live in different places, he in Beijing and me in the Gobi Desert, and meet for 15 days once a year, according to the government regulations. There were tens of thousands of couples in China leading a life like this, which was called *liang di feng ju* — a married couple living in two places, or 'marriage of separation'. And if there were children involved, they either lived with one of the parents or were looked after by relatives. By the time Pine and I divorced, I had lived like this for five years, and during the entire time of our marriage we stayed together for no more than two months.

On the New Year's Eve, he disappeared after dinner without telling me anything. I waited and waited for hours. I stayed up in the dark room since the lamp was turned off after dinner to save oil, and it was cold since there was no stove in the whole house; the only heat was from the kitchen when meals were cooked. I sat on the *kang*, sad and lonely and worried. Three hours later he returned. Excitedly he exclaimed, 'What a good movie, with battles!'

'Why didn't you tell me where you were going? I was worrying where you were,' I said, trying to be as gentle as I could.

He jumped up and shouted at me. His voice was a howl, his face hot, startling me as if a firecracker had exploded in my face. 'Why do I need to tell bloody you? You don't deserve it, a bloody physical labourer,' he sneered at me.

His parents heard his shouting and hurriedly ran to our room. 'Don't shout so loudly. It is New Year's Eve. Aren't you afraid of others laughing at us?' said his father.

'This is my own business and I am teaching my *lao po* (wife). I don't want you to give me lectures!' he snapped at the old man. Anger made me dizzy. My teeth were biting and making clicking sounds, my heart racing, my legs shivering and my whole body trembling. I pressed my body tightly against the wall to stay standing.

His father lamented: 'If you were not our son, I would not lecture you even if you begged me.' The old man sighed heavily and continued: 'I would beat your bloody bottom if you were not a husband!' Beating up your children was considered not only natural but necessary and was universally accepted. Every child, especially a son, grew up with his father's kicks and blows, but this kind of abuse would stop abruptly after the son married, since he was then the master of his wife and children. There was the saying *dang mian jiao zi, bei hou jiao qi*, lecturing your children in front of others (to show you are a strict, therefore a good, father), and lecturing your wife behind. Such was the domestic hierarchy.

Pine became scared at his father's words and suddenly threw himself onto the *kang* on his belly. 'She is no good for me, no good for me!' he wailed. His parents watched him weeping silently and then left Pine and me in the room alone. He was still spread on his front on the *kang*, sobbing. He looked so pitiful. I felt very guilty. I was no good for him.

When Enya was three months old her grandparents and I had a fancy ceremony for her, which was called *guo bai sui* — One Hundred Days Celebration. The day before Enya was one hundred days old, Granny made dough out of five kilograms of wheat flour. The dough was made to be as hard as possible by using only a little bit of water in it. With various wooden moulders, she made all sorts of fairy-tale shapes — flowers, birds, fish, butterflies, dragonflies, chubby babies and so on — and then she baked them in the big wok over a very low fire for hours until they became cooked and solid. Granny used some special dye — bright green, fresh yellow, glittering red — to make the bread colourful. The next day baby Enya was dressed in a new yellow cap, red jacket and green trousers. Her little face was pink and white, as pretty as a spring rose. A round willow basket was covered with a piece of new scarlet cloth and books, buns, thread and needles were placed in it. Grandpa held the baby and let her jump on it three times, so her life would become prosperous, intelligent, affluent with food, and hardworking. Pine's nephew Health, a young lad living with Pine's parents, tied a long string of hundreds of red-skinned firecrackers to the end of a long bamboo pole and set light to them. Cracking sounds broke out like beans jumping on a metal plate. Villagers were summoned up. Young and old, men and women, all hustled over and gathered outside our courtyard, waiting. Baby Enya was carried by Grandpa who stood on top of the courtyard wall on a ladder. On another ladder, our young nephew Health climbed up to the top of the courtyard wall, settling down himself, and chanted:

West gods bless Baby tall and strong;
East sun blesses Baby healthy and fun;
South winds bless Baby kind and pretty;
North clouds bless Baby living long.

After each line, the crowd chanted it in unison to a nice tune. Grandpa was down and up the ladder again, holding a big round wicker hamper with the fancy bread. Helped by Health, he threw the pieces of bread into the air and they danced and flew like colorful drops of rain into the hands of the watchers. Everybody chanted *Chang ming bai sui, chang ming bai sui,* may your baby live to one hundred years. Afterwards relatives came and presented crabs and garlic, which in the area were considered to offer blessings of longevity. The garlic and crabs were plaited into a long rope by a special kind of seaweed. Some of the crabs were still alive and were trying to crawl along the seaweed.

The next day I wept and the baby cried, as if she knew Mum was leaving for the Gobi Desert.

I took the train via Beijing to Ulumuqi. I stayed in Beijing with Pine for three days. He treated me like rubbish, and criticised me all the time. Putting his hands into my travel bag, he took out a package of imitation lotus root starch, food for Enya before the nanny-goat was bought. 'Why not let me drink it?' He put it under his arm, yanked his hand again into the travel bag and took out the garlic. 'Oh, garlic, I like garlic,' and he stuffed them into his pockets until my bag was empty. My heart sank, not only because this was precious food in my poor Gobi Desert life, but also because it showed his lack of love for me, grabbing the desperately needed food from me while he had never spent even one cent on me or on our baby.

We walked in the streets of Beijing to the railway station. Seeing I was watching a woman in a checked red and black jacket, he sneered, 'Do you like that kind of jacket? Do you want me to buy one for you? Kneel down in front of me and I will buy it for you.' I formed a bitter smile. In the waiting hall of the railway station, amongst the crowds, he kicked me hard with his leather boots. In the train, he poked his finger to my nose and jeered, 'You bloody woman, born to be bullied!' And he left me without saying goodbye.

Back in the Gobi Desert I searched my mind, exhausted, trying to find ways to change myself in response to Pine's criticism. I supposed he liked a wife with few words; I retrained myself not to talk. He disliked the way I walked; I tried to walk differently by minding every step carefully. I converted myself from a left-handed person to right, and for months I became the slowest eater and often didn't have enough time to finish my meal. I was criticised as 'stupid', but how to become a clever person I had no idea; as far as being born to be bullied, he might be right. I was too soft and too trusting, but it would take me many years before I learned how to deal with bullies. I was confused and unhappy about myself and tried to be a different person. I hoped I would make Pine happy next time. And how hard I worked to make presents for him.

There was a shop in our camp but the goods were scarce. Every time when the cattle-cart arrived from Caijiahu, we all crowded in the shop, fighting and shoving in front of the counter. Fired up by love, I fought like crazy. 'I need material, I need material!' I shouted, pushing hard with all my might. I was going to make ten presents for Pine, all with my own hands. I knitted him a woollen vest and a scarf; I bought some camel wool from a nomadic Kazakh and twisted the wool into thread, inch by inch, and then knitted two pairs of especially warm socks; I wove a cute green deer with plastic thread as a key-ring decoration; I made a cover for his bike seat, black outside and red as the lining; I sewed a pair of trousers for him; I made a pair of shoe mats with a coloured pattern; a white wallet with red linen; a carrying bag knitted up by plastic. Thinking how happy Pine would be when I showed him the ten presents, I smiled from the bottom of my heart. I sat on a little stool, bending my head, focusing on my busy fingers, pushing in and out my needles, beside the peanut-like flame of the oil lamp in the quiet night. Everyone else in the room was asleep so that I could be close to the lamp-light for a little more time, even though I was scolded by my room-mates for wasting oil.

He broke my heart the first second he saw me at the gate of his factory in Beijing. He didn't appreciate my loving effort. As soon as he saw me, he growled, 'Why do you come? I don't want sex at the moment!' I couldn't believe my ears. Was that how to greet your wife, or anybody? And then I heard him howling, 'You haven't changed a bit despite what you said in your letters. Look at your ugly way of walking. I don't want to be with you in the street. You make me lose face!'

My way of walking was wrong indeed. Imitating my mother when I was a little child, I walked as if I had bound feet. My feet muscles didn't relax and my toes didn't spread. With arched feet I didn't grip the ground with my toes properly, as if they were swathed by wrappers. And my knees were bent as if to relieve pain from the feet. I moved my legs with small, awkward steps in a stiff way since the muscles around my legs were not relaxed. Pine was right with his criticism, but if only he knew how to communicate properly and not hurt my feelings so badly.

During the fifteen days I stayed in Beijing, Pine treated me rudely. He despised me as a Gobi Desert labourer; he put me down in front of others;

he looked at me with loathing; he lost his temper again and again. He never failed to remind me that I was not worthy to be his wife and, most hurtful of all, he repeatedly said he wanted to divorce me.

I had a year of dull resignation after this visit. I no longer hoped I could please Pine. Instead, I was disgusted by myself and I criticised myself harshly. I tried to find how I could change myself completely.

Although I was shunned by Pine, I still yearned for his letters, the only emotional comfort I could get in my desert life. Day after day, week after week, I looked for his letter to arrive. Every afternoon after work I would stride at speed to the team office. There on a makeshift table was the mail for the day. I was excited before I got there, and nervous while searching amongst the dozens of letters for Pine's familiar handwriting. Most days, of course, I didn't get one. I will never forget the painful disappointment each time when I failed to find a letter from him — the agony was almost unendurable. There were always others in the office and I would try to hide my feelings but I could hardly conceal my crestfallen face. Walking on the deserted space in the grim dusk, totally dispirited, I would tiredly sit on my little wooden stool beside my bed in the dark cave on the earth floor, eating my meal; mending my clothes, making my shoes, sobbing silently. Things didn't improve until bedtime when, lying in bed, hope would rise in my heart. Maybe, I consoled myself, tomorrow probably, less than twenty-four hours later, I would get a letter from him. How happy I would be then! Hopeful dreams helped me as one lonely day after another, hundreds of them.

Another year passed and it was time for me to have the holiday of 'married couples living in different places'. I wrote to Pine to let him know about my holiday permit. To my surprise, he answered my letter with uncharacteristic promptness this time, but I was knocked headlong after reading it. He ordered me not to see him since he had used the holiday alone and he didn't want his boss to find out as the holiday was for the couple, not just for him.

Sadly I went to his parents' place by myself. The double door of the courtyard opened with a slight twisting sound and there was my baby Enya. Her pretty little head covered with thick black hair, she looked at me in surprise. Enya was two years and eight months now, a beautiful little girl with clever language skills. When she called me 'mum', tears welled up in my eyes. I felt sad, shy and excited. This was the first time I had been called 'mum', yet my baby was already nearly three years old.

One day we were playing in the garden, picking up mulberries on the ground and eating them, when her playmate Sanba came. Enya stood up, running quickly in her little blue top and yellow short pants, mouth red and purple from the mulberries, and shouted at him, 'Sanba, you dare not to come. This is *my* mum!'

A few days later I was ready to take Enya to visit her maternal grandmother. While I was packing up her clothes, her Granny baked peanuts and dried dates for her. Again and again, Granny said to her, 'Don't forget to say hello to your *laolao* [maternal grandmother]. See you later, dear darling.'

Standing at the gate of the courtyard, Grandpa and Granny watched us leave. It was the last time they would ever see her.

My mother was living in Crab Village again after two and a half years in Sunge Village. Superb had managed to use a connection with a member of the Public Security, and with his help Mother was allowed to go back to Qingdao and regain her pension; Main got his teaching job back, and they rented a house with four rooms in a row. Main, my mother and I were very grateful to Superb and regarded her as a family hero, but it was not enough. Every now and then she would throw a tantrum and accuse us of treating her poorly. 'You ought to offer me seven dishes and eight bowls as I am the empress of the household!' she would scream.

Enya and I arrived in Crab Village in the dusk. 'Where is my Granny? I cannot find my Granny,' she wailed as she walked around the courtyard in confusion. She was looking everywhere for her paternal grandma and crying until my mother called to her and held her in her arms.

Listening to my child's frustrated crying, my heart broke. I felt a dark omen: I knew something tragic would happen in this house, especially after I saw Superb's insincere smile.

Little Enya cried herself to sleep soon. I was lying beside my mother in the room at the east of the house and Superb and Main were in the room at the western end. There was the kitchen and the guest room in between. I thought it was safe to talk to my mother and that I didn't have to worry about anybody else hearing — but I was wrong.

Sobbing bitterly, I told my mother that Pine didn't respect me and I was hurt by his rude and bullying ways: 'I never imagined I could be treated by anybody so badly. Why didn't you teach me how to be a proper person, *niang?*'

My mother listened to me attentively and silently. She was weeping in her heart, I could feel. I knew she understood me. After I got everything off my chest, I felt much relieved and fell into a peaceful sleep. I had no idea that all the time I was talking to my mother, Superb was clinging to our door, listening.

The next day, she arranged to have a serious talk with me. 'You are wrong to trouble Mother's mind with your own problems,' said Superb frankly. I was surprised that she could have known about my private talk to my mother. How did she do it? Ears flattened to the door, bottom up, back bending, legs spreading, shivering in the dark night — wasn't it hard work for something that was nothing to do with her? I didn't realise it was Superb's major business to ruin others' lives because of her jealousy; neither did I know that to pretend to be frank was just her tactic to win trust from others. What she said made me believe she meant to be considerate to my mother, and I willingly forgave her for listening in on my private talk. She then said in a very caring voice, 'I suggest you divorce Pine. I always knew Pine was no good. You are much better than he is. Don't you know how pretty you are? I am sure you will find happiness as long as you listen to me. I will help you to find a much better man and you will be happy forever.'

I never had thought about divorcing Pine. I still had strong feelings for him. All I wanted was to get his love and respect. Although the last thing Superb wanted in the world was to see me happy, I didn't know that until I fell into her trap. She spent lots of time talking to me, admiring me, making a new blouse for me, confiding in me and praising me. Her compliments warmed me tremendously at a time when I was suffering from an inferiority complex in and out of marriage, and I was eager to win friendship and respect from anybody.

In the following nine months I experienced one of the most devastating times of my life. I travelled between Crab Village and Beijing, doing whatever Superb directed me to do.

In October 1971, Superb took me to Beijing to ask for a divorce from Pine. At this stage I was quite sure that he would agree to the divorce since he had told me again and again that he wanted to divorce me. But nothing was further from the truth.

I went to Pine's dormitory to find him. He was lying in his bed, legs and boots up on the bed rail. At the first glimpse of me, he lifted up his head and roared, 'Why do you come here? Didn't I tell you not to come? Get out! You bloody stupid woman!'

'I come here for a divorce, Pine,' said I, calmly.

'Don't be silly. Get out!' He jabbed his finger to the door, stretching the whole length of his arm and glaring at me. Suddenly all the rage and humiliation built up during the last few years burst out. Before I realised it, he was dragged up by my small but strong hands trained in physical labour in the Gobi Desert. Like a hawk grabbing a chick, I pulled him to the door, hit his head on it, and spoke clearly and firmly. 'Listen carefully. I come here for a divorce. I've had enough of your bullying. You don't deserve my love. Go find your boss and tell him I want a divorce!'

To my great surprise, Pine's attitude changed one hundred and eighty degrees. His voice softened and he smiled. I was nudged to his bed and pushed gently onto it. I turned my back to him but he sat behind me and caressed me. 'Well, you are angry. Please don't be. Let's talk in peace.' I ignored him and pulled myself away. I repeated, 'Go get your boss here. I want to talk to him, not you.' Eventually Pine recognised the seriousness of the situation. He said to me in a honeyed voice, 'All right, I will go find my workshop director, but you wait for me here. Don't leave, okay?' I was shivering with frantic emotions and all I could do was nod my head. Within a few minutes he came back accompanied by Mr Gao, the director and the head of Party branch of his workshop, a young man called Big Wave who was the head of the Youth League group, and a third man who was the head of his working group. Superb followed them in. Mr Gao said to me, 'I presume you are Pine's wife. I was told you've got some domestic problems. It is not always easy to lead a life of marriage in separation. I am sorry we haven't done a good job for you. We are here to listen to you.'

Pine said, 'I was unhappy with her because she had a relationship with another man before she married me and I am distressed.'

Superb interrupted him and said calmly, 'Pine, you are wrong. It was because of her deep love for you that Weijun left Bliss for you.' At these words, as if they were magic, Pine suddenly became subdued and looked very remorseful. Seeing Pine silent and beaten, I was very grateful to

Superb and I thought: How stupid I was to suffer Pine's bullying for so long and not to know how to confront him. How clever and capable my sister-in-law was! Only a few words from her had sorted Pine out and saved me from many years of humiliation by him. I was grateful to Superb and I took her as my great saviour from that moment.

Mr Gao gave the order to the other men and they quickly arranged a guest room for us. This was a special treat as factory guest rooms were always full, occupied by 'the married couples living in two places'. Normally a few weeks' notice was needed.

Pine had bought a package of egg sponge for Superb and me, a rare treat at the time. This was the first time Pine had ever bought anything for me since we had known each other. After Superb and I had the egg sponge as our supper in his dormitory, we went to the guest room and there I told Mr Gao and his colleagues about our torment. They showed great sympathy for me and criticised Pine: 'Your wife loves you and she is so nice to you; you should feel very lucky to have such a pretty and nice wife and should look after her well.'

In Mao's China, everyone's private life was talked about, watched, commented on and interfered with by others; a workplace was like your home and the heads of your workplace were like your parents and took every aspect of your life under their care. Your workmates were your family members and they had the right to have a say on your personal life.

The director and his colleagues gave a lot of advice to Pine, who could say nothing but nodded all the time in agreement. By the time they were ready to leave it was pretty late and Big Wave, the head of the Youth League, said to Pine, 'We'll have a meeting tomorrow to help you.' Pine looked scared.

After the men were gone, Superb immediately left the guest room to catch the late-night train to Qingdao. She said it was none of her business now since Pine didn't want a divorce. After she left, Pine asked me not to divorce him: 'You are so good-natured. I could never find another person who treated me so well. The public will blame me and no woman would like to marry me if you divorce me.'

I couldn't be more confused: Why had Pine changed into a different person within a few hours? Was he honest or was he playing a trick? I didn't know whether I should believe him or not. Thinking hard, I decided to listen to my sister-in-law. I asked him to leave me alone and, lying in the guest room by myself, I found my mind was in chaos. In the early morning I left the guest room and caught the train to Qingdao.

Back at Crab Village I received loving letters every second day from Pine while Superb gave me frequent and long lectures. She said I was wrong to love a person like Pine. 'I would never marry a man like him,' she said. 'You are much better than he. But you are not as reasonable as I am and I know you won't listen to me.' With these words, she gave me a contemptuous look. I felt belittled and wanted to rise to her standard. She continued, 'If I were you, I would marry Simple, who loves you truly. You could stay in Qingdao instead of going back to the Gobi Desert, if you marry him.'

Simple was a man Superb had recently introduced to me. He was in his middle thirties, working as an officer in a government office. He had a gentle personality and was fond of me. He assured me, 'Weijun, once you divorce that bastard, I will marry you and take care of you with your daughter. You will stay in Qingdao and need never go back to the Gobi Desert.'

Directed by Superb, I stayed in Crab Village and listened to her hours-long talk analysing my mistakes and weak points. The more I listened to her, the more I felt I was wrong to love Pine and I should try to love Simple. Superb pointed out to me, 'You should love the one who loves you. I am sure Simple loves you, so you should love him.'

At one stage in the nine-month-long divorce struggle, driven by my own feelings, I went to Beijing and reconciled with Pine. Upon hearing the news, Simple burst into loud sobs just like a child. (Later I learned that this performance was directed by Superb.) I felt guilty when my mother told me about it. Manipulated by Superb, my poor mother blamed me: 'You lured Simple and then you abandoned him. It is immoral.' I was torn between morals and emotion, love and duty. The situation was like a double-edged sword stabbing my heart ruthlessly. When I stayed with Pine, I kept on criticising myself with Superb's words. When I stayed in Crab Village, I missed Pine and felt miserable. I kept on criticising myself as weak and immoral for loving the wrong man, as my sister-in-law had pointed out.

After months' of hesitation, doubt and hard mental labour, I decided that I loved Pine and wanted make peace with him, but I failed. By this time Mr Gao and his colleagues had become impatient with me, and everyone thought I was a naughty woman. I was told later that Mr Gao was going to make us live together by shifting both of our jobs to their branch factory in Shanxi province, a backwards area. Pine was not happy about that because he did not want to leave Beijing. He asked for a divorce at the end of the nine months' emotional trauma.

On March 7, 1973, accompanied by Big Wave as the representative of his workplace to show that they took it seriously and that they agreed with the divorce, Pine and I met in the law court of Chaoyang District of Beijing. I cried for the whole previous night, I was so reluctant to get divorced. I actually decided to say 'no' once I was in the court.

The official in the court was indifferent and impatient. He interrupted me when I started saying a few words. Big Wave was also impatient: 'We have tried our best to persuade them to reconcile but she doesn't listen to anybody. As the representative of Pine's workplace, I say she is hopeless.' Tears welled up to my eyes. I choked, and I could hardly breathe. Before I could open my mouth again, the official announced, 'As the duty judge of Chaoyang District Court, I hereby give a divorce permit for you two right now.'

Walking out of the court, Pine said to me calmly, 'Do you want me to see you off at the railway station?'

All I could manage was to shake my head and avoid looking at him. 'Goodbye, then,' he said light-heartedly and was gone, with his short figure in a dark blue uniform. I stood in the bustling Beijing street and watched him stroll away chatting with Big Wave and disappearing at the corner of the street. My tears poured out like a stream.

In the train from Beijing to Qingdao, after crying for hours, I tried to see the bright side. There was hope in my future. I was free now to marry Simple, who had promised to support me and Enya. I didn't have to go back to the Gobi Desert which lightened my heart a bit. However, when I saw Simple at the railway station I was so anguished that I couldn't bear to look at him. I especially could not bear to make love with him. Was it for this mean and petty physical pleasure that I had sacrificed the deep and long-time spiritual love I had had for years? It didn't make sense. I was torn apart by heartbreak when I saw Enya. Her little figure reminded me it was my fault that she had become fatherless.

Superb's lectures stopped after I had the divorce, her previous lectures started fading from my mind, and I was no longer bewitched. I could see I had made a terrible mistake, trying to fight love with reason. But I thought that I would become better once I settled down with Simple. We would have a peaceful life and Enya would benefit from it. So I tried to control myself and be nice to Simple. After all, he was innocent and he loved me and he would look after Enya and me. Again nothing was further from the truth.

Somehow Superb became unusually close to Simple at this stage. Every time he came to visit me, he would pay a pilgrimage to Superb in her room first. Superb kept telling me that what a nice man Simple was and how much better he was than me.

Bad news came a couple weeks later when Simple decided to withdraw his promise. He told me in a guilty voice, 'Weijun, I don't think it's a good idea if you stay in Qingdao just now, since you don't have the registered residence, and nor does Enya. It would be difficult for me to support the three of us. I think you should go back to Xinjiang and we will try to move your job to Qingdao later, after we get married.'

I could not believe my ears. The shock made me so angry that I could say nothing — I was numb. Superb listened attentively to Simple as he talked to me and she was watching my response with great interest. What was she thinking? Was she trying to help me and make me happy as she claimed, or was she taking satisfaction in my misery?

I took Enya to Beijing because I wanted her to see her father once more. We stayed in Beijing for ten days, homelessly strolling in the streets of Beijing, but we didn't have a single chance to meet him. He was hiding from us.

After Pine and I divorced, Enya lived at Crab Village with my mother, who offered plenty of love to Enya. It was difficult for Mother because she was not free to love Enya. The old lady and her little grandchild were thrown out of the house whenever Superb was agitated. Cold and hungry, the old and the little wandered in the streets, trying to find shelter. When they grew too tired, they would sit at the roadside, sobbing. To comfort Enya, Granny would tell stories. 'Cinderella' and 'The Ugly Duckling' were Enya's favourites. Wiping tears from Granny's wrinkled cheeks with her little hands, Enya would say, 'Granny, when I grow up, I will become a swan and carry you to a far, far good place.'

It would be Enya who finally brought Granny to New Zealand.

Three years later, in 1976, after I had become a teacher in the leather factory of Ulumuqi, I was called to see Mr Shen, the head of the personnel office of the factory, who told me a piece of sensational news: Pine had written me a letter via my employer and he wanted to remarry me. I walked as fast as I could to my dormitory, a thousand waves of emotions washing over me. As soon as I arrived at my room I threw myself on my single bed, my tears were pouring like a fountain. I hadn't forgotten Pine, nor the years-long passion for him, the hurt of his denying me, the sweet times when I dreamt of him, the short but truly happy days after we got married. These strong feelings flooded my heart and soul. But I didn't say yes to him. Twenty years later in 1993, Pine, a divorcee from his second marriage, come to Qingdao and asked me to marry him again. I refused. My feelings for him were no more than a little pile of ash.

CHAPTER NINE

I returned to the Gobi Desert with a broken heart. I felt cheated, betrayed and destroyed. Traditionally in China, any woman who served more than one man was degraded and not accepted by society. Marriage was a life-long affair, especially for a woman. Although divorce was legal after 1949, in people's hearts it was still an infamous thing for a woman to do. Superb held strongly traditional views and she had successfully made me a *liumong*, a very sharp Chinese word for a wanton woman or hooligan man. I hated myself so! Why was I so obedient to others? Why hadn't I accepted Pine's hand when he showed remorse? Why hadn't I stood firm in the court? How thick-headed I was. I was such a hopeless obtuse oaf. For years Pine was my hope for love and my dream of escape from the Gobi Desert. Now the hope and the dream were gone forever.

As a divorced woman, I was a *harijan*, a non-person in the Gobi Desert society, not only in No. 14 Team but in all fourteen teams in No. 103 Regiment. I could hear children swear behind me: 'She's a fucking divorced broken shoe, a *liumong!*' I was the top topic of gossip for a long while. To make it worse, nobody believed me when I told them that I had asked for the divorce in the first place. Materialism and hierarchy were the dominant mindset in China and feelings were not considered. Nobody could understand the pain I felt from Pine's disrespectful manner, or why I should ask for a divorce, since he was better off in hierarchy terms than me because he worked in the big city and he was a university graduate.

All the traumas pushed me to the edge of life's cliff. Life to me now was uglier than ever. It was dreadful, false and cruel. I found myself trapped in the dark hole, confined in the den, helpless and hopeless. It seemed the only solution to stop the unbearable pain was to finish my life.

In my spare time, I sneakily visited the hemp fields and cut off some plants. We grew hemp for making ropes but few knew it was a drug. Once a man who had been a military officer before 1949 stole some flowers, trying to make a cigarette. He was reported and was kept in detention for weeks.

I peeled off the skin of the stem and made myself a thick rope. I hid the rope underneath my pillow and when night came I would gaze up at a thick rafter and think of hanging myself on it. I tried to open my eyes wide and avoid sleep. I waited for the other three in the cave to fall asleep so I could get up quietly and hang myself. The thick rafter in the highest place on the roof of the cave should be strong enough to hold my weight.

Thanks to my young and healthy body, I always fell asleep quickly. Actually I bore the name of 'sleeping champion' for years. It was difficult for me to keep awake. I was exhausted from the long hours of heavy physical labour, especially since I was the one doing the heaviest task while others in my dormitory were favoured by the headman and got some light jobs to do. Night after night I failed to take my life. When the day dawned I was in the collective working team and another depressing day would come and pass in despair. Many times I would have a nightmare that groups of rats jumped on me and gnawed at my toes and ears. They laughed and screamed at me: 'We rats are better than you. At least we don't have to work like a beast of burden in the fields every day.' It was true that my life was nothing but the life of a beast of burden. Every minute was a long agony, everything dark and ugly.

Days passed. Weeks turned into months and I was still alive. Time is the panacea for anything and gradually I recovered from the torment and the desire for death. Getting through this period of feeling suicidal matured me and strengthened me so much that I never thought of killing myself again, even in the most depressed situations of my later life. The experience turned me into a serious person with a deep mind and an animated spirit. It stimulated my brain and enhanced my soul. I started to look at life with a new perspective. I discovered that the most difficult thing in life was personal relationships. Other people brought both joy and hell to you. I realised how little I understood about myself and about human nature. I wanted to work it out. I checked myself, observing others and absorbing. The knowledge from wide reading, which had lain dormant in my subconscious mind, helped me to develop the habit of contemplating, analysing and understanding. This new hobby not only matured me but also brought me huge pleasure. As Balzac once pointed out, 'Thinking is the biggest pleasure of a human being.' Thinking was such a handy hobby — you could do it anytime. It didn't need any special environment, any equipment or anybody to do it with, and a person who likes to think would never feel bored. I was thinking at the railway station when I was in the queue for tickets, in the train, on the fields, when I was eating — whenever I needed to fill in a boring moment. It made my desert life much easier to bear when all I was doing was moving my torso and limbs mechanically in the same rhythm all day, and I had all the time in the world to exercise my mind. Thinking offered me a rich mental world and the bleached desert life became bearable.

It was then that I made myself change from being a shallow-minded, vain young woman into a mature person with an independent mind. I no longer merely accepted what others said but searched for a deeper meaning. It was at this time that I learned to use books for guidance to solve problems.

For almost eight years, I didn't have any chance to read any books apart from Mao's works. Now I hit on some good luck: my new dormitory mate Daisy lent me a book called *Help Yourself*. Daisy's sister Rose was an opera singer in the city of Hangzhou, and used to be famous as the actress playing the male hero Bao Yu in *Dream of the Red Mansion*, the classic romantic novel of Chinese literature. During the Cultural Revolution the Red Guards denounced her as a 'feudalist worm' and put her under arrest in a house next to the library where they stored the books they had confiscated from homes, workplaces and libraries. In this lonely time of house arrest, Rose would climb through a gap in the wall to the library and sneak out some books. The book Daisy lent to me was one of them. Daisy was also a divorced woman and sympathised with me, which was the reason she dared to lend me the book. All books were forbidden at the time except Mao's works and it was a big risk to read any books other than his *Little Red Book*. *Help Yourself* was written by an American and translated into Chinese in the 1940s. I don't remember the author's name but it was a great book. I was captivated from my first glance at it and wanted to read it again and again. However, I was allowed to keep the book for only three days. The longer you keep a 'poisonous grass', a forbidden book, the more risk you took. I decided to copy all of its contents into my notebook, in secret.

Darkness and silence descended on the Gobi Desert. Everybody was sound asleep but me. Getting up quietly, I lit the oil lamp and started my project. Sitting on my little wooden stool, I used my bed as a desk and copied the book one sentence after another. It took me three nights to copy the entire book but the effort was worthwhile. *Help Yourself* became my Personal Mentor and I would read it again and again whenever I faced challenges in life. My personality and my mind were never the same after I had this book. I became self-confident and motivated.

Instead of accepting misfortune submissively, I made myself sprightly and optimistic. 'Everybody likes a youth who is lively with a high spirit', my Personal Mentor taught me. People were attracted to me little by little and I started to make friends, which made me no longer so lonely.

In 1973, I initiated an activity which made me popular in the team. In order to entertain myself as well as others I became a storyteller. Using my memory and imagination I told stories to my workmates in the fields. As you can imagine, in a place without any kind of entertainment, everybody wanted to listen to interesting stories. Even the headman had a bargain with me: 'Please, Tall Liu,' he called me by my friendly nickname, 'today's job is quite tight. Could you work a little bit faster?' He knew if I worked faster, others would follow me, otherwise they couldn't hear my stories. I virtually became the 'head sheep' of the working team.

As well as becoming a popular storyteller, I became a hard worker too. It had taken me about five years to get used to the heavy physical labour. Once I got used to it, I loved it. Day after day, month after month, year after year, I was doing the same things and eventually they became a habit. No matter if it involved clutching my fingers, flinging my arms, stooping my back, moving my shoulders, twisting my waist or kicking my legs, nothing was too hard. My heart would beat strongly with the rhythm of the physical activity and my whole body felt vigorous and exuberant.

I tried to be creative to amuse myself. When I tied up the wheat stems, instead of making a knot, I twisted the stems around each other, which was quicker and fun. I used my mind to find the way to rip off the maize ears with fewer movements and to work out how to throw them accurately into the basket on my back. I worked out how to save one movement around my fingers to collect the opium sap, and my collection was always more than others.

I became tough and strong, and no physical job was too hard for me. My muscles, after years of exercise, had become lithe and enduring. Love of physical work had grown in my blood and bones, and I enjoyed working in the fields far more than staying indoors. I overcame my indolence: the desert life made me a hardworking person, which has benefited me all the rest of my life.

My favorite job was to work through the night in summer. We worked from eight in the evening till five in the morning. Standing beside the combine harvester to husk the wheat, I would absorb the whole sound, light and motion with my heart: the roaring machine, the gleaming sweat, the flinging arms and the flying spades. At midnight the break came. Sitting on the dried-wheat straw, smelling the warm and cozy fragrance, the summer breeze cooling my hot skin, was heavenly.

Sometimes we would work with the tractor to harvest alfalfa. The forage grass was in full blossom, dark purple, blowing in the silver moonlight. I worked with a wooden fork behind the tractor with another woman in turn. When it was my turn to have a ten-minute break, I would lie on the freshly cut alfalfa, dozing off and having some beautiful dreams, inspired by the perfumed and refreshing night air. I liked to gaze at the Gobi Desert sky. The empty land gave way to the blue sapphire sky and it looked so close, portentous and beautiful. The stars would glow, the moon a delicious orange cake. When dawn came, whitish mist rose on a tossing sea of clouds, pink, red and purple, embracing a luminous sun on the horizon. It seemed to purify my soul.

At about one in the morning we would have our night meal. We walked back to the public kitchen and had warm noodles. I had a cunning way to get more out of the wok: I would make my bowl half-full for the first time and suck the noodles in fast. When I filled my bowl for the second time I would pile the noodles as high as a little hill and take my time to enjoy them. The free meal made everyone like a night-shift job.

In 1973, I was selected as head of the woman's group due to my popularity as a good storyteller as well as being a hard worker. The promotion would help me greatly later when I made my escape from the Gobi Desert.

The desire to control my life had never been so strong. My resolve to improve my life had never been so steely. I didn't want to be a labourer in the desert all my life; I wanted to be a teacher. Although at that time no schools or universities were open, I didn't believe any nation could afford to neglect education forever. Teachers would be useful and I'd better get ready for it. There were times that some well-intentioned people accosted me. 'There, Weijun, find yourself a husband in the Gobi Desert and bring your daughter here. One must be realistic,' they tried to persuade me. I became enraged and I shouted silently. 'Over my dead body! I will never marry in the Gobi Desert. I will never let my daughter suffer the Gobi Desert life!'

I took out the English textbook which had hidden underneath my bed for years. Some of my friends heard I was learning English and asked to join. Thus a little English learning group was formed with four students and me as the teacher. All came from 'black element' families: Ocean, Luck, Solid and Rock had experienced the same trauma as I had and the same fate made us close and understand each other.

The English lessons went smoothly to start with. Three evenings every week, I went to their dormitory and the five of us would sit at the makeshift table and have the lessons. I was a patient teacher and they were hardworking students; we would read aloud and had a few laughs at each other's pronunciation. They would thank me by offering me watermelons they stored under their beds. (The climate in Xinjiang meant that water-melons could be stored in the soil for as long as half a year.) On a cold winter's night, to eat precious and delicious watermelon with my friends was great fun.

A few weeks later, when we were having a quiz, a young man named Peace came in. He was one of those regarded as 'reformed black youths' coming from a black family but regarded as reformed. He was very revolutionary and followed the Party's calls closely. He had the task of watching other 'blacks' and reporting to the Party representatives. Seeing us talking in a strange language, he asked, 'What are you doing?' He looked over and saw our English textbook: 'Well, you are learning English.' He cast us a scornful glance and left.

The next evening a mass meeting was held for all. The Party branch secretariat of our team gave an angry speech: 'I was told some of you were learning a foreign language. Why do you learn a foreign language? You are Chinese. Have you learned Chinese well? I bet there must some wrong motives behind it. It is the sign of a new class struggle. The enemies will use all sorts of ways to upset our proletarian motherland. We must crack down on the reactionary action. English is not allowed to be spoken or learned in my team!'

The next day big character posters were on the walls of the public kitchen. I was condemned as the head of the 'black gang' and was denounced as a traitor and a spy for the imperialist countries and for Russia the revisionist. They said I was going to run away to Russia to sell China's secrets. They didn't know that Russians don't speak English.

Our English course came to a sudden halt and our learning group was dismantled. This event hurt me so much. How mean it was that a few innocent young people were humiliated only because we used our spare time to learn something harmless. My determination to leave this place was never as strong as it was then. For two years from 1973 to 1975, I tried all possible ways to leave the Gobi Desert.

I decided to make my English study an underground action.

The silence of night fell on the Gobi Desert. Everywhere was quiet as if the whole globe was asleep, and it seemed I could hear the air flow. I quietly got up and put on my clothes. I took out a torch, a pen and a piece of paper and put them in front of me while I was in bed on my knees. I covered myself with a quilt to make sure the light didn't show, and my night study scheme started. I would read, write and recite for one hour, and at the end of the session I would copy a few new words and sentences from the textbook onto a piece of paper. I chewed some dried bun or chilli to stop sleepiness. The next day in the field I would take the note out from my pocket, quickly scan it, then try to remember the words. During the break time I would leave the chatting people and pretend to

With little Enya in the Gobi Desert, summer 1974

have a pee behind a bush. I would sit on the ground and used a stick to write English words on the ground. I was nervous all the time, but I had no option. It was easier when we worked in the maize fields. The tall maize plants provided a natural screen and I could boldly recite the sentences out loud. I carried on my underground study scheme for two years. I didn't learn much but I could read and write some English and I improved my vocabulary by about three hundred new words.

Whenever I had a chance, I took a trip to Ulumuqi and visited schools and asked them if they wanted me as a teacher. I was treated more like a beggar than a job applicant. However, I was not discouraged but continued to knock on school doors. What else I could do? At least it offered me a chance to train my character to face challenges.

In early 1974 I went back to Qingdao and met Rich, a tall, handsome electrician one year older than me. He had difficulty finding a girlfriend because he was from a landlord's family. By the time I met him he was living with his aged mother, his older brother, his sister-in-law and their three children. They were all nice to me and I was fond of Rich.

I had been on the train between Qingdao to Ulumuqi so many times that I grew sick and frightened of the trip. I hated the traumatic time when I left my home town at the small, barren Cangkou railway station: the old concrete buildings, the empty waiting room, the boring noise of the train wheels and its high-pitched siren, a lonely homeless tramper sent off to the far end of the world leaving my mother and child behind. Now I had Rich to see me off and I was much happier. Moreover, I didn't have to suffer the pressure any more of being a divorced woman.

The year 1974 saw the political situation in China ease with the death of Lin Biao and the succession of Deng Xiaoping as premier. Deng gave orders to open schools and universities after nearly ten years. After so many years of non-schooling, there were few people who could read or write in English. Teachers of English were in great demand. I saw this as a chance to change my life.

One day in early 1974 while we were working in pairs in the fields, my friend Mrs Yang told me the shocking news: Minister Young was dying and his funeral was being organised in Ulumuqi.

Mrs Yang had connections in Ulumuqi as her husband used to work in the city. Mr Yang was an educated man with an artistic interest in calligraphy. Soon after the Cultural Revolution started, he lost his position of deputy team head and was condemned as a revisionist. Thus his life changed; from being a popular head of the team with people all around flattering and fawning, he became a lonely person whom nobody even bothered to talk to. I liked to make friends with unlucky people and it was at his lowest time that I became a friend of his, so whenever we needed to work in pairs in the fields, I would have Mrs Yang with me.

Minister Young had had a bad time during the Cultural Revolution and now, just when the situation turned to be a bit in his favour, he was dying. Sympathy welled up in my heart and I wanted to pay my condolences before his death. I had learned to be considerate and sensitive from adversity.

I rode my newly purchased bicycle, a 'Flying Dove', its trademark declared, and set off for Ulumuqi.

It had taken me more than three years to save up the one hundred and fifty-four *yuan* to buy my bicycle. Flying Dove was a very popular brand made in Tienjian and I had waited a long time for it. How happy I was when the first time I rode it back from Caijiahu to the door of my cave to receive comments and congratulations from my friends. I rode it to the fields and never had to walk on foot for the long distance from the camp to the work site, forty minutes away. I was almost the last person to buy a bicycle in our team: only one walker was left, a teenage girl who had recently lost her mother and was the oldest of the five motherless children.

Now everybody rode to the fields. I took the motherless girl on the back of my bicycle and it seemed even lighter with her sitting there. We shot along the winding path and down and up the slopes like a real flying dove, my heart jumping excitedly and my friend at my back screaming joyfully. The Flying Dove became my best friend and I was attached to it emotionally as if it was a living creature. Every morning the first thing I did was to look at it to make sure it was all right, and every evening after work I cleaned it. In my eyes it was so pretty and so lovely and I was full of appreciation towards it. I decorated its racks with bright red plastic ribbon; I covered the seat with crochet handicraft, black outside with red lining. I made sure the wheels were always shining.

It didn't take me long to find out which hospital Minister Young was in since his condition was big news in Ulumuqi. He was lying in bed in the hospital's special ward, unconscious and moaning. His situation was very serious and he could not talk nor recognise me. His wife met me in the visitors' room and told me the story.

The Youngs and their children had been exiled to a remote camp near Shihezi under custody for eight years. Three weeks ago Mr Young received the good news that he was reinstated. He and one of his colleagues, Mr Liu, the previous Political Director of the Corps, went to Ulumuqi to attend a conference and the same day they were offered a new Beijing jeep as their transport to go home a hundred miles away. The driver used to be a truck driver, and was not used to the jeep. (Cars, even jeeps, were considered a capitalist luxury, and during all the years of Cultural Revolution nobody was allowed to use them except Mao and his close followers.) As he was not familiar with the new vehicle, the driver made a fatal mistake. He pushed the brake instead of the accelerator when his passengers told him to hurry. The jeep jumped up to the air, flying more than ten metres and dropping in a deep ditch. Mr Young knocked the roof of the jeep open with his head, flying out of it, and dropping on the ground where his head hit a rock. He lost consciousness immediately. Mr Liu, a smaller figure, flew out of the jeep, following Mr Young through the same hole.

It turned out that Mr Young lost seven hundred millilitres of blood from his head alone, a huge trauma. Mrs Young's hair went grey overnight when she heard the news. She thanked me for coming to visit them from far away. I left the hospital with a heavy heart.

Several weeks later, surprisingly, I received a letter from Mr Young, asking me to visit him in Ulumiqi. This time he looked much better and he could sit up and talk. He told me a dramatic story.

After he was condemned at an early stage of the Cultural Revolution, his positions were taken by revolutionaries, commonly known as 'the New Ones'. The New Ones, of course, were not happy to give up their power when he was rehabilitated. On hearing that he had had the accident and was dying, they excitedly prepared his funeral and wrote an elegiac couplet — but then something unusual happened.

Minister Young had a long-time friend, Wang Zhen, with whom he fought shoulder to shoulder in the war. Mr Wang was one of the Deputy Premiers in the Party's central committee. When Premier Wang Zhen heard of Mr Young's trauma, he gave a special order, 'Try to do your best for Comrade Young.' He offered his private plane to carry rare and effective medicines for Mr Young. He asked for daily reports about Mr Young's condition and paid very close attention to his medical treatment. Nobody dared to neglect him under Premier Wang's close watch.

Minister Young was saved. He took me to a private room and had a talk with me: 'When I was sent to that remote place to be a shepherd, I sometimes met people I promoted in the past but they pretended not to know me. You are good-hearted. Thank you for visiting me when I was dying.'

Knowing about my sad career situation, he said, 'Don't worry, I will help you.'

A few weeks later, when I was walking in a street in Caijiahu, I was stopped by a Miss Zu of the personnel office. With an indifferent attitude, she said, 'I suppose you are Liu Weijun. I want to tell you that your dossier has been sent back by the School of the Leather Factory, Ulumuqi.' After these words she carried on her walking, leaving me standing like a log of wood. I stood there for a long while trying to think about what had happened, what lay behind the woman's words. People were walking around in the earth road amongst muddy houses. This was a place containing administration offices for all the farm teams in the regiment. There was a shop, a hospital, a secondary school, a post office, an inn and a factory. This place in our eyes was a town and we envied the people who lived and worked here. The Caijiahu residents looked down upon those of us from agricultural camps, the farming labourers, with an arrogant air, as Parisians do upon the provincials. There was no way for a person from any camp to transfer his or her job to Caijiahu unless they married somebody who worked there.

After thinking hard, I realised that it must be due to Minister Young, that he had tried to help me and had introduced my dossier to the school at the leather factory. It had been sent back probably because they didn't like what was written in my dossier, about being from a black family and divorced, and so on. It was a crucial moment of my life. If I accepted the present situation, I would be lost forever. It would be very difficult to change the decision, but I had nothing to lose if I took it as a challenge.

As depressing as the news from Miss Zu was, I was grateful to her. If she hadn't told me, I might have lost the chance forever. How lucky that she knew me, even though I had never talked to her before. For the winter season in the last two years, I had been selected as a member of a performing troupe and had been on the stage of Caijiahu to play Shandong opera, which was a sensational success and so I became well-known.

Any positive thing you do can become the key to open a door to a new life.

I quickly walked around in nearby streets trying to find a way to go to Ulumuqi. There was a truck leaving for Ulumuqi in a few hours and the driver said yes to my pleading for a ride. Eating a bun at the roadside, I waited patiently beside the truck for a couple of hours. At six-thirty in the evening the truck was on the way to Ulumuqi with me sitting on top of it. The day was getting dark and the temperature was dropping rapidly. Soon I was as frozen as a dead fish, numbly half-lying and half-sitting in the open tray of the truck. I couldn't even move my fingers. I hadn't prepared for this trip and all I wore that day was a thin padded jacket. Luckily the driver was kind and he offered me a woollen coat. It was midnight when we arrived in Ulumuqi. I thanked the driver and ran in the cold dark night to a friend's place. She was the only person I knew in the city. I wouldn't have dared to knock on somebody's door at midnight if I had not been inspired by my Mentor Book: 'Be brave when you make a decision and never regret it. If you decide to cross the river, you must do it and never regret it even if you end up drowning in the water.' And: 'A successful person will get what he wants and isn't stopped by any obstacles on the way.' Reciting these sentences from my Mentor Book in my mind, I squeezed myself in my friend's bed and lay awake until dawn. I didn't allow myself to fall asleep. I had to keep myself as alert as an owl so that I could think about the business of the next day. I prepared the conversation with Minister Young and the people in the leather factory and then I recited the words one by one in my heart until I could say them fluently without thinking. I knew that one wrong sentence could ruin everything.

In the cold early morning I left my kind friend and stood in the middle of the road and stopped a truck. Ignoring the driver's anger, I made some jokes to cheer him up and off we glided to the other side of the city. There I headed for the hospital where Minister Young was staying. In his room I sat with my back straight, facing Mr Young, his wife and his son, and, as confidently as I could, I started talking. The words I had recited the night before came out of my mouth without hesitation and I put into them all my heart and enthusiasm. My goal was clear: to make Mr Young willing to contact the leather factory and recommend me to them again.

My talk must have been successful since nobody from my audience stopped me even once during the half hour. When I had finished, Minister Young said to me: 'I am not in charge of the personnel affairs now but I could talk to Minister Dee, who is in charge of it at the moment. Fortunately he is also in the hospital. I am not sure if he would agree to help you but I can try. If he doesn't, I will do more to help you when I am recovered.' He then said, 'It would only take me one breath to appoint a divisional commander in the past. Nowadays it is more bloody compli-cated even to appoint a schoolteacher!'

Minister Dee was a tall, serious man. I was nervous when I saw him, this very high-up and powerful man who might control my destiny. I could hardly breathe when I tried to tell him my story. Fortunately Minister Dee was in favor of me after Mr Young had introduced me to him. He wrote a letter to the personnel officer of the leather factory:

Personnel Officer of Leather Factory,

I hereby recommend Comrade Liu Weijun as an English teacher for your school. She is happy to take some trial lessons for the teaching job. Please support her.

This letter carried a lot of weight since every cadre's job in the entire Corps depended on Minister Dee. He could allocate you a good job or he could shift you to a poor place if he liked. Now I had won the first step for my adventure, but there was still a long, long way to go.

CHAPTER TEN

In the bus to the leather factory, I was observing, thinking and searching, trying to find as much information as possible. I talked to several passengers in the bus and finally I found an old man with silver hair, who worked at the leather factory. I got off the right bus-stop with his guidance. I relaxed a bit and started to feel confident that I would achieve my next aim, which was to persuade the personnel officer of the leather factory to allow me to give some trial lessons at their school.

The weather was cold, the sky was crystal aqua. I walked in the frozen street of Ulumuqi, following the man with silver hair after we got off the bus. The factory was a huge place with a shop, a public bath, a hospital and a school of its own. The whole factory was about three square kilometres, with more than ten thousand workers, officers and their families. I followed the old man and looked around. At one stage I passed the school. I stopped at the gate and looked at the red characters on the top of the gate. They looked so beautiful in the blue sky. The characters of 'The School of Leather Factory' made my heart jump. How much I longed to be a teacher here.

'Silver hair' took me to the centre of the factory and showed me some buildings. 'The personnel office is in there,' he said, pointing to one of them. He wished me good luck and left. I stood in front of the building and thought through the situation. It was not a good idea to go right now to see the personnel officer. I decided to go to the school first. It is always wise to have as much information you can before you see an important person.

I strolled around in the big courtyard of the school and saw a few offices with white wooden boards at the door. I searched for a while and found one that read: Office of Middle School. Obviously the school contained both primary and middle-school students. Inside the office there were pairs of desks and chairs. A little old man, sitting at one of desks, was writing strenuously with his thick glasses standing right on the top of his nose. I greeted him in the most polite manner I could and he answered me warmly: 'Who are you looking for?'

'I am applying for the job as an English teacher.'

'Oh, welcome!' His face brightened. 'I am a retired teacher from the neighbourhood school. This school lacks English teachers and they asked me to help for a short while. Now more than half a year has passed and they still haven't found anyone who could teach English. You are most welcome. I am longing to have a rest if you can take over my job.' What important information, I thought. I thanked him happily and turned to the personnel office.

Mr Shen, the head of the personnel office, was a tall, gloomy man with pale yellowish skin. He asked me who I was and then said indifferently, 'I am sorry, we don't need any English teachers at the moment. Our upper authority has allocated us two more teachers recently and that's enough. You can go now.' With these words, he looked at his junior, who opened the door for me. I stood at the door, straightened up my back and said: 'I have just been to the school and was told that you are lacking English teachers.'

Mr Shen coughed dryly to conceal his embarrassment. For a while he didn't know what to say. This was my moment. I threw off my long scarf and seated myself gracefully. I started the conversation I had prepared. The flow of words was so smooth and fluent that it was hard for anyone to interrupt. Mr Shen and his junior had no option but to listen to me. I talked from all sorts of angles to get my goal — to get permission to give some trial lessons. Seeing Mr Shen was not very much persuaded by my words, I used my last tactic: I showed him the letter from Minister Dee. After reading the letter from his superior and confirming it was genuine, Mr Shen said reluctantly, 'All right. We'll arrange some trial lessons for you.'

I was happy but puzzled. Why did a short letter have so much more power than a person's honest words?

I was taken to the school and introduced to a young English teacher named Culture, who offered me a textbook, a notebook and a ballpoint pen. It was decided that I would give an English lesson the next morning. Then I was shown to the factory guest house and left on my own.

Cold night fell. I was frozen in the dark guest room. The stove didn't work. There was a power cut and the candle I was offered was poor-quality and smoked a lot. The room was damp and cold. I felt very tired with a splitting headache. I touched my forehead and realised I had a high fever. I tried to sit up but my back was sore and my whole body was screaming in agony. I had to go to see a doctor immediately.

In the dark and slippery snowy road I wobbled up and down trying to find the hospital at the corner of the factory. The female doctor on duty was alarmed at my high temperature but she refused to prescribe me medicine when she found out I was a visitor. She smiled apologetically and said, 'We don't offer injections or antibiotics to outsiders because they are rationed tightly. I can offer you some Chinese herbal medicine instead.' Chinese herbal medicine? It worked slowly but I needed to be well for the next day, a crucial day in my life. I was disappointed but couldn't say anything with my trembling lips and muzzy head. Accepting the black balls of processed herbal medicine, I went back to the guest room. It was full of smoke from the stove as well as from the candle. I was coughing and aching while I gathered myself together to try to prepare the lessons at the table which was covered by dark soot. I hadn't given English lessons — or any lessons — for eight years and the next day would decide my future. My health situation was desperate but I had to try my best. By the time I finished the preparation it was well past midnight. I silently recited some quotations from my Mentor Book and managed some sleep before dawn.

The young teacher Culture came to fetch me at seven-thirty in the morning and I followed him into a classroom. Contrary to what I expected, it was not full of students but half-full of adults. They must be the headmaster and deputy headmasters, the cadres of the factory and some selected teachers from the school. Mr Zhang and Culture were there, of course, and I supposed they were the only ones who could understand English, but the others could have some ideas about my teaching skills and classroom manners.

Somehow my nerves calmed as soon as I stood in front of the classroom, arranged my notebook on the rostrum and grabbed a piece of chalk. The forty-five minutes passed quickly and I felt good about my lesson. But I had to wait before I could get the result. The waiting time, with the flu and high fever attacking me, was tedious and almost unbearable. At last in the afternoon Mr Shen came into the guest room and said that I was regarded as a 'basically' competent middle-school teacher. I was nearly jumping with joy: 'Oh, I've won. I will be a teacher!' But the next second, my excitement was dampened by Mr Shen's unenthusiastic words: 'We'll try to shift your job here if we can.'

As soon as Mr Shen left, I quickly set off back to the Gobi Desert. I had left my team without a permit for two days and I had to hurry back as quickly as possible. I took a long-distance bus to Wujiaqu, which was a forty-minute ride. A cold wind was attacking Ulumuqi and I was sitting right beside the door. The wind came through the gap of the double-door, blowing in like a thin knife slashing my flesh around my back. My thin cotton-padded jacket felt like nothing in the spiteful wind. This started the arthritis around my back and lasted for more than ten years. It was the price I paid for my limited triumph. After the bus trip I hitched a ride in a truck to Caijiahu, and then rode on my bicycle back to the camp in the middle of the night.

Life began again in No. 14 Team, but it was even more depressing with the backache torturing me whenever I needed to stoop. I was expecting a letter every day from the leather factory and then I could say goodbye to the Gobi Desert. But I was disappointed one day after another. The letter never came.

One and half months passed and there was no news from the leather factory. I was angry and depressed. I felt as if I had been cheated and somehow it seemed that I hadn't given a lesson at the school and it was merely a dream.

The short winter days in Gobi Desert were more dull and boring than any other time of the year. It became dark at three-thirty in the afternoon, yet we had to work till five. After we finished building the ditches, we began moving a sand dune. Sand dunes appeared and disappeared here and there all the time according to the direction of the wind. This year a huge dune was sitting in the middle of one of the maize fields. The whole team went there every day to remove it. I was always the first one to arrive at the work site and the last one to leave, since I was the head of the women's group. I got up in the dark and pulled the cart with spades, shoulder poles, woven baskets and *kantuman*, the special tool in this area for scooping fine soil, to the field; and after work I collected them and pulled them back with a cart to the camp after everybody else had gone. By the time I arrived, the meal in the public kitchen was a little pile of cold greyish leftovers and the hot water was nearly frozen.

One day I made an excuse and got two days off. Riding on my bicycle, I set off for Ulumuqi again.

The Gobi Desert life, especially our life in No. 14 Team, was so poor that it was inevitable that everybody wanted to flee the place. To No. 14 Team, every place on earth was better, even No. 12 Team, which was a camp for rehabilitated criminals. They had more meat dishes for festivals and they had a big cave for meetings, with several pillars to support the roof, while we had to hold meetings in the open air no matter how cold or how hot it was. Some of us had asked for a job shift to No. 12 Team and been refused. It made us very sad that ours was even worse than the prisoners' life. Everybody wanted to leave No. 14 Team. There was furtive and strong competition about who could leave the place first. Each person's leaving meant another person's failure since the number of the workers for the team must be steady, decided by the authority. I knew my action must be conducted in extreme secrecy otherwise I would face strong objections from my colleagues as well as from the authority, and I would never succeed. Everyone's movements were watched tightly and I had to be very careful when I took days off to go to Ulumuqi to arrange my new job. I worked hard to make sure my excuses were credible. Sometimes I made up stories that I was meeting a friend in Ulumuqi. Other times I said that I wanted to see a specialist for my backache. Luckily it was not too difficult for me to get some days off as I was the head of the women's group and was in favour with the team head.

In the vast snowfields of the Gobi Desert, a tiny black spot was moving along in the endless snowy terrain. It was me, strenuously riding my bike. I was determined to face every challenge in order to escape from the Gobi

Desert. A green khaki handbag was on the handle, with three buns in it. When I was hungry, I took one out of the bag and had a few bites while I was still riding. When I was thirsty I got off the bike and hand-scooped some snow into my mouth. The distance from my camp to Ulumuqi was about sixty kilometres and it took me eight hours to ride without stopping. Sometimes the day was bad and I couldn't make the whole journey, and then I would stay in a kind of guest house at Wujiaqu and finish the rest of the trip in the early morning. When I arrived at the leather factory, my appearance caused a sensation. One day I met the head of the factory, Mr Li, when I had just arrived. Seeing the dirty mud all over my shoes and pants, and sweat running down my forehead, steaming out in the air like a cloud around my forehead, he was most impressed. He told Mr Shen, the personnel officer, 'We should accept this woman. She must be very hardworking. Even a man would be beaten in her situation.'

'You might be the head of the factory but I doubt you know any of the regulations about shifting jobs. Our factory, as our level of hierarchy is the same level as No. 103 Regiment, doesn't have the right to give orders to No. 6 Division of Agriculture to shift their workers. Only the personnel department of the Corps has the right,' said Mr Shen.

This was the truth. If only he could have told me earlier! Mr Shen turned to me and barked, 'Don't you know Minister Dee? I am sure he can help you.'

The hierarchy of administration in China must have been one of the most complicated phenomena in the world. As a common person, I had no idea about it. Hearing what Mr Shen said, I was very worried and thought that I could have no way to reach the personnel department, the top and most powerful layer of the Corps, in charge of millions of people's job positions. Still, I decided to see Minister Dee.

I went to the hospital but I was told that he was at home. The next time when I could find an excuse for two days off from my labour team, I rode to Ulumuqi and found where Minister Dee lived. To my disappointment, he said he couldn't help me: 'I have been on a long sick leave and The New Ones hold the power. I could do nothing about it but to blow your case if they knew I was helping you, since I am their rival.'

Hearing this, I was despair and cried out, 'Please, Minister Dee, tell me what I should do.'

'The present Minister of Personnel is Minister Han. If you can get support from him, you win.'

How difficult it turned out to be to find this Minister Han.

First I went to see Minister Young but he said he didn't know this Minister Han at all. 'He is a bloody New One and I have nothing to do with them,' he muttered. I tried to talk to some of the officers who were staying in the hospital but they were not helpful. Minister Han's position was so superior that nobody wanted to introduce an inferior Gobi Desert labourer to him. Sometimes I followed the wives, who came to the hospital to visit their husbands, trying to make friends with them. It was embarrassing but I didn't mind as long as I could get help. I contacted dozens of people but nobody could offer me an introduction to Minister Han. Weeks passed without any progress, I was more and more anxious but my determination was strong and I was not going to give up. At last I decided to see Minister Han without an introduction.

On a cold snowy day, I arrived at Wujiaqu and stayed overnight at the guest house. I had a permit for two days off and the excuse I had used this time was to meet someone from Qingdao who had brought some food from Mother for me. In the early hours of the morning I took a bus to Ulumuqi and then walked around the streets. The city was luminous with lights but I was cold and lonely. I wandered along streets amongst forests of concrete buildings for a long while until at last I got lucky — I met his son by chance. The little boy of six was skating on the snowy footpath when I stopped him and asked him the question I had asked so many times before: 'Where does Minister Han Hong-ru live?'

'He is my father. Our home is at the first door in the second row of that building.'

I was overjoyed and would have bestowed a deep bow on the boy if he was not too young to understand it. He shot away with his home-made skating gear before he finished his last word. I ran over and caught up with him. 'Is he at home now?'

'No, he isn't. He has just gone to work.'

I rode for a long distance and at last I found where the General Headquarters of the Corps was located. At the entrance of a grand building I stopped a man on his way in and asked where Minister Han was. He jabbed at a tall figure in a green woollen military uniform and said, 'There he is.' I looked up and saw Minister Han walking with a soldier's steps towards one of the big buildings. I ran as fast as I could and when he was merely a few steps away from the door, I called out, 'Minister Han!'

He was astonished and turned his head. 'Who are you?'

'I am from No. 103 Regiment of No. 6 Agriculture Division. I want to shift my job to the leather factory of Ulumuqi.'

'Go back and talk to your team head,' Minister Han said while he was still walking. He entered the room and closed the door on my nose. I found myself looking into the hall through one of the windows and saw him giving a speech to a big audience.

The next morning, I waited in the cold open air at the side of the building where Minister Han lived. I waited and waited. I had to keep walking and jumping to stop myself from freezing, while keeping my eyes focussed on the door. At last I saw him walk out. I shouted, 'Minister Han!'

He was surprised: 'Oh, it's you again. Go back to your team! I don't have time to look after every individual in the whole Corps.' As soon as the words were out, he was on his bike and shot away. Another failed trip to Ulumuqi.

I understood Minister Han and I knew he must be very busy but I had to save myself. 'Politeness is of the least importance when you are desperate to run away from ill fate,' I recited from my Mentor Book and decided to take a bold risk.

A few weeks later, just as I was about to recover from the fatigue of the long cycle ride, I managed to get leave for another two days. I could sense that some people had become suspicious of my frequent leave and I realised that time was running short. I must be quick and more efficient.

In the early morning I arrived at the door of Minister Han's home. I knocked on the door and Minister Han himself opened the door. As soon as he saw me, he murmured, 'It's you again. Go back.' Bang! The door was shut before I had a chance to say a word. I hadn't prepared for this and I lost my confidence to knock on the door again.

Back at the camp, I thought hard and decided what to do next. I was going to make Minister Han say yes to me, come what may!

Several weeks passed in the Gobi Desert and I mentally prepared a conversation with Minister Han. When the time came that I could have another permit for leaving without raising much suspicion, I got on my bicycle again.

Luckily my friend Ocean had recently married and his wife was working at a coal mine company belonging to No. 103 Regiment in Ulumuqi, and Ocean had managed to shift his job there as an electrician. They offered me generous free meals and accommodation whenever I needed to stay overnight. The coal mine was fifteen miles away from the city and I hitchhiked on the trucks. The only trouble was that each time I had a ride on the truck, coal dust covered my face and made me look like a comedian.

One night when I stayed with Ocean and his wife, I had a sincere talk with them about my job-transferring challenge. Ocean offered me an important piece of information: the PCCX was going to be unified by the local government and the situation would become tense. I had to hurry.

I was at the door of Minister Han's house again in the early morning on January 9, 1975, which was a Sunday. I took a deep breath before I knocked on the door. Minister Han came to the door, holding it with one hand and was about to shut it, when I quickly slid myself underneath his arm and entered the room.

CHAPTER ELEVEN

The minister frowned and reluctantly seated himself on the sofa opposite me.

'Your business has finished. We couldn't find your papers,' he said as soon as he was on seat. I was shocked but not surprised. Doing my mental homework I had imagined all the possible responses and answers from Minister Han and I had prepared replies to all of them. I pretended I hadn't heard him and gave no response to his remark. Then I started my spiel.

In the years of the Cultural Revolution nobody wanted to be a teacher. Being a teacher was almost a symbol of torture since teachers had suffered more than those of any other occupation. But I realised that the way to get what you want was to do what others didn't want to do. The schools had now been reopened and teachers were needed. Although hardly anybody wanted to be a teacher since the bad memories from the Red Guards were still fresh, I saw it as an opportunity. One day, the direction of the wind would change and teachers would get what they deserved. My way was wide open since there was little competition.

I told Minister Han with enthusiasm how much I longed to be a teacher and how much I loved teaching, ignoring his expression of disbelief. I told him about my perseverance in teaching myself English. I told him how hard I worked in the desert, and how I'd been selected as the head of the women's labour team. Somehow I knew it was all right to take a little risk and I deliberately but subtly mentioned Minister Dee's role in my project. To my surprise, despite Minister Dee's warning, I found that Minister Han was impressed by the fact that Minister Dee was involved in my job search.

He became more attentive to me, and this encouraged me to be more confident.

Words flowed freely out of my mouth like a stream. Occasionally, I looked at the palm of my left hand to see the next point I needed to say, but my speech had been carefully prepared and recited again and again so it came easily. At the end of my talk I used a psychological tactic: 'Minister Han, I know only you are powerful enough and capable enough to solve my problem; and if you do it now, I won't come to bother you any more.' His eyes brightened. From his body language I could see he was touched by what I said and he realised that I, such a determined woman, would not give up unless he said yes to me. Now I reached the final point. I said, 'Please, Minister Han, write a few words to the personnel office of the leather factory. I know they are working today.' To save power, a rotating working system was used and the leather factory worked on Sundays and took a day off on Wednesdays. I took out a pen and a piece of paper from my pocket and offered them to Minister Han.

He had listened to me attentively for forty-five minutes and now he answered without hesitation, 'Don't worry. I will ring them.' Deeply grateful, I said goodbye to him and left cheerfully.

I arrived at the leather factory in the afternoon and was met by the head of the factory, Mr Li, who told me they had received the information from the personnel department of the Corps and the permit for my job transfer had been issued. However, the happy moment didn't last long, for he said, 'I will collect the members of the Party's committee of the factory and discuss your case.' This meant I couldn't relax yet but faced a further battle. If anyone in the committee made an objection, all the effort I had made so far would have been wasted. I decided to stay at the leather factory and to find out everything I could about each of the eight committee members so that I could talk to them face to face, one at a time, to get their sympathy, support and help. I spent the whole afternoon and evening collecting the information I needed — where they lived, what they looked like, what kind of position they held, and so on. I slept a little, and planned to start my lobbying of the members the next day.

It was just dawn when I arrived at Mr Liang's house. He was the main deputy head of the factory, so I chose him as the first person to lobby. He sat in a low easy chair, eyes half-closed, head lowered, listening in silence to my long spiel. At the end he opened his eyes and said slowly, 'Last night the committee members discussed your case and we have made the decision to accept you as an English teacher.' I wanted to jump up, to hug him, to tell him, 'You silly old man, if you'd told me earlier I wouldn't have wasted so much breath!'

The same day I obtained my signed paper from the personnel department of the Corps to take to the No. 6 Division in Wujiaqu. I rode on my bike for more than four hours and finally I arrived at the personnel office in Wujiaqu and showed the officer the paper. Mr Ma, the head of the office, a man in his late thirties, told me coldly, 'You can come this afternoon. We are having a political study, which is *lei da bu dong*, nothing will stop it even if the building is hit by lightening.' After the lunch break I arrived at the office punctually but the door was locked. I wandered nearby for a long while but the door stayed locked. I realised it wasn't going to open for me and I decided to find Mr Ma's house. In a shabby muddy building I found Mr Ma and his sick wife. His wife was a very thin woman, sitting at the corner of the double bed, which occupied most of the space of their single-room home, like a little kitten dying. I exchanged some sociable chit-chat with them and left. I realised I must do more to win over Mr Ma.

A week later I rode to the personnel office in Wujiaqu again. On the back of my bike I carried a big piece of mutton that I'd managed to buy from the shepherd of a nomad group in the Gobi Desert. It was frozen and difficult to manoeuvre, so it took more than seven hours to ride my bicycle to Wujiaqu. In the cold and gloomy dusk I arrived at Mr Ma's home again. I was holding the big piece of mutton with both hands when he opened the door. I said, 'This is for your wife. I hope she becomes well soon.' Mr Ma accepted the mutton and smiled at me.

The next morning I went to the office and Mr Ma cordially offered me the paper for the job shift. It was a formal document and he pressed a round red stamp on it. Holding the precious paper, I hurried back to Caijiahu and handed it in to the personnel office of No. 103 Regiment. Here I received another round red stamp on the paper.

Now came the last step: to get a permit from the members of the head group in my labour team. There were five of them, the headman and four deputies. I waited patiently once I'd handed in the paper. I knew it would be no use to rush them now because it was too big an issue. I went to work in the field as usual and worked as hard as a donkey. I told stories and jokes to the others, as if nothing was going to happen in my life. But my nerves were tensed and felt as if they could snap anytime. I couldn't sleep at night. Hundreds of thoughts constantly raced in my mind. What if any of the heads didn't like me and wanted to stop me? What if one of them leaked the news to the public? What if some nasty people told lies and ruined my chances? I remembered a story Ocean had told me: his niece had told a friend that she was going to transfer her job to Caijiahu from her original team. This friend of hers was jealous and spread wicked lies to the team head, so the niece was stopped and never managed to leave her team.

I spent a whole week in a state of extreme anxiety waiting for the news. Sometimes I was confident that I had worked hard and I was favoured by the team head, so I would be permitted to leave. Other times I was pessimistic when I recalled that there had never been a single person in our whole division who had moved out of the Gobi Desert to Ulumuqi by his or her own effort.

I was absolutely exhausted when finally the head of the team came to me and handed me the paper. There was a third round red stamp on it. They would allow me to go. The headman said, 'I argued that it's easier to find a labourer than an English teacher.' I flinched. They must have had a debate about my job shift and someone *did* want to keep me in the desert.

That night everyone in No. 14 Team was talking about me. I heard expressions of surprise, jealousy and disbelief everywhere. There was some kindness too. I was stopped by a workmate, a big woman with a husband and three sons who were often short of food. I had offered her ten wheat-bun tickets once. She invited me to her cave for lunch. She had a precious dish, stir-fried eggs — three eggs from the hens she raised. But three eggs could only make a little pile at the bottom of bowl and she put salt into it and more salt again, to make it stretch further. It tasted pungent and salty but her three little sons ate it up in no time. Now she stopped me in front of the public kitchen. 'Dear group head, how capable you are to shift your job to Ulumuqi. I will miss you so,' she said, tears streaming down her face.

The next day, on March 15, 1975, when I was busy moving my stuff onto a cattle-cart, my room-mates gathered at the door and chanted in unison:

> Cattle-cart tossing up in the Gobi Desert,
> Weijun was thrown on to the dusty road,
> The sun was sharp and strong,
> Her toes and soles were upside down!

And then they laughed. I understood. They felt betrayed by the fact that I had got myself this huge job but nobody knew about it until the last moment. My friend Mr Yang was up and saw me off. His sincere face wore a bitter smile. He wished me a good life ahead. When I was on the way to Caijiahu, the driver of the cattle-cart made it run so quickly that I was covered by thick dust. My dried chillies bounced up in the air but I was not allowed to pick them up. The driver was jealous too, and he didn't think it fair that I was going to Ulumuqi while he had to stay in the Gobi Desert.

In the guest house at Caijiahu, however, a group of my friends from other teams saw me off with emotion and congratulations. They admired my feat and said, 'How wonderful that you could escape from the Gobi Desert. You've taken such a huge step and it's just as if you've departed from hell to seventh heaven.' Mr Zhang, the big boss of the regiment, happened to be there, too. He said to me, 'Weijun, can you help me leave too?'

'But you are the big boss and should be happy here.'

'I'd prefer being a small soldier in Ulumuqi to being a head of the regiment in such a disgusting place!'

In the residence registrar's office in Caijiahu, I got a signed paper and shifted my residence from Caijiahu to Ulumuqi. It was a big deal, as vital as a life-line, as it decided where you could stay legally. After that I went to the Grain and Cooking Oil Administration to shift my rations away to Ulumuqi. But the man in charge was not there and he would not be back until the next Monday. It was Saturday now. Should I wait for him or not? I recalled what Ocean had told me the other day: the local government of Xinjiang was going to unify the Corps. Rumours were spreading that during the take-over period no person from an agricultural area could transfer their jobs to a non-agricultural area, and my labour team was in an agricultural area but Ulumuqi was not. I could not run the risk of being trapped at the last moment. I decided not to wait for the papers for my grain and oil ration. If I had to starve, so be it. I had to settle my job and residence first.

I rode the forty kilometres from Caijiahu to Ulumuqi in a hurry and managed to arrive at the leather factory a few minutes before they finished work. I registered my work permit and residence permit with the personnel office and relaxed on Sunday.

On Monday I went to the personnel office and told them I needed a day off for a trip to Caijiahu. They said, 'You can't go now as the Corps has been taken over by the local government and all transfers have been frozen indefinitely.' Beads of sweat broke out on my forehead. I had been just two days ahead of the deadline!

I didn't have my ration of grain and oil for nearly two years, which was stressful as it meant that I could be sent back to the Gobi Desert at any time. Every month I wrote a note of debt and borrowed grain and oil from the leather factory. Later, when I eventually got my grain and oil ration transferred, the No. 103 Regiment paid them back.

In March 1975, a few months after my thirtieth birthday, I realised my goal and became a happy teacher in the big city of Ulumuqi.

I was ecstatic, intoxicated. I was in seventh heaven. No words could describe my happiness. The sound of horns from buses in the street made my heart leap with excitement. The variety of food, the library, the electricity, the films, and living in a proper house were all so amazing that I was in a state of perpetual joy. Nobody can imagine the feeling if they haven't lived in hell and then moved to heaven by their own efforts. I was so happy that I could hardly stop smiling.

I would start the day with a brisk walk from my dormitory to the school and on the way I would be greeted with reverence by many students. I answered them happily, tender feelings welling up in my heart. Time passed easily in the classroom: there were two classes every day, and the rest of the day I spent in the office reading, preparing lessons and marking homework. I studied English grammar with great zeal by analysing every sentence to find the function of each word. I recited new words even when

I was having lunch, which I had in the office. Comparing this with the long hours of harsh labour in the Gobi Desert, I felt unbelievably idle. During the evenings I would read in the library, chatting with my students in the English group. My life was one happy day after another and I was on top of the world.

I enjoyed my academic life to the full, especially the library. My reading had expanded from fiction to biography and autobiography, genres which have remained my favourites. Enchanted and empowered by others' personal experiences, I was transported to another level of maturity.

I taught four classes, each of fifty students. I was proud and happy to be able to offer what I knew to two hundred youngsters. The young faces with bright eyes made me feel rejuvenated.

The whole year of 1975 was one of endless elation for me. Then came 1976, and the political wind changed. Just about half a year before he died, Mao Zedong initiated another political upheaval. In his senility, following his life-long habit, he was ready to denounce somebody again. This time he chose as his target Deng Xiaoping, who was doing a good job as the prime minister. Mao wanted the nation to denounce Deng as a 'Capitalist authority', who was trying to improve the people's standard of living. Mao didn't like Premier Zhou Enlai either, as he enjoyed a high popularity amongst the people. Fearing the nation would spin out of control without Zhou's administration, however, Mao couldn't condemn him openly. Instead he called on the whole nation to denounce Zhou Gong, a man who lived two thousand years ago, also surnamed Zhou. To confuse people and conceal his plot, he called on them to criticise Confucius together with Zhou Gong, to show their enduring hatred of the intellectuals. The popular slogan of the time was the ridiculous 'We prefer proletarian grass to capitalists' rice.' As had happened in the early stages of the Cultural Revolution, naïve school students were the first to be manipulated by Mao, only this time nobody took it as seriously as before, except the new generation of students, the junior-school kids. Madam Mao and Mao's close followers called them Chairman Mao's Little Red Guards, a glorious name to boost their egos. They enjoyed the anarchy — no discipline, no timetables and no schoolwork to do. They threw away their textbooks and notebooks as 'glorious revolutionary little generals' were supposed to do. They believed that Deng Xiaoping was plotting to turn China into a rotten capitalist nation and that the people would suffer in poverty, like in the stories we had heard about America and Taiwan. Under the *you qing fan an fen*, movement of political counter-current, China became turbulent again and teaching, especially English teaching, was again under threat.

The Gang of Four, headed by Mao's wife Jiang Qing, controlled the media, spreading the absurd words of Mao, a dying and neurotic tyrant. Nobody believed the propaganda except ignorant school kids. Some of my students turned against learning English, believing that it was one of the 'stinky ideas' from Deng. 'Why do we learn a foreign language? Do revolutionaries need English? Our parents never knew how to read and write even in Chinese, and it hasn't stopped them being revolutionary workers.' The classroom became a hooligans' playground and the students were free to contradict the teachers; dozens of voices yelling, cursing and screaming at the same time. Holding a huge bamboo broom, boys would jump on the desks, sweeping them in the air. A dusty storm hovered over the desks and chairs. In the centre of all the chaos and noise, standing by the rostrum and speaking as loudly as possible, I tried my best to read English and call them to attention. Some students were still keen to learn. I remember a small girl of thirteen who had to move her desk near the blackboard, no more than three feet away. Placing both her hands behind her ears, she shouted constantly, 'I can't hear. Please teacher, speak louder!' She was the smallest of all my students with a very thin face, her thick glasses seeming so heavy. She would bend down to her notebook, so close as if she was trying to fall into it to reject the chaos around her.

One day I was teaching a little rhyme, which turned out to be my downfall. The rhyme went:

> Good, better, best,
> Never let it rest,
> Till good is better
> And better, best.

All through the lesson, I couldn't help but notice a pair of ferocious eyes, glaring at me. The owner of the enraged eyes was a girl called Red, a popular name during the Cultural Revolution. (Red was regarded as revolutionary; black was reactionary; and white was revisionist.) No matter where I went and what I did in the classroom, I felt Red's eyes following me.

After class I was visited by Red and three other revolutionary girls. Each one wore her hair in two bunches on the top of her head, which shook violently. They growled at me, 'Why good, better, best? Are you trying to teach us to seek a better life such as from potato to rice, then rice to meat? You are instigating us to be greedy. How filthy it is. You are against Chairman Mao's teachings. Chairman Mao teaches us to be thrifty and here you want us to have a better and best life.' And then they shouted, 'Downfall to you, counter-revolutionary! We are here to inform you that tomorrow we Little Red Guards will hold condemns on you and you must confess your stinky thoughts.' Necks stiff, heads high, they marched out of my room. The next day I saw big-character posters on the walls in the school denouncing me as a 'reactionary intellectual', but not many people read them. The Cultural Revolution had gone too far and was well past its popular peak; adults had become tired of the endless 'revolutionary actions'. Only the young and innocent were taking it seriously, but to all effects it was merely playful.

A few years later, in the winter of 1978, I had a special guest in my dormitory, my previous student, Red. She came to my room, sitting in silence, modest and humble, and then left. I didn't realise she had come to apologise until later I received a letter from her:

Dear Teacher Liu,

Now I am a happy university student and I am sincerely grateful to my teachers who helped me pass the university entrance. I am especially grateful to you, my English teacher. You worked hard to help me and you don't mind what I did to you during the Cultural Revolution when I and my classmates condemned you as a 'capitalist intellectual'. I have been keen to express my sincere apology in person but I was too guilty to say it to you face to face. Please accept my apology.

CHAPTER TWELVE

The year of 1977 saw me a sad, hopeless and miserable women. Rich came to Ulumuqi to visit me with the intention of fathering a child. However, instead of becoming pregnant, I turned into an insomniac because of the emotional stress. Rich kept accusing me of infidelity, which upset me a lot. Every time he saw me talk to a male, whether he was a colleague, a friend or merely a neighbour, he would swear. He made up stories and then took his stories as evidence that I was unfaithful to him. He barked, 'Don't think I am blind. Your sister-in-law has told me all about what you are!' Once he even said, 'I would have divorced you if your sister-in-law wasn't so nice to me.' Superb knew how to boost his ego.

I had little knowledge or experience of marriage and of men. I had a silly idea: Rich would become loving to me if only I could give birth to a child for him. So I crazily fought against my infertility. I had seen countless doctors, both authentic doctors and traditional Chinese herbist. I had taken countless different medicines; some as common as vitamins, others as weird as insect shells or snake skin. I made friends with a gynaecologist and borrowed her professional books, and read them one after another. I learned that hormone deficiency could cause infertility and that problematic sleep could deplete hormone levels. I must sleep and sleep well! Unfortunately the more I tried, the more I drove sleep away.

On October 10, 1976, just one month after Mao died, exciting news came through. There had been a coup in Beijing, led by the senior military marshal Ye Jianying. Madam Mao and her colleagues in the Gang of Four

— Zhang Chunqiao, Wang Hongwen and Yao Wenyuan — were summonsed by a false message from Hua Guofeng, Mao's successor. When they arrived at the meeting room, Ye and Hua were sitting in their chairs, smiling. As soon as the entire Gang of Four had arrived, armed guards burst in and the Gang of Four were captured without a fight, except for Madam Mao's screaming and protesting.

As has happened time and again in Chinese history, the woman was made the scapegoat. Soon after she was arrested, Madam Mao was brought to trial before the Supreme Court with half a billion people watching on TV. She was sentenced to life imprisonment. In Qincheng prison in Beijing, one of the most horrendous prisons in the world, she stayed for thirteen years until she committed suicide in 1989.

The night when the news came that the Gang of Four had been arrested, the whole of China was overjoyed. Beer, wine and spirits were sold out in no time, and everywhere — households, restaurants and parks — noisy parties were held to celebrate the people's real liberation. The favourite dish was four boiled crabs — three male, one female, indicating Madam Mao and her three male colleagues.

China was entering an era of renaissance and resurrection. Souls reviving and minds reactivating, the whole nation was happily reborn. More freedom brought more hope, and everybody was optimistic and hopeful.

I could hardly contain my happiness when I realised the dark time was in the past and a new time was coming. Deng Xiaoping was in power again and he called on China to stop class struggles and to focus on economic development. China started a new policy of economic reform, modernising and opening up to the world. One of the results was that learning English became popular and my teaching job became easier. I reformed my teaching method — instead of criticising the slow students and praising the better ones, I encouraged the better students and praised the slow ones. No matter how poorly they did in their study, I could find some good points in them, such as their sitting quietly, finishing their homework on time, working hard to clean the blackboard . . . No deed was too little for a teenager to be encouraged. I became a popular teacher. My students enjoyed my lessons and after class they liked to visit my dormitory and chat with me as to a friend.

People's minds were becoming liberal little by little. After ten years of dull garments, fashionable clothes started to appear in shops, in markets, in the streets. Young women, although still not daring to wear showy clothes, discreetly put on some of the new fashions, something other than the grey, brown and dark blue clothes they had worn since 1966. Liberal articles appeared in newspapers and magazines, and those engaging in 'capitalist thinking' faced no opprobrium, which was inspiring and encouraging. Pretty clothes and hairstyles became popular. Young women with permed hair walked in the streets. Flat heels were replaced by heels a little higher, then higher and higher still. The bright colour which used to show shyly around the collar and the edge of the blouse now took up more space. Some girls even started to dress in brightly patterned shirts. It was an exciting time for the whole nation. After more than a decade living in a stifling heavy mood of dread and dullness, people's senses were stimulated and became extraordinarily sensitive. The desire for aesthetic pleasure in these newly liberated hearts was immense. Any hint of prettiness, no matter how negligible, would ignite the senses and set a fire in the heart.

I was in my early thirties and still slim. I gathered up my courage and bought myself a new fashionable outfit: a blue jacket with a little high collar. Its style was plain and simple, not much different from the famous Mao suit, but it had a fitting waist.

Every time I stepped into Class One, I would feel a pair of eyes following me everywhere. Even when I was facing the blackboard, I could sense them at my back. It made me excited, just like I felt in my early days when others stared at me with admiration and appreciation. But I was puzzled, too: who was the owner of the lusting eyes? Why did they follow me? Was it possible that I still had some attraction when I was not that young and my looks had been more or less ruined by my hard life and poor health?

The special looks came from Field. He was an outgoing boy, talented at sports. He was very clever and great fun, often making the whole class laugh. At first I didn't believe that it was romance approaching me, since I was feeling humble and unlucky. But Field had different ideas. He told me later that he would go to his friend's house every evening to stare at a photo of me in which I was standing amongst boys and girls as their class teacher.

Me, sixth from the left, second row, with my class students at our graduation ceremony, 1976; this is the photo that attracted Field – every day he went to the house of his friend, Xin-jan (behind me), to gaze at it

Field was from a factory-hand's family. He and his older sister Dew were adopted. Both of his parents were illiterate but his father was a model worker, a very kind and respected man. Unfortunately his adopted mother used to be a prostitute. As an unfortunate girl from a poor family, sold to the brothel, she had a twisted personality and Field had lacked motherly affection.

One winter afternoon, I was pushing a two-wheeled cart to carry coal for our office. The metal handles of the cart were frozen and I had to clutch my bare hands to my mouth to warm them. Suddenly I saw a pair of cotton gloves dangling in the air. I looked up and saw it was Field holding them. He was wearing an olive-green suit and a dark-brown fur hat, which made him look taller. He put the gloves gently but firmly into my palms and said, 'Put them on, Teacher.' He blushed and then whirled around smartly, skimming along the icy ground like a flying swallow. I put on the gloves and my hands warmed up. A magic feeling arose in my heart. After so many years of loneliness, it was the first time I had been cared for by another heart. The affection was wonderful for my lonely soul.

The most difficult time for me was in the evening when the sun was down, the light was dim, the birds were going back to their nests and everyone was returning home. No one came to me, no one at all. The long and lonely evenings that I spent by myself, sitting and gazing at the emptiness in silence, were miserable. Since I had developed insomnia, I didn't know how to laugh, and every laughing sound from others was a torment to me, a sick and lonely woman. I didn't understand why others could laugh and be joyous.

One Sunday evening Field and a couple of his friends, Border and United, came into my dormitory. The dormitory was a small room I shared with two other women, Ms Yi and Ms Song. Their husbands worked and lived in the city centre and most nights they didn't stay in the dormitory. I was the only permanent resident. Our room of twelve square metres was damp, dark and shabby. The only window was on the same side as the door facing the public lane, a very narrow lane less than two metres wide. The unpainted mud walls were rough and the earth floor was damp. There was no ceiling beneath the roof. Particles of dust and other material often dropped down and blinded me when I was lying in bed. The whole place felt gloomy and pathetic — just like my mental state at the time.

Field looked around the room while his friends were chatting away with me. Suddenly our talk was interrupted by Field: 'Teacher, don't you have a clothes hanger?'

I didn't have any clothes hangers. They were expensive and most house mistresses had their hangers made by their husbands, but I didn't have the strength nor the skill to make them. So my towels, underclothes, trousers and bits of rags were hanging on a rope in the middle of the room.

The next Sunday the three came again. Field, like a magician standing in the centre of the room, brought out clothes hangers one after another from the collar of his shirt and placed them on my bed. There were eight altogether. 'I am sorry, Teacher, I wanted to make ten but could only find enough wire for eight.'

Later on, I would come to know that his 'shirt pocket' was a magical treasure bag and fancy gifts one after another came out of it for me, bringing endless pleasure and wonderful feelings. To make the shirt pocket, he had tied up his underwear with his belt and created a handy bag. Items from his parents' home shifted to me without notice when he crossed the long path from the other end of the factory to my place.

With a beautiful smile he made a proposal: 'Teacher, we three want to make a ceiling for your room.'

'Thank you for the hangers, but the ceiling would be a difficult job.' I replied. 'Why not forget the ceiling and repair the wet ground? I cannot bear the damp ground any longer.'

The floor was damp because the level inside the house was several inches lower than the outside. I had already developed arthritis and my knees were so painful that it added to my troublesome sleep. I desperately wanted to fix the earth floor but could never find the energy or the skill to do it.

'Don't worry,' Border said, and they looked at each other conspiratorially. With twinkling eyes Field said, 'Could you trust us to be in your room alone?'

'Yes, of course I will,' I said. Leaving the room, I looked back over my shoulder and met Field's eyes; they were glittering with feeling, making my heart tremble with tender sweetness.

When I came back that evening, the three boys were just finishing the job and getting ready to leave. The ground now looked dry, firm and clean. It had been repaired with chalk, cinders and clay, a common way to build up earth floors at that time; and the ceiling was completed, made out of clean newspapers over a network of wire in many small squares.

I couldn't believe my eyes! The room looked so different from the one I'd left in the morning. Now it was new, clean and neat. I was full of appreciation and kept on looking at the ground, then the ceiling, then the ground again and didn't know what to say to express my gratitude. Field was looking at me with a lovely, lovely smile. They collected their tools and said goodbye, and as they left Field looked back over his shoulder with a fire in his eyes that warmed me to the bottom of my heart.

Little by little I found myself longing to go to work, to get into Field's classroom and to see he who would always smile at me. As I lay in bed and closed my eyes, Fields' face kept floating in front of me. He had a handsome face with a perfect complexion, patches of healthy pink on his cheeks and eyelids. His nose was straight, his lips were full. When he smiled, he showed his small white neat teeth. His hair was black and shining. The mental picture of Field would mesmerise me into sleep and I had no more fear of horrible nights.

But I felt guilty about Rich and I decided to fight against the temptation of passion. During the winter holiday between 1976 and 1977 when I was staying with Rich in Qingdao, I kicked myself hard each time when I thought of Field. I was determined to forget him.

When I came back to Ulumuqi after three weeks' holiday, I did my best not to have any contact with Field. I didn't smile when I gave the lessons to his class, I didn't look in his direction and I didn't stay in the classroom for even one second after class. I would quickly gather my stuff and run away as fast as I could. This resistance lasted for a couple of months until one day United, Field's close friend, caught up with me when I was walking alone from the school to my dormitory. He said to me, 'Teacher, you have changed. You are no longer as happy as you were. Field is sad and he says he dreams of you frequently. In his dreams you wear a red jacket and smile happily.' Hearing this, I could hardly keep back my tears. I was very sad and lonely just then. I had just received a letter from Rich, and it was very hurtful: 'It is better for us to have a divorce since you are not be able to give birth to a baby for me,' he wrote. Rich's heartless attitude made me ponder. Was it worthwhile to keep my allegiance to him? If I did, I was not being fair to myself. From this moment I made up my mind that I would take a dangerous road. This would be my protest against Rich's abuse, showing my contempt for the people who made the cruel and absurd system of 'marriage of separation'.

CHAPTER THIRTEEN

Field was nineteen years my junior. The age difference between us didn't reduce any sweetness and happiness for us; rather, it was a perfect haven for protecting our secret friendship since nobody would suspect it. It was the only possible way for me to seek emotional comfort as a married woman without a husband. Field came to my house every evening after supper. The time spent waiting for him to arrive was pleasurable as I knew he was always punctual. On cold days, we stayed in the room and I would sit on the edge of my single bed beside the door, he on Ms Yi's bed opposite mine. We'd talk and laugh away the time until my bedtime, then he would say goodnight. I would go to bed in delight, thinking about him: the loving from his dark eyes, the beauty of his youthful face, his shining hair, his caring talk, his humour and his singing. How pure he was. He had no vanity at all, and he loved me so deeply.

In summer we would go out in the moonlight and sit under the trees, chatting away. And how I could talk! Walking beside me and listening attentively, Field was the perfect listener. I could talk for ages about books I had read, stories I remembered, and my hopes, dreams and thoughts. When I talked about my family, I always talked about Superb with great admiration. Later, when her true colours showed, Field laughed at my naïvety.

I was surprised I could have so much to say. For years I hadn't had anybody who would listen to me so patiently. I talked and talked. We didn't touch each other and for three years we were celibate, although we were very much in love. On my side, Field's presence was enough to make my heart leap with satisfaction and happiness. On his side, he loved me so tenderly and was too respectful to do any physical invading. How beautiful our spiritual romance was.

The years of 1978 and 1979 saw me an absolutely different person. I was ardently in love. My heart, full of sunshine, was wafting in a land of roses. My life was content with a pleasant teaching job during the day and romantic enjoyment in the evening.

One Sunday morning in spring, Field and I planned an outing. To avoid people noticing us, we travelled separately and met at the other side of the hills behind the factory. The sunshine was warm and bright, the hills were covered with drifts of wild flowers in white, yellow and blue. I strolled in the valley alongside a brisk stream. Bees danced over the pink-and-white wild rose bush at the bank over the river, and I felt entranced as if I was slightly drunk. There wasn't a single soul around. I was so happy that I felt I was eighteen again.

At the foot of the hills there was a small bus-stop where Field was waiting for me. Sitting on the ground, lost in contemplation, he looked a bit sullen but as soon as I saw him, his eyes gleamed.

He sprang up and said, 'Let's go.' I followed him and soon we were walking in an avenue lined up with sand-date trees. I revelled in the sweet fragrance of the warm air. Sand-date trees are famous for their ability to live in dry places and for the fragrance from their small pale yellow flowers. Then Field disappeared. I looked around, distraught. Suddenly I heard him call me. To my amusement, he was sitting in a tree, hiding himself in the dense flowers, grinning mischievously. The next moment, I saw him standing in front of me, holding a big bunch of flowers. He handed the flowers to me and at this moment our hands touched accidentally. It was a heavenly feeling. My eyes met his; he blushed. Everything was intoxicating. For hours and days the magic feeling of touching his hand stayed in my heart.

Holding the sand-date flowers, we walked down the path along the stream side by side. We sped up down the valley, singing, laughing and running — just like two teenagers. At the bottom of the valley, making sure nobody was watching, Field stopped and said, 'You are my sunshine.'

A few days later we arranged to meet at a cinema one mile away from the leather factory. The evening air was cool and the sky was like brilliant satin. I walked briskly and my heart jumped with passion. I was keen to meet Field and to see the movie. After Mao's death, old films made before the Cultural Revolution were screened again. After ten years without seeing a film apart from Madam Mao's *Eight Standard Revolutionaries* movies and Peking operas, the public was crazy for real artistic works and old films were extremely popular. I had been to one not long before on my own, but it was a disaster. Hundreds of men and women fought each other at the gate, trying to get through first. I managed to get as far as the entrance, but then I was pressed onto the bar and was stuck there. People around me were pushing, shoving and elbowing. My stomach was crushed, my wallet stolen and my watch scratched. It was a 'Made in Shanghai' watch, the most popular watch at that time, and had cost me ten months of saving. I dared not to go to cinema after that.

'You have me now,' Field said gallantly. 'I will take care of you.'

Holding two tickets in his hands, Field was waiting for me at the gate. 'Follow me,' he said and began moving into the heaving mass. I clutched a corner of his coat, trying to push forward in the pressing crowd but was soon separated from him. I craned my neck but all I could see was an endless sea of dark heads. Just when I began to panic, Field elbowed his way back to me. He held me in front of him and bulldozed through the crowd, elbowing, pushing and shouldering. Moving into the middle of the cinema, which had been converted from a conference hall, Field showed me two stools in a good position — God knows where he'd got them from. Soon the movie, *Old Woods Revived*, started. What a good choice to suit the joy in my heart! But I couldn't concentrate on the screen.

Field was sitting beside me on my left, and I could feel the warmth from his young body. I wanted to touch his hands. The beautiful feeling I'd had on the day when our hands touched accidentally was seducing me again. From the corner of my eye I saw his right hand on his hip, pink, healthy and shapely with youthful tone. How much I wanted to touch it. My heart was beating fast. My head was spinning. The desire was so strong that I wanted to take a risk. Brave, I needed to be brave. But what would happen if I was caught? People were everywhere. On my right was a middle-aged woman with a big gossipy-looking mouth. If she saw anything unusual the whole community would know. But I did want to do it, to touch Field's hand, to nourish my soul.

Very, very slowly I moved my left hand a quarter of an inch, half an inch, one inch . . . Once I had started I didn't hesitate. I touched his little finger, and he quickly gripped my hand and moved it towards him. Two grabbing hands were hidden in the gap between us. I held my head up high and Field did too. We were looking at the screen attentively, but all we could feel was the sweetness of our hands touching.

Weeks and months passed. The happiness brought by the hand-touch stayed in my heart, producing endless romantic feelings. We still met almost every evening. I was not a poor lonely soul any more. Field had changed my life completely. We didn't touch any more after the hand-holding. Who needs physical stuff if the heart is happy? I didn't know if Field was controlling his desire or not, but for me, I enjoyed aesthetic beauty and poetic romance far more than physical pleasure. After all, we were more spiritual creatures than animals. We had minds, hearts and souls, which produced much enjoyment through thinking, dreaming and imagining.

One summer day I went to visit Pearl, the daughter of my desert friend Mr Yang. Pearl was a studious girl and had passed the entrance examination to a medical institute in Ulumuqi when the university reopened in 1978, and she became the glory of No. 14 Team. We talked and talked until late afternoon and then she insisted that I should stay with her overnight so that we could chat some more. We were rambling in the campus garden after dinner. The summer evening was cool and the lilac spread its subtle fragrance in the air. I told Pearl about my exciting romance. 'How lucky you are. To love and be loved is the highest bliss in life,' she exclaimed.

It was late morning when I returned to the leather factory and I missed Field all the way back. Thinking of his beautiful face, his affectionate eyes and his smart figure, my heart was filled with bittersweet emotions. I wanted to see him right now; I couldn't wait any longer. How I regretted staying with Pearl overnight. I started to count the hours before I could see Field in the evening.

Arriving at my dormitory feeling a little depressed, I turned the lock and opened the door. I couldn't believe my eyes! Field was in the room, sitting on my single bed beside the door. He smiled at me when I stepped in. He jumped to his feet, exclaiming, 'I missed you so much,' and he dragged me towards him and kissed me on the lips. His lips were soft and full, a gentle touch of velvet, and his breath was as fresh as newly baked bread. I tasted a heavenly enjoyment. He told me he had walked back and forth dozens of times near my dormitory the evening before but saw the metal lock on the door. I was amazed when he told me how he came in: through the air hole, a small opening by the window. 'Love makes me capable of anything, even turning into a cat,' he said, and he embraced me and kissed me ardently.

Summer holiday of 1978 came and I went to Qingdao for the vacation. I kept dreaming about Field. In the dream I was in heaven walking on clouds. Field came up to me and we walked hand in hand to a place where I saw a big watermelon, fresh and shining; its dark green skin had impressive curved black stripes. Field cut it open for me. The ripe texture was the most beautiful rosy colour with a few shining black seeds in it.

Still in a happy mood, I woke up, thinking about the dream. Soon I realised that this was not an ordinary dream but a special message: the very next day I was confirmed pregnant. How nice it was that I would become a mother again and I supposed Rich would be happy now.

Nine weeks of summer holiday passed slowly and at last it was time for me to go back to Xinjiang. I waved a red handkerchief at the window when the train was slowing down in Ulumuqi Railway Station. I saw Field and his friends running one after another excitedly when they saw the red handkerchief, the signal we had agreed before I left. Field was wearing a new shirt, a pale blue one, just as fresh as his young face. He had grown taller and broader during the last two months.

As I got off the train, our eyes met. We both had great difficulty concealing our love. Arriving in my dormitory accompanied by Field and his friends, to my great surprise, I saw a big watermelon on the wooden bench in the room, exactly the same as I'd see in my dream. What a miracle! United told me an impressive story. Worried that the watermelon season might finish before I returned, Field had hidden a couple of watermelons in a hole beside a fountain in the fields. He covered them with straw and went there to check them twice a day.

After I told him about my pregnancy, Field made a big fuss of me.

Often I would see a couple of red apples, a packet of sweets or a bag of roasted peanuts lying underneath my pillow. I never knew when he placed the presents there but they made me very happy as if I had touched his secret loving hands, and they caressed me into sleep. In the morning when I opened the door I often found a piece of tofu, a package of eggs or a jar of milk. Those foods were rare and you had to fight in the crowds to buy them. I would never have had them if I didn't have Field's love. One more sweet memory: on a fine Sunday we had an outing. Using a glass jar, he caught many small fish, each no more than an inch long. Back home, he washed and gutted them one by one and helped me to fry them. Then he watched me eating all of them with an air of contentment. They were the most delicious fish I had had in all my life.

When it was snowing and the ground was icy he would walk cautiously just half a step behind me. He would say, 'I am preparing in case you fall down. If I see you falling, I will fall first so that you can land on me.' From his expression I knew he was serious. Was there another person in the world who could take so much care of his sweetheart for her husband's baby? Only a pure young person is capable of such unselfish love. How lucky I was!

In the eyes of people around me, I was a poor, lonely pregnant woman without a husband or any family around to take care of me. In reality I was cared for and content, with a gentle and compassionate sweetheart — and the secret was exciting too. My pregnancy was going very smoothly without any morning sickness or ailment. Surprisingly, I slept very well without any symptoms of insomnia during the whole nine months.

CHAPTER FOURTEEN

Every evening I had my simple dinner in my dormitory, washed my face, combed my hair, and waited for Field. He always came at around six-thirty in winter and seven-thirty in summer. Sitting on my bed, I read a book and waited for him peacefully, many happy memories warming my heart.

We would have a long sweet kiss behind the door, a place safe from intruders; we would embrace at the edge of my single bed beside the door and then we would go out for a walk, or see a film in summer; in winter he would make the fire roar and we would chat the time away. He always left for home at around nine-thirty in winter and ten-thirty in summer. He was full of gallantry and never failed to show his love, concern and consideration for me.

In the open-air cinema when seats ran out, he searched hard to find some bricks and brought them back, let me sit on them, stood behind me and smiled with satisfaction, as if it was him seated not me.

One day we were strolling around the city and I was wearing a new pair of high-heeled shoes which hurt me a lot. Taking off his sport shoes, Field put on my red high heels. He looked so funny and he ridiculed himself and made me laugh. My heart was tenderly touched. His loving deeds like this happened all the time: encouraging me, warming me, comforting me. It seemed as if he was my eternal source of happiness.

However, things later became a bit difficult. He was watched more tightly by his parents, and there were days when he had to run the mile from his home to my dormitory just to say that he had to stay at home, and then he was gone again. His coming to me every day had alerted his parents and it worried them a lot. It would be a huge scandal and their names would be ruined if it was found out that their son was dating a much older married woman. While understanding his parents, I was desperately in love with Field and couldn't give him up. My heart was torn by conflict.

The day became darker and darker. It was well past the usual time but Field still hadn't come. If only I could hear his voice I would be fine, but there was no way I could call him.

The weather was getting bad. Huge flakes of snow were circling in a wild storm, whistling, ghostly. I was becoming 'an ant on a hot wok', very restless and anxious. Agitatedly I began walking to and fro across the room, neurotically waiting for bad news. At one stage I tried to lie in bed but it was too difficult to close my eyes. Time was moving slowly and I was desperate.

Suddenly I heard a knock at the door, a faint sound, almost lost in the storm. With a whirl of cold wind, Field rushed in, covered with snow. He held me and kissed me passionately. My lips, cheeks, eyelids and neck were covered by his frantic kisses and I could hardly breathe, but I felt a huge joy.

Then, answering my enquiring eyes, he told me he had been kept in the house by his parents and his father had whipped him with a belt: 'This is the first time in all my life my father has beaten me. I don't mind it that much as long as I am allowed to see you. I got up from the dinner table and quickly walked to the door only to see my father was standing at it like a guard, with a severe face. I tried to run away from him but he caught me by my arm. Holding a belt, he beat my bottom which hardly hurt. However with each blow I screamed loudly to make a fuss. My father took pity on me and set me loose. After lying in bed for a short while I jumped up and ran out of the house. My father, aroused by anger, caught me and took me back. He locked me in the firewood hut where I stayed for a couple hours, then I made a hole in the door and slipped out.'

There were a few cuts on his face, made by the cracks in the wooden door. He didn't care about his scars but was more concerned about my anxiety. Gently wiping away my tears, he soothed me by telling jokes, pulling faces and dancing comically. I couldn't help but burst into laughter although there were still tears in my eyes.

Despite increasing conflict with his parents, Field still managed to come and visit me almost every day. Once he wept, when his father became so stressed that he had a heart attack. His father was a nice man with great love for Field even though he was an adopted child. Field felt conflict between caring for his father and romancing me.

Rationally I wanted to fight against love, but my soul was breaking and my heart bleeding. One day I summoned my courage and told Field we must not see each other again. He responded with more kisses: 'I will love you forever, even when the rock becomes rotten and the sea becomes dry.' Tears came to my eyes. My heart was aching.

I tried really hard to stick to my resolutions: to avoid seeing Field and to promote my job transfer. Every evening I went to the home of Mr Zheng, the head of the personnel office, and taught his son English. I deliberately stayed there until late so that Field would have no chance to see me. Life became lonely, dull and unbearable again, but I was not going to relent. I must listen to my rational mind and keep my resolve. I looked forward to the baby's birth and wanted to take care of my relationship with Rich. Surely Rich would be nice to me when I was his baby's mother?

In February 1979, I wrote to Rich informing him that I would soon go back to Qingdao for the baby's birth. He wrote back, 'Everybody knows when the baby should be due and if it is earlier, it is not my baby.' I was outraged and could never forget the hurt of his ruthless words. I didn't take the trip until it was only a couple weeks before the due date. When my baby daughter Nini was born, I developed depression and couldn't sleep after Rich visited me and said in front of several women in the ward that he didn't like babies. My insomnia came back, even though I'd been perfectly healthy during the whole pregnancy and had had no problem falling asleep anywhere or at any time.

Sleeping poorly and eating little, I lay in bed in the cramped small room I shared with Rich's aged talkative mother and wept frequently. I was concerned for Nini's well-being. Would I have to leave my new-born baby behind again?

The baby's birth didn't change Rich's attitude; rather, he was annoyed because I'd given birth to a girl instead of a boy. 'Damn it, I will never have a son at this rate,' he complained. He hardly came to see me after the baby was born.

One day I gathered all my courage and called Rich to my bedside: 'I don't want to leave the baby alone. I want to stay here and try my best to shift my job from Xinjiang to Qingdao.'

'What about money? If you stay here, a lot of money will lost. No. You must go back to Xinjiang to work and earn money!'

As if he was afraid I would stay too long, Rich urged me to leave when Nini was only two months old. The night before I left, lying beside my baby, watching her tiny sweet face, my tears flowed with no stopping. It was arranged that Rich's mother would look after Nini and I would take Enya to Ulumqi.

My heart breaking, I took Enya in one hand and the travelling bag in another, and walked out of the room where baby Nini was sleeping, smiling in her dreams. She had no idea Mama was leaving, for money's sake, for 46.5 *yuan* ($US5.50) a month.

During the five-day train journey, I wept and wept. Many times I wished the train would crash and I would be killed, to save me from the unbearable pain of leaving my new-born baby behind.

In my dormitory, little Enya shared the room with me and the two other women. As poor and crowded as it was, she was very happy and enjoyed herself. The fact that she was living with Mum for the first time in her nine years was good enough for her to feel elated. After a few months' turbulence between mother and child, we developed a close relationship and became dedicated to each other with unconditioned love and support.

Disappointed by Rich, I allowed Field to become part of my life again. I now realised that Field and I had no option and would share a powerful and painful destiny.

With Enya living with me and sharing my meagre income, our material life was very difficult. Field helped us a lot — repairing the roof, brushing the wall, carrying coal, cutting firewood and building the stove. He spent almost every Sunday doing some heavy jobs for us. I don't know how we could have managed without his help. When Enya's only pants wore out, Field, who had never touched a sewing machine before, sewed a pair of pants overnight and delivered them to us in the early morning, just at the time when Enya was weeping about being unable to go to school without pants.

Field and I were still chaste and we still met almost every day, although we couldn't have our kiss in the evening since Enya was there. The only time we could manage it was in the daytime behind the door. To avoid being discovered, we nervously kissed for a while then separated, listening attentively to any sound outside, and then came back to kiss again. Anybody's steps could induce a panic in both of us. Red-faced, we'd look at each other, smile, and then go back to kissing again. Sometimes we were interrupted by Ms Yi or Ms Song, my dormitory mates, whose steps were familiar to us. Hearing them approaching, we would quickly separate — I would sit on my bed holding a book, pretending to read, and Field would stand beside the stove as if he were tending the fire.

In the summer of 1979, Field left school and became a worker in the leather factory. His father had recently retired and, according to the regulations, Field was allowed to take his father's position. Field was reluctant since he was hoping to go to university. But his father's wish had to be obeyed. Soon after he took the job in the foundry, Field developed a knee problem and needed an operation.

Surprisingly, the operation initiated our first sex adventure.

It was nearly three years since we had fallen in love and our love was mature and ripe, eager now to fruit. The separation during the past few days when he had been in hospital was the catalyst, pushing our feelings towards lust.

It was an autumn Sunday in 1979, with Enya playing with her friends somewhere, I was at home alone, missing Field and worrying about his operation. It seemed that three months instead of three days had passed since he had left for the hospital. It seemed I could feel the pain in my knee as if the doctor was cutting my own kneecap open. I was actually shivering with the pain created by my imagination. Suddenly, in came Field, limping. He was wearing a scarlet sports jacket and a pair of olive-coloured trousers. On his right knee, I could see the round curve of the thick bandage. Excitedly he told me he had escaped from the hospital: 'I just want to see you for a second and then I will be all right and leave.' He smiled at me, hardly able to stand up. One of his legs touched the ground; the other one in the air; he was shivering. He leaned forward to kiss me and collapsed on top of me. I felt the warmth of his youthful body, the lissomness of lean muscles. I felt his heart beating hard, a prelude to action. We clasped and kissed fervently. With his healthy knee supporting him, he managed to take off his pants halfway while moaning from the pain of his operated knee. He then pulled up my blue skirt up with his hand and took off my underpants. The next second, it happened so naturally, our two bodies joined together. Our bodies were as hot as flames, and Field's painful bleeding knee was like a mute inspiration, reminding me of his true love for me and it brought more passion into my heart. His penis, pink and hard, touched my belly. My skin was on fire. At my entrance he hesitated; maybe he didn't know what to do as a virgin, or he was waiting for me to make the decision. I said, 'Go,' and in he thrust. When he was inside me and making adept waves with his flexible body in spite of his painful right knee, my whole body became sexual cells, each one screaming, shaking and impassioned. The joyous feeling was phenomenal and unforgettable. After three years of chaste romantic love, it tasted hilariously sweet and its beauty had produced enough inspiration to nourish me, heart and soul, for many years to come.

It had lasted only a couple of minutes but it was enough for an eternal memory. It was delicious and heart-wrenching. We were rewarded for our three years of celibate and spiritual love. But what a mess his right leg was in! Blood was on his trousers, the bandage was red all over, and drips of blood were running towards his ankle. 'I am sorry,' he said, but his eyes were filled with excitement as if he had discovered a new continent.

I was both happy and remorseful afterwards. I had now committed adultery and I was ashamed and scared. If anybody got to know about it, I would get into deep trouble. I would lose my job as a teacher and also get a bad record in my dossier that would follow me all my life, and my name and future would be ruined forever. It was bad for Field too. After all, he was nineteen years younger than I was. The misalliance between us could make him the most scandalous young man in China.

We had to stop seeing each other, I decided, in case the same thing happened again.

I wrote many letters to the authorities, both in Ulumuqi and in Qingdao. I also visited Mr Zheng and pleaded with him again and again. Under my coaching his son had passed the examination for university entrance and he was grateful to me. Another positive point was that English teachers were in great demand everywhere in China, and the fact that my husband worked in Qingdao was helpful since Deng Xiaoping had given orders to unify separated husbands and wives, to let them live together.

At last, one day in August 1980, I got a permit to shift my job to Qingdao. I had been dreaming of this event for the whole fifteen years since I left my hometown in 1965. However, I couldn't feel any gaiety about it; rather, I became jittery and neurotic. I would lose my temper with Field one minute and then weep bitterly the next. Tears fell whenever I contemplated life without Field. I ordered a dress from a tailor, thinking that Field might like it, forgetting that I would be leaving in two days and he would never see me in it. Even on the top of the truck to the railway station, with many students to see me off, I was fussy and picky towards Field and blamed him for his 'wrong looking'. At the railway station after I shook hands and said good-bye to each of the thirty-odd students, I got on the train and seated Enya and myself beside the window. Suddenly I burst out crying. Field, his head held up high, standing underneath my train window, stared at me with incredible emotion. His eyes were gleaming with tears, full of despair and sadness. And how painful and agonising the train journey was. Throughout the entire four nights and five days, I was weeping and sobbing. Uncountable times I wished the train would go towards Ulumuqi instead of leaving it further and further. More than once I wondered if it was possible for Enya and me to get off this train and get on one running in the opposite direction. But I was confined by the job-shifting documents, all my belongings were in another carriage, and we would have no practical base to live in Ulumuqi. Holding my copy of La Dame aux Camellias by Alexandre Dumas, I was reading and weeping. I shared Violetta's tragedy with my own broken heart. Forced by a strong and invisible power, we were destined to give up love. The end for Violetta was death. What lay ahead for me in the unknown future? I knew it would be no less painful than Violetta's tormented ending.

Against my will, it was impossible to face Rich without thinking about

Field: his personality was a far cry from Field's loving, lively and good-natured demeanour. I had made up my mind that I would try my best to reconcile with Rich, but reality is always more difficult than what we hope for.

To start with, Rich and I had a big row over where I should work. He wanted me to work in Licun and he had built connections with an official of the educational bureau. A position had been kept for me in a primary school at the town centre, but I hated the town life there. In the last decades the once-quiet suburb had changed. The river in the middle of the town was now a dry, dirty ditch. The orchards had been replaced by concrete buildings. The whole place was noisy, ugly and filthy. Its people were an absurd mob who had changed from earthy, simple-minded peasants into conceited and self-important townfolk. I said I would work anywhere but Licun. The official who had kept the position for me was outraged. 'You don't know what a favour I've done for you. That single position is sought after by dozens of teachers!' he shouted indignantly. 'There is one vacancy for you outside Licun, which is in Beijai.'

Beijai was the poorest area in the whole county of Laoshan, a suburb of Qingdao, but I decided to go and have a look. It was an hour's journey by bus, and the last stop was Da Lao Village. I found myself in an exquisite valley surrounded by high and stony mountains. I started to walk towards Sunjia School, my future workplace. Strolling on a little winding path shaded by poplar trees, I enjoyed the country scenery. The air was refreshing, the breeze was cool. There were a few peasant women selling pears and apples on the side of the road. The women were healthy and good-looking. A few peasants were working in the vegetable gardens, where the Chinese cabbages and Jiaodong turnips were lush and vigorous. The uphill walk took me about half an hour and at the curve of the road I saw the school, a small two-storey granite building with a red roof and a playground in the front of it. A brisk stream, singing and flowing, circled the school; its water was clean and clear, with white and pink sand visible at the river bed. Many trees were growing in the water — it was all picturesque. Behind the school there was an ancient-looking stone bridge, curving up towards the road and the deep mountains, at whose foot I saw bright orange wild lilies and walnut trees. Herbs covered the ground, their mauve flowers spreading a pretty smell that made me feel light-headed and intoxicated. It seemed I was in a different era, and the hustling and bustling of modern life seemed distant and vague.

I fell in love with the place. While nobody else shared my zeal, my mother was greatly impressed by the beauty from my description.

I happily accepted the position at Sunjia School and immediately became the centre of gossip. People expressed their surprise to me and behind my back about my bizarre choice. After all, life in the town would have been much easier. Rich yelled at me, 'You could have made 50,000 *yuan* by exchanging the job in town with a job in Beijai!' Even my new colleagues at Sunjia School, kind and simple as they were, took pity on my eccentric behaviour and thought I was naïve and ignorant. 'Life here is very poor and inconvenient. If you have official connections, it's better to leave as soon as you can,' they said. I didn't budge. My way of thinking was anything but mercenary. I simply longed for a simple and peaceful life close to nature. My soul was yearning for it.

I tried to persuade Rich to shift his work to Beijai so that we could reconcile our family life, but all I got from him was a sneer: 'I'm not as crazy as you are!' Once he'd helped me to carry my belongings for the bus trip to Sunjia School, he never came again.

Sunjia School had built a house as a teacher's residence on the bank of the river but there was nobody living there at the time I arrived as the construction was considered too poor. The school found me a peasant house belonging to an old woman and I stayed there instead.

I started teaching at once. My students were in the third and last grade of junior-middle school, about fifteen and sixteen years old. They were the most diligent students I had ever known. They were children of various villages with their homes as near as Sunjia Village and as far as Swallow's Nest village ten kilometres away. No matter how far away they lived, everybody arrived at school before six-thirty in the morning and hardly anyone was late. Their future depended exclusively on how well they did at school. To pass the entrance examination to technical academic schools was the only way to leave their village life and obtain a city residence, which was a much better life with benefits provided by the government. The competition was extremely harsh and they had to work extremely hard. The second choice was to pass the examination for high school, but then they had to face even harsher competition for university. If they failed these two options, the only future ahead for them, for most of them, was to remain in their original village for life, as their parents and ancestors had for centuries. My teaching career was never so fulfilling and appreciated by my students, and I got a tremendous response from my industrious students to every effort I put into my teaching. I enjoyed my job at Sunjia School to the full.

The parents of my students were almost all peasants who lived simple and primitive lives in the mountains. In Mao's time, after they lost their own land, their lives became poorer with little money or freedom. They had enough food, though; this was the area in which the least number of people died during the Three Years' Starvation in the 1960s, since they had vast mountainous areas providing edible weeds, leaves and roots, and in the deep mountains they could collect wild fruits and nuts. Fountains and streams with top-quality water were dotted over the mountains. Fertile land was scarce, though, and didn't provide enough food for them. To make a few *yuan*, the men went up to the mountains and cut the granite rocks and sold them for construction; the women raised goats and hens, selling the goat milk and eggs in the market to buy necessities.

On Sundays I went back to Licun by bus to stay with Rich overnight in his small flat and dined at his brother's place. Nini, Enya and six of Rich's relatives were living in the two-room house. I felt sorry for my two little girls but the lack of housing was a hellish problem everywhere in China at that time.

I missed Field terribly. After school all the students left and the whole place was empty and eerie. My sleep became worse and my appetite was poor. I felt I could survive if only I could see Field once more to get rid of the dreadful foreboding that I had lost him forever. The choice I had made, leaving him and letting the passion die down, had turned out to be so difficult. The distance of more than 10,000 kilometres from Qingdao to Ulumuqi was as far, in my mind, as from Earth to the moon. Field and I were separated by time, space and social code. I believed that I would never see him again. How anguished and lonely I was. From his letters, which arrived once a week, I knew that Field was missing me bitterly, too. He put his emotions into his diary every time he missed me and on Mondays he gathered them and posted them to me. He described how much he missed me. Once his legs carried him to the roadside where we used to meet under the poplar trees in the evenings. He saw a woman's figure and in reverie he thought it was me. He ran as fast as he could, his heart leaping with excitement, but the reality was cruel: it was somebody else. He was knocked back hard. Tears poured from my eyes when I read about it. In the dark small room, by a dim light when the old woman was asleep, I wrote to him and wept.

The living conditions were really harsh without cooking facilities. All I could get to eat was steamed buns and a little salted vegetables from the school kitchen at lunch time. During the night I was constantly woken up by hunger and dogs barking. Soon I became exhausted due to malnutrition and poor sleep, and had to take sick leave. I stayed at Crab Village since I felt so uncomfortable with Rich. There was no cooking facility available in his flat and his brother's place was too crowded. I was allowed to take Enya with me, but not Nini. At Crab Village I fell ill and had a high fever, but nobody looked after me since my mother was confined to bed for weeks, suffering a bad backache. Superb and Main pretended not to hear me even though I could hear their talking and laughing clearly. Lying sick in bed, I had a daydream of Field and his apparition kept on floating in front of me, driving me crazy. I want to see him, if only once!

Staying at my brother's place was humiliating. I was a nuisance and I could see the loathing on the faces of even Superb's children. I was like a pauper, nobody there cared for me and the one who cared was too far away. I was in despair.

On January 25, 1981 a telegram arrived. To my great surprise, it was from Field! He was coming to Qingdao to visit me. No words could describe my happiness — I had not lost him after all. Oh, dearest Field, you've saved me.

Field arrived at the railway station of Cangkou in the evening after I had waited for a couple of hours, which had seemed a century. The happiness the moment we saw each other was so huge we couldn't speak. Maybe you don't want to speak at such a special moment. In silence I let the rapture flow through my veins. We looked at each, sparks jumping in our eyes.

Field told me about his trip. On the eve of the Chinese New Year, after carrying six buckets of water to the jar for his parents and his sister, he left a note underneath his pillow informing them that he was going to

Qingdao for a few days, and off he went. He carried a small, tightly packed bundle, two woollen blankets, and famous products from the leather factory as presents for me. His toilet gear was in his shirt-and-belt pocket. He had seven days off for the New Year holiday but it wasn't enough since the return train journey alone would need ten days. He was prepared to be late for work for one week, which meant that he could stay with me for only three days. How short it was. But what else could I expect? All I had wanted was to be able to see him again. And now he was in front of me, real, alive and loving. How grateful I was.

Superb and Main had built their new house with the help of my mother's pension. The house had four rooms in a row, in the style of the rural houses at the time, with a square courtyard surrounded by tall brick walls. Mother had lost all say over her money. Superb kept mother's registered document for pension, the pensioner's book and her stamp with her name officially carved on it, the two things you needed to get your pension from your previous workplace. Every month, Main went to get the fifty-one *yuan* (later it became seventy-three *yuan*), an enviable income in the neighbourhood, and then would hand all of it to his wife. Superb would give my mother ten *yuan* and, for the rest of it Mother had no say. Although Superb liked Mother's money, she couldn't get along with Mother. She wanted to throw the old lady away while keeping her money. She was just waiting for the right moment.

According to Superb's arrangement, Field stayed in the bed shared by my Mother and Superb's two daughters, Bell and June. Next to my mother's was a room that acted as dining room and lounge. Further up was the room where Enya and I were to stay. Main and Superb's bedroom was at the far end.

Superb behaved nicely to Field. She offered him warm food and made polite conversation with him, and then it was time to go to bed. Lying in bed beside Enya, I was in an ecstatic mood, half-asleep half-awake, enjoying the fact that Field was only next door to me. Suddenly I heard a noise and the next second I was aware that Field was with me. He had covertly slipped out over my mother, who slept at the edge of their bed, and come to me. He pulled up my quilt and lay beside me. I was fully awake instantly. He clasped me in his arms and we kissed and cuddled and then lay quietly to feel the intimacy, so close, warm and sweet. I heard my mother call Field's name in an angry voice but we clasped even tighter. My body was shivering with both excitement and fearful anticipation.

The next morning we got up before everybody else and set off for sightseeing in Qingdao. We had spicy bean-curd soup in Pichaiyuan, a famous traditional food lane built in the 1920s. We strolled along Zhongshan Road, the busiest commercial street, with all sorts of fancy shops. Field enjoyed the art and handcrafts shop the most. He sighed happily, 'These works are so beautiful and eye-opening. I am very lucky to have a chance to see them.' My heart sang in great joy and appreciation. How lovely he was. We rambled along the beach and the pier and visited Luxun Park with its ancient-style aquarium and sea-products museum, their red, yellow and blue tiles shining in the warm and gentle winter sunshine. There were fewer people in the streets, mainly the ones wearing their festival best, carrying boxes of presents and visiting their relatives or friends, the major activity for the New Year season. There were also people returning from a feast, drunk and wobbling with red jolly faces.

When we arrived home in the evening according to Superb's invitation to have dinner with the family, we found the atmosphere tense. Everybody was silent except Superb, who was over-excited. Main's face was dark and forbidding.

Main had always been my mother's darling and he acted towards me in a superior manner, edged with a spoiled temper. He had had a hard life because of being a 'son of black elements'. He was prevented from attending university even though he had sat the entrance examination three times. The ordeal in the Cultural Revolution and his reluctant marriage didn't help. It had all made him a bitter person. After he married Superb his life went down another slope, because he became controlled and intimidated. To take over the power in the family, Superb had gone to extremes. She shrieked at Mother for hours, saying Mother didn't love her enough. She had shat in the bedroom and ordered Main to scoop it up with his hands; at nights, she scratched and kicked, not allowing him to sleep; she had slapped Mother's face when she was upset at seeing her taking care of Enya; she had been to Main's workplace to tell his boss and colleagues how nasty Main was and how nice she was; she had cut off Main from all his friends; she would act sad, miserable and pitiable as her last weapon if all the other tricks didn't work — and she always won.

187

Main was subdued by his wife. Superficially he looked light-hearted to please her, but beneath this false gaiety he was enraged by his low self-esteem and the loss of his self-respect. He would show his anger towards Mother and me, the more vulnerable ones, whom he was not afraid of. He was encouraged in this by Superb, who was keen to harm me and get rid of me.

'I don't like your brother's home,' Field said while we were walking towards Crab Village. It was true that the atmosphere was uneasy and our tremendously happy time was overshadowed by it. Main was constantly holding a hunting gun in and out of the house with a gloomy and brooding face. My mother looked nervous and she avoided my eyes.

At midnight on the second day, I heard my mother call, 'Field!' I then heard her walking to my room. Field was standing beside my bed. On hearing Mother's voice, he quickly lowered himself to the floor and hid underneath a table like a curling dog while my mother was angrily yelling, 'Where is Field?' I was so nervous that my breathing nearly stopped. Mother searched the moon-lit room while Field crawled soundlessly around her feet. Under her nose he walked on all fours to the courtyard. Mother went back to her bed. Finding no Field there, she came back to me and yelled, 'Where is Field?' Field, in his summer singlet and short pants, came in from the courtyard and answered, 'Do you ask for me? I've been out for a pee.' His voice was amazingly calm, even though he was shivering in the below-zero temperature. My mother came back to me, standing in front of my bed and scolded, 'You are a bad woman!' My mother, with a loving heart, understood my ordeal of emotional loneliness, but she was nervous that if our affair was made known, people would be scandalised and Superb would use it to ruin me.

The next day when we were out of the house, Field had a good laugh at the game he played with my mother: 'I was just at her feet and if she moved her feet one inch more, she might have kicked me.' I was laughing with him. The grim and gloomy air in my brother's place seemed nothing and not worth thinking about so long as Field was here with me, so long as I loved and was loved.

In the afternoon we took the bus to Sunjia School and I showed him the teachers' residential house at the river bank. The house was in a pathetic state. The windows were broken; dog shit was on the earth floor;

tiles were missing on the roof . . . Who could imagine that the very next day, my mother, my daughter and I would come and live here?

Another day came, the day that Field was leaving us for Ulumuqi. As I was putting on my clothes, I heard Main yelling from my mother's room, 'Weijun! Come here!' I walked to him and flinched when I saw his angry face. Suddenly I felt two heavy smacks in my face. 'You woman of depravity, get out of my house!' howled my brother in a wild rage. As he was about to strike a third blow he was stopped by Field, who ran quickly and planted himself between us. Main whirled to the other side of the room and yelled at Mother, 'Get up! Go away with your bloody daughter who has lost face!' My mother had suffered from back pain for weeks and had been out of bed for only a couple of days. My poor old mother was struggling up from her bed when Main rolled up the bedding and threw the entire pile on the floor and screamed at her, 'You get away from my house with your bloody daughter! Hurry up! Otherwise I will kill her!'

Superb could hardly conceal a malicious, satisfied smile. She said airily, 'Okay, I'll go to find a rubber-wheeled tractor for you.' (These were the only kind of transport in the village.) Within a few minutes she was back and a rubber-wheeled tractor was outside the house. Bewildered, I started to move my few possessions onto the tractor with the help of Field and Enya. At this moment, I heard Superb call me: 'Come in, Weijun. Leave Field to do the job. I need to have a talk with you and Mother.'

In the room, my mother, suddenly enormously aged, was sitting on a chair with her head shaking and her hands trembling. It was as if all the hundreds of wrinkles in her face had become sad streams and sore liquid was running out of them. Main, standing beside Superb like a guard, was severe and attentive. Obviously he knew what the talk was to be about and was ready to give us women a hit if necessary.

'Weijun, Mother, now Main has decided to let you go. I am his wife and I have to agree with him. It is all right for Mother to live with Weijun, but her pension should not be taken away with her. We all know that it was me who worked hard and brought Mother back from Changle. If it was not because of my superb job, she would definitely be dead by now. Therefore, her pension should belong to me for my old age. Do you agree?'

My mother's wrinkled face twitched. She wanted to say something but couldn't — she was too shocked by her son's inhuman stance. Seeing there was no objection, Superb carried on: 'But I am an excellent person with a golden heart. I will look after Mother's life. We will deliver thirty *yuan* every month and I will take the responsibility to make clothes for Mother. As for the remaining forty-three *yuan*, I want you to help my children. You have shown lots of love to Enya and it is time for you to show love for your son's daughters.' Main was nodding agreeably as if he also believed that Mother didn't love his children.

My mother and I were actually relieved when we heard that all that Superb wanted was money. Money was never my major issue and I kept quiet. Mother was not a money-lover and her favourite saying was, 'Losing money is not as painful as losing friendship or health,' a statement by William Wordsworth. Both my mother and I thought that thirty *yuan* plus clothes provided by Superb was enough for Mother's monthly expenses.

Facing no objection, Superb was on cloud nine. She was singing happily and walking with a dance in her step as she watched Mother, me and Enya — three generations of miserable women — getting ready to leave.

Outside in the courtyard, Field was busy loading and arranging our belongings on the tractor's trailer. All we had were Mother's bundle of clothes and her chamber pot, a makeshift table and four bowls Superb had offered to us, a makeshift metal bed and two packing boxes I had brought back from Xinjiang, two quilts for Enya and me and the two woollen blankets from Field. Field made space for me and Enya to sit amongst the piles on the small trailer of the tractor, and he accompanied my mother to take the bus for Da Lao. Little Enya, holding her schoolbag with both arms, waited at the side of the tractor patiently while the adults were in turmoil around her. She looked serious, contemplative. It must have been then that she made up her mind that it was her responsibility to protect me, her poor mother, and she must study hard and be strong so that we would not be bullied like this when she grew up. (A few years later when Superb's daughter Bell came to my place, trying to strike me for her father sleeping with another woman, Enya caught her and gave her a good kick. Bell never dared to come around to make trouble after that.)

I said to Field, 'I am sorry I can't see you off at the railway station. Please go and leave me here.'

'How could I leave you like this?' he exclaimed. 'I will go with you to Sunjia School.'

Sitting on top of the snail-speed tractor, suffering in the stormy wind from Siberia, my body was as frozen as my heart. My brother's brutality hurt me tremendously and I couldn't understand why he had become so cruel. Main had been a simple-minded person, with a bad temper occasionally. He had not been particularly close to me but he had not acted so relentlessly before, especially to Mother. I realised then that a family fight was the most hurtful trauma in life.

One hour later, Mother, Field, Enya and I arrived at the house of Sunjia School at the river bank. It was divided into four family flats but they were all locked. I had to find the key. Leaving my mother and daughter in the cold open air, I set off for the key, which the headmaster kept. Field caught up with me: 'Let me come with you. I worry about your safety in the empty road and I can do nothing to make Mother and Enya warm.'

Searching for the headmaster turned out to be difficult. It was the Spring Festival (Chinese New Year) time and everyone was visiting, eating and drinking. Field and I searched two villages before we found the half-drunk headmaster eventually. Mr Li was very astonished and sobered up immediately after he heard that my old mother and child were sitting at the open air waiting to move in. The kind-hearted man promptly left his host's house in the middle of a feast and hurried home for the key. He asked, 'Why are you moving on such a cold day in the festival time?' He didn't insist on an answer when he saw how embarrassed I was. He wrote a note to the teachers on duty at the school and handed me the key to the second door of the house.

It was more than two hours before Field and I at last arrived at the school house again. Back at my new home, I was heartbroken. My old mother of seventy-six was sitting on a little wooden stool in the empty space in front of the house and her grey hair, like dried grass, was flying about wildly in the high storm. Her body was scrunched tight, hands tucked in her sleeves, as if she wanted to shrink into a ball to keep out the coldness. Why was life so unfair to my mother? How could Main, her only son whom Mother loved so dearly, throw her out of his house on a cold day during a festival time, and not even come to see if she was still alive or dead?

Little Enya, standing beside her granny, nose running, cheeks red and lips blue with cold, was jumping and shivering. To my surprise neither Mother nor Enya showed much sadness. Rather, they looked quite patient and resolved. They must have felt comforted by the idea that we had our own home at last. Shabby and poor as it was, it was a home that could offer precious independence and set us free from the cruelty of our relatives.

With the help of Field and my colleagues at school, our home was gradually made liveable even though the first few weeks were really harsh. There was no electricity and the windows were covered with paper. The earth floor smelled of dog shit; the tiles on the roof were so poorly arranged, and there being no ceiling, snowflakes floated freely in the room when it snowed outside. It was too cold to sleep at night, and the water in the bucket turned into a solid block of ice overnight.

One very cold day when the temperature was eight degrees below zero, my colleague Glitter, who lived at Sunjia Village, came to help with the leaking roof. He climbed up on top of the house in the high wind and stuffed mud into the gaps between the tiles. His fingers were blue and green by the time the job was finished several hours later. The soldiers, who lived a hundred metres away in what had been the summer villa of a rich family before 1949, carried drinking water for us since we had no access to it — all we had was river water. The soldiers were a great help and would kindly bring anything — vegetables, cooking oil, fruits, even cement — to help us. On Sundays some of the young soldiers would come to help with hard physical labour, such as building the footpath, carrying coal and so on. The school students, led by their class teacher, helped us with other heavy jobs, such as digging the stony land into vegetable gardens and cutting firewood. What good luck to have such kind people living around us.

Three days after we arrived at Sunjia, after he helped me to set up the stove and carried coal from the shop two miles away, it was time for Field to leave. He was already very late for work. My tears falling, I saw Field's train going further and further away until it was merely a black dot in the misty horizon. Bless you, my dearest boy; I would never bestow my love on anybody else but you, beautiful young boy with a pure and deep loving heart. You have brought the deepest love to me. You have shown the virtues that a human heart could have. I would wait for you forever in solitude.

A letter arrived soon after Field was back at Ulumuqi. His father, worrying that he might stay with me permanently, had reported him to the authorities about his Qingdao trip. Within a few days rumours were spreading around the leather factory. Wherever he went, he heard people talking scornfully about him. He became the laughing stock of the community, 'the young man who runs away with a married old woman'. Nobody wanted anything to do with him — his friends deserted him and their households would not welcome him. His pay rise was cancelled, and he was even refused permission to attend a short English course. For the first time in his life he realised no one was free in an interfering and conformist society, that the 'collective spirit' was the dominating principle and everybody had to do what society expected you to do. Individuality was not accepted, and you would be punished by the mass if you did something unacceptable to the social conventions.

After a few months of confusion and shame, Field became submissive and accepted his position. On one hand he still had strong feelings for me; on the other hand he was beaten down by the relentless reality. And he gradually changed.

I loved Field even more after he took the risky trip to visit me. His bravery showed his unselfishness and true love. 'Love is a great tutor that makes us develop,' as Gustavo Flaubert wrote. I developed to another level in my life.

CHAPTER FIFTEEN

The teachers' residence, a simple concrete house, long and low, a tiny spot amongst the mountains, was our home now. Two years later three other families moved in; five years later another house was built in front of the first one, and a community of eight teachers' families was formed. But at the beginning of 1981, my mother, aged seventy-six, little Enya, aged ten, and myself, aged thirty-six, were the only residents, occupying one of the four flats of the house. White Sand River was at the back of the house. The river curved around the house against an upright granite rock shaped like a dragon horn. The rock was called Dragon Rock. The river underneath it was Dragon Pool and our house bore the same name.

Dragon Pool was surrounded by high mountains. They looked stern, serious and silent. To the west was Sunjia Village and to the east was Lying Dragon Village. The low granite bridge linked our residence to Sunjia School, one hundred metres away. A narrow, clean, sandy road in front of the house led to Dalaoguan, a Taoist Temple a couple of hundred metres away. This temple used to be a popular place with many worshippers coming from far and wide during the Bright and Refreshing Festival in spring, the Middle Autumn Moon Festival, the Chinese New Year and the Lantern Festival. Now its glory was gone.

At the time we moved in, a small factory was using the temple buildings to make machinery parts, and two years later it was converted into a state-owned garden hotel. Officials from all over the country would come in summer for a peaceful holiday.

Further up along the sandy road, ten miles away, was the beautiful

Beijiushui Sanatorium, famous for its tonic air, water and forests. The whole area, from Dragon Pool to Beijiushui, was an ideal holiday place. The local people were wonderfully good-looking and long-lived. You could see old men in their eighties, slim and energetic, walking up the mountain like brisk goats. You would see beauties in the village, beside the river, in the fields and mountains. Almost all the young girls were smooth-skinned with good figures, even though they lived a poor life and had to do heavy physical labour for survival. They seemed to have some special remedy to enable them to remain young and healthy. No wonder both Taoists and Japanese loved the place and wanted to live here permanently. The Taoists had built temples there throughout history, and the Japanese had wanted to build a Shangri-La in the area in the 1940s when they occupied China.

Living in Dragon Pool, my aged mother received wonderful benefits. Within one year, her health had improved tremendously. Her backache was gone. She no longer needed to hold a little wooden stool, stooped to the ground, as she moved about slowly and with difficulty. Her head was no longer shaky. Her bronchitis, which she had suffered from for decades, had almost disappeared. She used to have pulmonary emphysema which caused difficult breathing and now this symptom was gone too. Walking freely and energetically, she got up early, going out for a walk, coming home with a bunch of wild flowers in her hand, and then she would happily do the cooking and other light household chores.

In March, wild azaleas, pink, mauve and purple, bloomed on rocks and roadsides. In April cherry blossoms floated in the air, dancing on the river water, rolling in the green fields, covering the white granite bridge. In May, there were flowers from the trees of apple, peach, pear, apricot, plum and date. In June the wheat fields turned golden and the air was full of a warm aroma. August was the rainy month and floods from the mountains filled the river. Yellow water roared and rolled as if a thousand horses were stampeding, but within a couple days it calmed down and the water turned crystal-clear. We would walk on the granite bridge bare-footed and let the water run along our skin and caress our hearts. September came with a mature beauty; silver-coloured little fish swam in the river and herbs from the mountain spread their perfume. October was even better — the fields were waiting for harvest, like a pretty woman expecting her baby, happy and content. Apples, peaches, sweet potatoes, peanuts and chestnuts would be delivered to my house by the villagers. They wanted my mother to taste them first. It was the custom that the aged were the most respected. Even winter in Dragon Pool had its charm — the sunshine was golden and pure, the most beautiful sunshine I had ever known; the fields were covered with a green carpet of young wheat plants with snowflakes on them, serene and silent.

In spring and autumn Enya and I went deep into the mountains and walked in the dense fir-tree forests. In summer we bathed in the Dragon Pool. The winter holiday was the festival season. We played house games and entertained our visitors. My colleagues and I would be invited to many households and received warm hospitality and good meals from the parents of the students who had passed the entrance examination to a higher educational institution.

Dalaoguan used to have many devout worshippers during the festival season. Sedan chairs as well as cars would cover the square of the temple and 'red men and green women', people from rich families of the town and the city, were dotted over rocky paths, strolling in cherry orchards, climbing up the mountains and kneeling down in front of the gods and goddesses. Incense smoke made the air blue, its rich aroma floating over the ancient buildings.

Dense wild forests used to cover the mountains, but in 1958 they were cut as fuel for steel mills. The damage was huge, with nothing left but bare rocks. Life was harsher for the local peasants: apart from selling stones, they had nothing provided by the mountains. As for us, the city residence holders, the remoteness, bad road and lack of transportation were the hazards. Apart from a tiny shop selling a few items and a butcher selling pork once a week, there was no way we could get food provided locally. Flour and rice had to be purchased in the Grain Station ten miles away and other food in Licun twenty miles away. Still, my mother was healthier, Enya was happy with peasant children as her friends, and I enjoyed the tranquillity and people's kindness. I had plenty of quiet time to think. Field's letters were my spiritual food, nourishing me and strengthening me to live the poor and lonely life forever, which was my plan. Modesty and humility were the local people's traits, which suited my single-minded and eccentric character.

The flat was twenty-six square metres, divided into two rooms by a brick wall. Mother's and Enya's two single beds were in the right-hand room with a desk on which Enya, with great willpower, would study hour after hour. In the left-hand room a wall divided the room into two parts. The front part was the doorway. There was a square dining table, a cabinet holding a few bowls and plates, and a makeshift bed from which my mother could watch the outside scenery. She could see the peak of the mountain opposite our place, shaped like a resting camel in the blue sky.

At the back of the wall was our kitchen. A mud stove was in one corner; a makeshift bed acted as kitchen bench in the daytime and at night I rolled out the bedding and it was my bed.

The two poorest people in the area, East from Sunjia Village and Laughing Lady from Lying Dragon Village, were the most frequent visitors to our house. Whenever East was starving, he came to us and my mother would offer him some steamed buns. Laughing Lady was a real character, outgoing and unpretentious. She would tell her sad stories with much laughter. She had lost her mother when she was a baby and was sold to an old man when she was sixteen. She was illiterate and for every major decision in life she listened to the blind fortune teller, who charged two *yuan* for each session and told her that her son's girlfriend was not suitable since her future daughter-in-law should be stocky, with dark skin, small eyes and thick lips, while the girlfriend was thin-fingered with wide eyes and thin lips. What a turbulent time when she tried to get rid of the poor girl. At last the girl left the family in torment but her son still had never found the 'right' girlfriend, or any girlfriend at all. Later he left home for Manchuria and Laughing Lady was so remorseful that she lost part of her mind.

In springtime, Laughing Lady and I would pick weeds in the fields and make *xiao dou fu*, a dish made of ground soybeans and weeds. We picked the weeds, cleaned and washed them; the soybeans were soaked in water for twenty-four hours and then ground into fine powder by pushing the millstones in Laughing Lady's courtyard round and round for hours. The whole process could take as long as one week. Once it was cooked, Laughing Lady and I would present it to many neighbours to much appreciation since it was so delicious and was difficult to make.

My favourite colleagues were Zang and Wang. Zang was a young teacher of politics. He was too honest for the subject and as the textbook told the bright future of Communism, Zang would say to the class, 'I don't believe it but I have to teach you according to the doctrine. Please forgive me for the hypocrisy.' Unfortunately he had an affair with one of his ex-students and the girl's parents asked for three thousand *yuan* from Zang as compensation for the loss of her good name. The whole team of more than fifty formed by family members, relatives and neighbours would cross the bridge to Zang's flat in a dragon-like formation, asking for the money. They would stay in Zang's place for the whole day. Poor Zang, how could he and his wife afford it when all they had was twenty *yuan* a month? The year before, they had tried to have a second baby and received a harsh fine. Their furniture, bikes and most of their wages were taken away. They had nothing left in the empty house and they had nothing to eat but salt and cornmeal buns. Unable to afford the three thousand *yuan*, Zang drank a whole bottle of spirits and hanged himself.

Wang, the deputy director of the school, was a sincere man, of medium build with a big belly. He was chosen as the director since he looked like a proper official. Wang's village, North Ridge, behind the mountain of Sleep Goddess, was the only Christian village amongst the tens of villages in Beijai, which was established in 1885. On Christmas Eve, Enya and I would visit their small church where the feeling of fellowship moved us a lot: ten people crowded on a bench for five, windows opened for more to listen to Christ's words, everybody, one after and another, jumping to the stage to sing and dance. Every guest received a present: some in the congregation had sold their precious belongings for the donation. The spiritual warmth impressed me a lot and it was a good remedy for my lonely life.

Time moved slowly in the quiet mountains, except every month my mother would be disturbed by Main. He came to deliver her pension but the amount was never the amount that Superb had promised.

Ever since we moved to Dragon Pool, Superb and Main had refused to give Mother's food and cooking-oil ration document to us. We three had to share two people's rations and we hardly had enough to eat. We all became very thin. Mother and I had kept quiet for two years and still we were not to be left in peace. Every time when Main came to deliver the money, he would argue with Mother and if I was at home he would hit me. He said it was his right as an older brother to educate me, like a father giving lessons to a child. I would have a bleeding nose and loosened teeth. Little Enya would be in fear and weeping. I didn't understand why my brother had become so cruel, and it was really painful to witness a family member turned nasty. I know now that it was Superb who bewitched Main and made him behave that way, but at the time I had no idea since it was always Main who took the action. Superb was never out in the open to show her real intention — to get rid of me so that they could enjoy Mother's pension exclusively.

While Main bullied me openly, Superb used subtler, more insidious ways. She knew that 'words can kill'. On gloomy days she would persuade me to visit various places with her where the scenery was depressing, and then she would tell me stories. All her stories were about lovelorn women committing suicide. She told the stories in such vivid way that I would become bewitched. After the storytelling she would conclude, 'Death is the best solution for a woman like you.'

Innocently I asked, 'What about my children if I die? They are so small. Enya is eleven and Nini is only one and a half.'

'You must think positively. They will grow stronger without a mother,' Superb answered.

One day Mother handed me a letter and asked me to post it in the post office of Beijai, the central village of the area. Television sets had started to appear and Mother asked Main to offer a little money to buy a nine-inch black-and-white set for her. This letter caused great conflict amongst the family. In reply, Main didn't bother to write a new letter but, using red ink, he put swear words and curses in the spaces between the original lines of Mother's handwriting, accusing her of being a disturber of the peace, a greedy old woman. He also threatened me, 'If you don't dare to show this letter to Mother, I will do something to teach you.' Both Mother and I were terribly distressed. When Main came to our place and bullied us again, Mother told him that she wanted to go to the court and get her pension document back.

The next Sunday, together with Main, Superb rushed into our place. Her hand over her mouth and nose, she sneered, 'What a stinky earth smell in your place!' And she refused to eat lunch. Main scolded me, 'Don't you have better food to offer us?' When I argued that they were unkind, Main hit me on the head with his fist. When they were ready to leave, Superb barked, 'Mother, Weijun, if you go to court for the pension money, you can get it but, in connections and relations, I'll let you lose all. Try, if you don't believe me!'

Next, Field wrote to me that his father and his boss had received letters from Main telling about our 'misalliance' and he was forced to cut off all contact with me. A family friend from Shanghai wrote accusing letters and said I would end up like Anna Karenina. Elegant and Grace, my friends of twenty years, exclaimed that they wanted to cut contact with me; another friend told me to end my life like Sister Yu — a lovelorn concubine who committed suicide by swallowing golden rings in the novel *Dreams of a Red Mansion*. My older half-brother from Taiwan abruptly stopped writing to me. My niece Phoenix in Changle turned her back on me . . .

A few days later Superb arrived at my school office in the late afternoon. She ordered me to call my colleagues: 'I know you are a popular teacher but I will tell them who you really are!' I was nervous and confused and didn't know what she was going to say, but I knew she was *li hai* — ruthless and harmful. I didn't want her to destroy my life at Sunjia School, the only peaceful place I had ever had, built up by hard work. I tried to be as deferential as I could — smiled to her, offered her tea and chatted politely to her — but she insisted talking to my colleagues. Luckily they were on my side and they didn't want to listen to Superb. One after another they walked away from the office until at last only a young teacher named Moral Liu remained.

Superb said to him, 'Could you please make the judgement for me?'

Moral interrupted her, 'Do you want my judgement? My judgement is you are wrong. You should let the old lady have her own money!'

'My aim isn't to get the money.'

'Don't you dare lie! You are shamelessly after her pension.'

Seeing the last of my colleagues walking away from the office, Superb looked pathetic and pitiful. Leaning on one of the desks, she frowned and said, 'Oh, my head aches.' She then said to me, 'I will not go to your house. I will stay here till dawn.' It was getting dark. The cold wind was blowing fiercely outside and I was worried about her. I said, 'No, my sister-in-law, you can't stay here. It's too cold and you'll ruin your health.' I suggested that she could stay with Teacher Tian, one of my neighbours if she didn't want to stay at my place. I was relieved that she agreed and I didn't think even for a second that she might play dirty tricks. I brought medicine for her headache and helped her settle down with the Tians. She smiled at me and I was happy we were friendly again. I trusted she would have a good sleep at the Tiens. How far it was from the truth! She didn't sleep at all. Instead, she vilified me in front of the Tiens until midnight — and then in the small hours of the morning she went to Wang's and did the same. She even showed them a stolen letter I had written to Field.

The next day was one of the most anguished of my life after Wang told me what had happened during the night. I was so shocked I could hardly believe my ears. How could somebody smile at you one moment and then the next turn out to be your enemy? Didn't she feel ashamed to break my trust? Being betrayed by someone you trust is the most painful thing in life. How stupid I was to trust somebody for so long and not know she was a wolf in sheep's clothing.

On March 3, 1983, Mother decided to go to court. Made desperate by the attitude of Superb and Main, she at last decided to take action. Mother was never a money-lover but she didn't like the way her pension was handled. She would like to have a say over her own money instead of receiving it from others' hands. She would like her son to appreciate her help, or at least not argue with her over her money. She used to say, 'My parents spent heaps of silver and golden coins to support and educate me, and I worked hard for decades to earn my retired pension. I don't like somebody else depriving me of it.'

Mother went to see the judge in Cangkou District and reported her misery: 'My son used to be nice but he has changed and become cruel to me. He and his wife promised to bring me thirty *yuan* from my pension once a month, but they don't keep their word. Moreover, they keep my registered food ration book. My daughter, my granddaughter and I are starving.'

Knowing this kind of family conflict was always difficult to solve face to face, the judge used a clever strategy. He called for Main to bring my mother's pension papers to him. 'We'll discuss the problem after I see the documents,' he said. After Main gave him my mother's pension documents as well as food and cooking-oil ration books, he wrote to her and asked her to come and collect them. When she saw the familiar old handkerchief she used to wrap all her precious stuff, she was as happy as a child. She said cheerfully, 'Weijun, come on, I'll take you to a restaurant to eat *jiaozi!*'

In the restaurant Mother was eating *jiaozi* happily but I could not relax. There was absolutely no saliva in my mouth. *Jiaozi*, a festival food, small, round and elegant, made of thin pastry filled with minced meat and chopped vegetables, stayed in my mouth and refused to go down to my throat. I could taste no flavour despite my mother's admiration of the chef's good cooking skill. My heart was beating irregularly. I tried my best to smile at my mother but my mind kept wandering; depressing thoughts were overwhelming me. How terrible my family was, ending up in battles over my mother's meagre pension. And I knew Superb and Main would not let Mother and me go easily now they had lost the money they yearned for so much.

Superb and Main were furious at us, especially at me. But Superb was slippery. She didn't want to have a bad image in public. She made Main out to be the one wanting to fight. This drove him to take crazy and stupid actions. He went to the court, banged on the desk and swore at the judge, 'You fool! My sister is a bad woman and my mother spoils her. Women like my sister should die, yet you look after them. You have no justice!' The authority of the law court went to his school where he was teaching and told his employer to lecture him. Main became even madder at me and Mother. He stopped his visits to Dragon Pool.

Another year passed, and for all those days and nights my poor mother waited for her son to come to visit her, but he never did. The poor old lady became sick with sadness. One day she decided to take the trip and visit Main in Crab Village. In the little shop at Da Lao bus-stop she bought a few bags of peanuts and some bottles of face cream for her beloved granddaughters. There was a happy smile on her face when she stepped out of the shop, holding the peanuts and face cream. She must have been thinking of the nice old days when she bought nibbles for the children and Bell, her favourite granddaughter, would laugh cheerfully.

When we arrived in Licun by bus, she said, 'You stay here. I don't want any arguments. I'll go to their place by myself. I know they hate you, not me.'

I stayed in the bus station of Licun and waited for Mother. With her bound feet and bent back, she bravely hobbled off to Crab Village and her silver head disappeared. I bought a magazine in the bus station and settled down, trying to fill the time. I reckoned it would be about two hours before my mother could be back. I drew a happy picture in my mind — Superb would offer Mother tea, and then she would cook lunch while Main and their two daughters chatted with Mother. But I could not relax. The bus station was noisy and crowded and I was continually disturbed by the manager's announcements, which were followed by masses of people running, shoving and pushing their way onto whatever bus was due to leave. There were thirteen smaller towns and hundreds of villages in the surrounding area of Licun, and the entire population used this single bus station when they were commuting, shopping and visiting.

Finding it difficult to focus on my reading, I looked around. Suddenly I was alerted by a small figure walking slowly towards me. Her head was drooping, her back was bent, and her steps were uneven as if she was suffering great inner pain. I didn't want to believe my eyes but it was my poor old mother. She had come back from my brother's place after merely half an hour. She told me the story later:

She pushed the familiar door open and saw Bell, her beloved granddaughter, playing in the big courtyard. She happily called, 'My little Bell, your nana is back. How much I miss you!' At this moment, she heard a noise and Bell instantly disappeared. Not knowing what to do, she stood at the door, waiting in puzzlement. Bell returned a short while later and yelled, 'Why do you come to our house? Get away!' The shock was so great that Mother didn't know what to do. Tears running down her cheeks, she sobbed, 'I missed you, Bell. I bought you some peanuts and some face cream. Where is your dad?' With shaking hands, she tried to place the presents and some money into Bell's hands. Bell grabbed them and threw them to the ground. 'Who fancies your stinky stuff? Go away!' As she walked out of the house, Mother heard a sound from inside. It was a sound that she could never mistake. It was Main's cough. Mother's heart was broken.

Mother became bitterly sad after that. She would cry at New Year's Eve, and she often lost her temper and screamed at me, 'You bloody woman, you made me lose my son and my grandchildren.'

I decided to go to see Main for a talk. To avoid Superb, I went straight to his workplace.

In his headmaster's office I burst into uncontrollable sobs. 'My brother hasn't visited my mother for nearly two years. Mother is very sad. Could you please talk him about it? He should visit his mother since it is only twenty miles away.' The headmaster kindly offered me a seat and a glass of tea, and then he sent somebody for Main. A few minutes later Main came in with a timid smile, but his expression changed immediately when he saw me. He grabbed a chair and he tried to throw it at me. He would have hit me if he hadn't been stopped by several of his colleagues.

When I walked away from the office I saw Main waiting at the corner of the school building. Fearing he might try to hit me again, I ran quickly past him. To my surprise I didn't hear footsteps coming after me. I looked back and saw him standing still, his thin face sour and sad. Slowly he walked to me and said in a mumbling voice, 'Sister, you don't know. . .' Suddenly the rage inside me melted. It was at this moment that I began to understand Main's misery — this poor timid, controlled man, he was not happy either.

'Superb! You wait, I'll make you pay!'

I was at the top of the highest mountain behind Dragon Pool, shouting until my lungs nearly burst. It was a gloomy dusk in winter and the sky was grey and heavy. There was nobody else around this wild world except me. I had visited this spot to pour my anger out more than once. Realising how much pain Superb had caused to my whole family, I was furious. I couldn't help but want to do something to easy my anger, as the Chinese proverb indicated: *yu si wang po*, break the net until the fish dies, get even, take revenge. Standing at the tip of a huge rock on the mountain, after shouting myself hoarse, I threw stones at the rocks. Hours passed and I became exhausted. Little by little, as the evening breeze lifted, a calm mood descended over me. With tired steps, I walked home, rolled the bedding down the board and lay in the dark.

I touched my pillow. Underneath it was a letter from Field. His letters came rarely nowadays; instead of once every ten days, I might receive one letter in a month if I was lucky. However, no matter how long it took to receive another letter, the current letter was always under my pillow and I would read it every evening until his next letter arrived.

Reading Field's letters comforted me a great deal, as I suffered from insomnia again, and at two in the morning I would wake up and stay awake until six, when it was time to get up. Students arrived at school at six-thirty to study by themselves. Although classes didn't start until eight, I liked to be with my students and help them when they were studying. When I couldn't fall asleep, I recited Field's letters. Words have a magic power — particularly for a lonely, sensitive heart. Several hours could pass easily for me with happy imaginings.

'Would it be worthwhile to sacrifice myself for revenge?' I asked myself. By now I had had a few hours of happiness, and I was calm and rational. I decided the best way of revenge was to have the last laugh.

I persuaded myself not to think about Superb. Instead, I engaged myself in learning and helping. There were always plenty of things to learn and there were always plenty of people I could help.

Sitting under a cherry tree, I played the violin, practised singing and recited English words. Leaning on a rock at the river bank, I wrote short pieces of prose and studied books on medicine and psychology. Working in my vegetable garden, I learned horticulture. Walking with Enya, I talked to her and encouraged her. In spring and autumn time, tourists would come and visit our mountains. Seeing others' happy faces, I would be inspired and feel the beauty of life, too. Watching them walking up from the little granite bridge, I greeted them and offered them tea or food. I would collect cherries in spring, green cucumbers and red tomatoes in summer. If I saw a silly young girl wearing a pair of high-heeled shoes to climb the mountains, I would offer her a pair of flat-heeled shoes. If people got down the mountain too late and missed the bus, I would offer them room in our house; poor and small as it was, they were always grateful that they didn't have to stay in the open air at night. Once, a group of university students got sick with food poisoning and they could hardly walk one more step in the dusk. When I saw those poor lads, I set off for a doctor, offered boiling water and made beds for them. Later, they wrote a letter of thanks to my work place.

Over the years, I helped countless tourists and although I never saw most of them again, I didn't mind. I helped others for pleasure, not for reward. Nevertheless, the reward came when I was least expecting it.

CHAPTER SIXTEEN

Whenever I could manage to get some sleep, I would have a dream with the same story, and it was clear and vivid. I was in a dark hole, looking up towards a stairway. On the highest step of the stairs, a lovely young man was sitting on the step and waving to me. He was Field's age but with white skin, golden hair and blue eyes. Summoned by him, I walked up the stairs. When I was at the top, I saw a tremendous space. I rambled here and there excitedly, and saw an exotic land. White clouds were floating in an impressive sky, and all sorts of food and clothes were on display. I walked around and met a middle-aged man, big, tall and handsome. He smiled at me amiably. His face was very relaxed. I had never seen anybody so relaxed. I followed him, walking along a creamy-coloured meandering road with colourful flowers on both sides. He held my hand and we walked shoulder to shoulder.

Only in my later life did I realise that the young man in the dream was a combination of Field and Bruce, who would appear in my life soon. As for the middle-aged man, he was actually my present husband, who would take me on his travels all over the world. We would visit fancy shops, exquisite restaurants and splendid buildings, taste exotic cuisines and stroll amongst the beautiful scenery, just like I did in my dreams.

When spring came in Dragon Pool, I was comforted by growing vegetables, which had become the best remedy for my lonely life. I planted spinach, rape and spring onions in winter; potatoes, green beans, tomatoes, cucumbers and eggplants in spring. I grew Chinese cabbages and *jiaodong* turnips in mid-summer, and sowed seeds of cabbages, broccoli and carrots in autumn. The climax came when the harvest was due. Arms loaded with golden potatoes, red tomatoes, green cucumbers and purple eggplants, Enya and I would show them to my mother with enormous pride. Mother would grin broadly and say, 'Well done, girls!'

The growing process was so fascinating it soothed my lonely soul. Watching little seedlings become young plants and young plants flowering and then offering fruits was a wonderful process and it gave me hope. I often sat on a rock beside my little garden and gazed at the plants for ages, as a mother tirelessly watches her baby. But autumn would turn to be winter and winter was dull. I could not grow vegetables any more. When the cold wind blew fiercely, the bare earth became frozen, the river iced up, and my heart became sad.

Our only relatives, Main and his family, had never come to visit us after Mother got her pension back. After finding himself a girlfriend, Rich divorced me and won custody of Nini through the court. I missed my baby daughter terribly and cursed myself for being a bad mother. Field's letters became rare as his father and his boss forbade him from writing to me. He had to write at midnight when everyone fell asleep. To receive my letters was even more difficult since he had to find a reliable friend out of reach of the leather factory to receive them first, and then he had to wait for a chance to collect them. For years I had relied on letters as my emotional comfort but now I hardly received any, which was unbearable. In such a remote, lonely and sad place, I badly missed Field and his letters. My teaching job became boring once I'd taught the same textbook for five years. I had tried to teach in a new way but this idea was rejected by the educational bureau.

The winter of 1984 saw me badly depressed and in poor health. I suffered some terrible symptoms — I had almost no appetite, slept poorly, was fatigued, and wept a lot. It seemed my life had come to its lowest point and there was no hope ahead. I felt as if I was in a pool of dead water and I was drowning. I would stand on the road at the end of the little granite bridge, looking to the east, looking to the west, longing for God to send somebody to save me.

'Teacher Liu, you have some guests!' I heard one of my colleagues call.

'Who is it?' I asked.

My mother and Bruce in winter 1993

'It is a luxury car and a *da bi zi* [big nose, a foreigner] at the river bank,' my humorous colleague answered.

'A foreigner and a car?' I puzzled. I had ridden in a car once when I was eight but other than that I had never even touched a car. How could a car, especially a luxury car, have anything to do with me? In Chinese we called a car *xiao jiao che*, little speedy sedan, and they were not for the likes of me. Curious, I strode down the stairs and looked to the river bank. There, beside the stream, I saw a grey-haired Western man in a brown checked jacket standing in front of a big black car, and a slender young Chinese man in a neat black suit standing beside him.

I recognised the foreigner: he was Bruce, whom I'd met briefly the year before on a fine Sunday in November 1984.

That day I was watering my vegetable garden in the early morning. The autumn breeze was refreshing. The magpies were singing at the tops of the cherry trees. In China we say magpies are happy messengers and bring joyful news. My Chinese cabbages and *jiaodong* turnips were growing so well. The dew on the leaves sparkled like hundreds of diamonds, pink, yellow, blue, red and green, as if in a fairy tale.

I was wearing a greyish-green shirt, the only shirt I had. My dark blue trousers were shabby and there were patches on my knees. My sockless feet were in a pair of old plastic shoes. Placing my bucket on the ground and wiping sweat from my forehead, I looked up from my cabbage patch and saw a strange figure. He was not a Chinese but a Westerner! He had grey hair — must be in his early seventies, I was thinking — and he wore a cream jacket; his shirt collar was white and clean; his blue eyes were bright and kind, and his big nose was impressive. Walking on the sandy path from the east his steps were firm and his legs straight. Beside him was Mr Wang.

'Hello, Weijun, how are you?' Mr Wang greeted me.

The day before, when I came home from school, Mother had told me that Mr Wang had visited her in the morning. 'He was with an old foreigner who speaks English, like a bird talking,' she giggled.

'Really?' I asked in astonishment. 'What a shame I missed the chance to see him. I'd like to have a talk in English.'

I had never talked with any native English speakers. All the words and sentences I learned were from reading and writing. I was very keen to practise speaking with someone whose native tongue was English.

'Don't worry. Mr Wang said they would come down the mountain of Beijiushui and visit us again,' said my mother.

Mr Wang was one of the talented intellectuals whom Mao hated. He was condemned as a rightist in 1957, and spent twenty-three years in humiliation and torment. His girlfriend left him, and he was still single now. Old though he was, he translated Russian poems, wrote poems in Chinese and taught himself English. He enjoyed his retired life as a freelance tourist guide and interpreter.

Mr Wang and the foreigner walked towards me. I shook hands with them and invited them in for a cup of tea. The Westerner's face looked benevolent, with a natural smile, very nice and relaxed. His bright blue eyes were smiling too, like a baby's smile, pure and happy. He and Mr Wang looked exhausted: dirt clung to their trousers and dust covered their hair. Their tired faces showed the result of a bad night's sleep, which was not a surprise since there was only one shabby guest inn in Beijiushui, belonging to the timber workers. Sympathy rose from my heart. Hardship and adversity had meant I could feel others' pain as my own and I was keen to help. This old Western man must be poor, I thought, if he didn't have money to visit the famous cities of Beijing, Shanghai or Guilin, and had to come to our remote mountains. He must be an unfortunate creature like myself. I was full of pity for him and I was ready to help him if I could.

I took Mr Wang and the foreigner inside our house and we sat at the dining table in the small space in the doorway. I offered them jasmine tea. The day was crisp and the peak of the mountains looked fantastic. The fresh air was floating lightly and I was excited by the fact that I had my first English speaker to talk to, probably the only one I would ever meet. I understood his name was Bruce and he was from New Zealand. I managed to form a few more questions but, to my dismay, I could not understand much of his English. Then I had a good idea. I brought a pen and a notebook and let him put his words in writing. After I introduced myself to him, I asked my guests, 'Have you had breakfast?' This was a question as common as 'How are you?' It might have seemed a surprising hospitality to Bruce to offer a stranger a meal, but to me it was perfectly natural since he looked worn-out and must be hungry. I saw Bruce's eyes brighten the moment I asked the question and I realised that he must need food for his aged body. I guessed they hadn't had a proper dinner in Beijiushui, and after walking down the rough mountain path they were exhausted and starved.

I started to organise some breakfast, which was a major effort in our life. With guests in the house I needed to try even harder. The only food we had was a little raw rice and some sweet potatoes. We also had some salty turnips my mother had made from our own harvest last year, which was the main everyday side dish for us three generations of women, but I didn't think I could offer my guest from afar the poor, leather-like salty turnip. In a panic I rushed out to the road, waiting for a while until a young man came over. I said to him, 'Little Stone, could you help me, please? I have two guests at my place and I am going to cook breakfast for them. Do you have time to go and buy a tin of fish and a tin of pork for me?' Tinned food was the only kind available at the shop. I gave Little Stone a five-*yuan* note. He laughed. 'You are extravagant. Spending five *yuan* for breakfast!' I earned only forty-one *yuan* a month, so five *yuan* for breakfast *was* a lot.

I asked Enya to wash the rice and the sweet potatoes in the river while

I set a fire in the stove. The stove, built by my own clumsy hands with bricks and mud, was small and inefficient. While I waited for the wood to burn, I mixed clay and water with coal powder, the only kind of fuel we were rationed in this area, and placed the mixture on top of the fire. Enya had cleaned the rice, and the sweet potatoes were washed and cut into cubes. I put the pot on the stove, poured the rice, sweet potatoes and water into it and came out of the kitchen to my guests. Wiping the tears from my eyes which were stinging from the smoke, I apologised to Mr Wang and Bruce for the delay in the meal.

Little Stone came in and said, 'Sorry, Teacher Liu, I could only manage to buy one tin of pork. They don't sell tinned fish.' Damn it! It meant I would have only one dish, the tinned pork, to offer my guests. By our local custom it was impolite to offer your guests odd-numbered dishes, so I had no option but to use the salty pickled turnip and, together with the pork, this made two dishes. The breakfast was so poor it made me very embarrassed. I cursed myself, 'Weijun, you bloody poor woman, the first time you get to entertain a foreign guest you shamefully offer him pickled turnip!'

Bruce was happy and easy-going and ate the rice and sweet potatoes heartily, although he didn't touch the turnip. He said, 'I like sweet potatoes. We call them kumara in New Zealand.'

We started a conversation after breakfast with Mr Wang acting as the interpreter. It seemed Mr Wang didn't understand Bruce so well either, since he translated some of the conversation incorrectly. One of these mis-translations was about Bruce's job in New Zealand. His words were translated to mean that he grew green peppers in New Zealand, which confirmed my guess that he was a poor man because only poor peasants grew vegetables for a living in China.

Full of sympathy, I insisted on putting some pears, the only snack we had, into Bruce's travelling bag. I also pulled out some turnips from my garden and put them into his bag too. When it was time for them to leave in the late afternoon, I carried both of their big bags, pretending to be strong and energetic. I accompanied them to Da Lao Village and then uphill in the direction of Youngkou, another scenic place in the Laoshan mountain chain, where Mr Wang and Bruce were to catch a bus. Several weeks later I received a letter from Bruce, thanking me for the breakfast.

I answered his letter with a few lines in poor English. Ever since, as one of the tourists I had helped, he was at the back of my mind.

Now, half a year later, he was in front of me again. I ran to him and shook hands with him. What a happy surprise to see him again. The young man in a neat black suit said to me, 'I am from the Fountain Hotel of Qingdao. I am this gentleman's tourist guide and interpreter. Mr Bruce Renton wants to invite you to the hotel for dinner.' I went back to the school and asked for a half-day off, then got in the car while all my colleagues and dozens of my students watched through the school windows. The driver mumbled complaints about the rough earth road as the car shot ahead with me sitting excitedly in the back seat. Over dinner Bruce told me the reason he'd come to see me again. Apparently he had arrived in Qingdao a few days before and he'd visited Mr Wang, but the latter had gone to Beijing for his honeymoon with his new wife. He said, 'Now you are the only person I know in Qingdao.'

After a very impressive dinner in the posh hotel I left Bruce and stayed overnight in a little inn nearby, and then came to see him again in the morning. In his room, Bruce was troubled with a loose button on his shirt and he looked stressed. I took his travel sewing kit and in no time the button was sewed up. Bruce smiled gratefully and then he started talking at a slow speed to make sure I could catch the words. 'Weijun, I have been to several big cities in China but I have never been to the countryside. Is it possible that you could find me a bed in your village?'

This question put me in a difficult position. China in 1985 wasn't fully open to foreigners, so I wasn't sure if I would be allowed to put up Bruce at my place. On the other hand I had a curious nature and liked to be adventurous, to do things my own way, ignoring conventions. I wanted to help Bruce. Didn't Confucius say that when guests come from afar, show hospitality with all your heart? And Chairman Mao always taught us, 'People from all over the world are our friends.' So Bruce was a friend from very far away and I ought to show hospitality to him.

I helped Bruce pack and brought him to Dragon Pool.

'It would be even better if the man was older — eighty, even ninety. A good life ahead for the woman after he dies . . .'

I heard my colleagues talking when I entered the office. Bruce's stay at my place became big news in the area and scandal reverberated far and wide. It was a typical Chinese mindset — if you put up someone of the opposite sex in your house, surely you would have had sex with them. So they thought I would sleep with Bruce. What dirty thinking. What about Field, then? How could I look into his eyes if I slept with another man? Loving Field, I found it impossible to bring myself to be interested in any other man. Actually, during the years that I lived alone, quite a few males, young and old, smart and ugly, had tried to take advantage or had designs on me. Nobody got what he wanted. To me, love was constant, permanent and unique; you did not bestow it on anyone but your true love.

I arranged for Bruce stay in the front space of the left-side room. On the first night Bruce stayed with me, I locked the door between the front space and the kitchen where I slept. The next day Bruce told me, 'I can see you are sensible about safety but don't worry, I won't do anything you don't want.' I thought that Bruce might be interested in me but I was too obsessed with Field to think about it. I told Bruce I had a young lover who was nineteen years my junior and asked him for advice: 'Is it right or wrong that I love a young man?'

'You have to decide for yourself. Whatever others say would sound wrong to you,' he said. I appreciated his sensible answer.

On the fourth day of Bruce's stay, I was called to the principal's office where a stern-faced member of Public Security, the police, was waiting for me. He looked serious and angry. 'We were told you have a foreigner in your house.'

'Yes,' I said warily.

'Why didn't you report this to us?'

Playing dumb, I answered him as calmly as I could, 'I am just a humble country schoolteacher. How could I know your rules?'

'You looked nervous when you first entered the room. Why?'

'Who isn't nervous seeing a member of Public Security?'

The policeman smiled. 'Okay,' he said in a softer tone. 'Go and look after your guest well. Don't tell him I talked to you.'

'Why not?'

'Just put yourself in his shoes and think. Would you like a member of Public Security after you if you were a tourist?'

It was my turn to smile.

My mother and I tried our best to entertain Bruce. He burst into roaring laughter when my mother cooked four fried eggs for him on the first morning.

'Too much — eggs are bad for you,' he said.

'Eggs are bad for you?' I was puzzled. We'd never heard of that. Eggs were considered a rare and fine food in our area and only sick people and new mothers could eat eggs in plenty. As was the custom in rural China, a new mother would be fed three hundred eggs in the first month after she gave birth. It probably was the only time in her life that a working-class woman could enjoy eggs like that. My mother no longer cooked four eggs but fried two for Bruce every morning. For lunch and dinner we would cook four dishes for him. This was over our budget, and soon I ran out of money. I borrowed some to keep the standard of hospitality for Bruce.

Every day after school I took Bruce walking in the fields or visited my friends while I continuously practised English with him. I carried a pen and pieces of paper, and every time when I didn't understand him I would ask him to spell out the word for me and I would write it down on the paper.

One day we were walking along the little path in the wheat fields. The wheat fields, dotted with wild flowers, waved golden lights in the late spring breeze. Birds were singing and the stream was dancing happily at the foot of the mountains. It was a beautiful evening and I enjoyed the opportunity to practise English with my foreign guest. However Bruce was not happy and my poor comprehension distressed him. 'Weijun, you are an English teacher, why is your hearing so poor?'

The fresh evening air must have inspired my subconscious mind and enhanced my intelligence. I did understand these words and I said, 'Bruce, if I had a chance to practise English in an English-speaking country, my English would be good enough to be a competent teacher, even an interpreter.'

Hearing this, Bruce fell into silence.

The next evening he handed me a piece of paper. It read: 'Dear Weijun, I have decided to invite you to New Zealand for one year to practise English.'

My heart started to pound excitedly and nervously. I had dreamt of going overseas but I was not fully prepared. My hard life had crushed my dreams and it had turned them into a sweet fairytale at the back of my mind, distant, vague and unrealistic. I was speechless for a while, and then reality intervened. I was now a daughter with an old mother, I was a mother to two young daughters and it would be hard for me to make the trip. 'Bruce, I am too old to be a student,' I said.

'One is never too old to learn.'

'What about letting Enya go? She is sixteen, a good age for learning.'

'It would be too much for me to look after a teenager.'

I fell into contemplation again. Suddenly I came to the most important issue and asked, 'How much would it cost for the plane tickets?'

Bruce took a pen and paper, wrote a figure on it and handed it to me. I looked at it with a sinking heart and started to calculate. Oh my God, it would take me forty-three years without eating and spending to pay him back.

'No, Bruce, it's too expensive for me.'

'Don't worry, I will pay for you.'

'I will never be able to pay you back.'

'I will never ask you to pay me back. I have received support from my friends in the past and they don't ask me to pay. Your friendship is the payment.'

I couldn't believe my good luck!

Later I understood that Bruce was not poor at all. He was very wealthy as an owner of a successful business — it was so successful that even after he retired and sold the business, the new owner kept the same name for the business: Renton Garage of Kerikeri.

Two weeks later, Bruce left us for New Zealand and soon he sent me a letter of invitation drafted by his brother-in-law Warren Freer, a Member of Parliament in New Zealand. Thus I started the process of applying for a passport, which was a long, difficult procedure at that time. There were many bureaucratic obstacles and it involved many bus trips to the city. I was the ninth person out of the seven million in Qingdao who had applied for an overseas trip after China opened up to the world in the late 1970s.

Finally after much endeavour, the Public Security of Qingdao issued my passport. Instead of contacting me directly, they sent a page-man to my school with the news. The page-man was so excited about somebody going overseas that he leaked the news all along his way. By the time he arrived at Sunjia School, almost everybody in the Beijai area knew that I was going to New Zealand. My furtive scheme had failed. Immediately my school campus was full of gossip, anger and jealousy.

My flustered headmaster called me to his office and lamented: 'Why are you planning such a big thing and don't report it to me? You are too free-thinking. You know you could make me lose my post. The head of the Bureau will have a talk with you.'

I arrived at the Bureau in Licun town and found they were very nervous. However they treated me quite differently as they knew I was a big shot now: the Public Security of Qingdao had issued me special permission and I was going to have a very rare document, a passport. The secretary of the big boss of the Bureau asked me to wait while an emergency committee meeting was held to discuss my case.

I waited nervously, alone in an empty room. Having seen the attitude of my headmaster and the serious look of the secretary of the Bureau boss, I reckoned my chances of achieving my overseas trip were nil. It seemed I might have to go back to Sunjia School, to do my old teaching job, only now everybody would know I had tried to 'abandon the motherland' — a scandalous thing to do — and my life would become even worse in Dragon Pool.

I thought hard and had an idea. Getting up from my seat, I went straight to the office where the committee meeting was on. Pushing the door open, I saw the Bureau boss at the end of the oval table, with a group of men sitting around. They all turned to me and watched me, astonished. Wasting no time, I said, 'Report! I have a piece of information to tell you. The invitation extended to me was written by the Minister of Foreign Affairs of the New Zealand government. Mr Warren Freer is an old friend of China. He has been to China for official visits fourteen times since 1953. He likes to play bridge with Deng Xiaoping.'

Without looking at any of the faces — which must have had expressions that would have frightened me to the bottom of my heart since they were my superiors in hierarchy — I quickly turned away and walked out of the office. Once outside I wiped my sweaty forehead with shaking hands. Ten minutes later the boss of the Bureau, Mr Gao, came up to me with a smile and said, 'The committee has issued the permit for you. You can leave any time with your full wages sustained.'

We have a common saying in China: foreigners are afraid of common people; common people are afraid of officials; and officials are afraid of foreigners.

CHAPTER SEVENTEEN

It was a great relief when I learnt that the authorities had given me permission to travel overseas. I went to the Public Security station in Qingdao and excitedly waited in their office for my passport, the precious document that would allow me to leave China.

When it was my turn, I nervously walked up to a young policeman. He handed me my passport and said, 'You can go to the New Zealand embassy for a visa now.'

'Why?' I asked, trying to be as polite as I could. You didn't confront a security policeman in China. They were powerful men from the government and their job was to crush anybody who dared to stand up for themselves.

'The passport is only a document allowing you to leave China. You also need a document to enter New Zealand.'

'Where is the embassy?'

'Beijing.'

Oh my God! I cried from my heart and almost collapsed. Thinking about my ordeal over the last six months, I was stunned by the thought that I might have to wait the same length of time again. After a sleepless night I got on the train to Beijing. After a seventeen-hour train journey I arrived into a snow storm in the evening. I went to a travel centre at the station. Waiting in the long queue, worried there may not be a place available, I moved inch by inch to the window and at last it was my turn. Standing in front of a hole in the wall no bigger than a square foot, I shouted to the woman behind the glass. She repeated my words: 'One person, two nights, two *yuan*, please . . .' A piece of paper slipped out of the slot, but before I could pick it up a hand gripped it. I turned around and saw a dirty-faced man running away from me, the letter of introduction in his hand. The person behind me impatiently pushed me away from the queue, grumbling, 'Away from home you must be very alert.' It was too late for me to wait in the queue again. What to do? I rambled in the square, in distress, amongst countless migrants, and then I was stopped by a woman. She smiled at me. 'Want to find a place to stay, sister? Where do you come from? Shangdong? Qingdao? Oh, what a good place. My grandma was from Qingdao. Come with me, I'll take you to a place.' I followed her through narrow lanes and arrived at the opening to an underground inn. A rotten smell made me feel sick. She talked to a man who said, 'One person one night? All right, you pay twenty *yuan*. Follow me.' I hesitated briefly but handed over twenty *yuan* and followed him. I saw a shabby ceiling, dirty walls and cramped small rooms full of inmates. Twenty *yuan* for this slum? It was worth no more than two *yuan*. I complained and asked for my money back. Almost like magic, men appeared from all directions and in no time they surrounded me with their fists clenched. I had to stay here.

Noise started very early in the morning. I opened my swollen eyes and saw a little girl at the side of my bed using my toothbrush to clean her teeth.

By the time I found the embassy in the big city, it was already late morning. With trepidation, I waited in the embassy hall. A young European lady came up to me. I stared at her curly brown hair, tall figure, long sky-blue skirt draping to her ankle. She introduced herself as the second secretary, accepted my passport and disappeared behind a grand white door. A few seconds later she came up to me again, holding my passport and the plane tickets that Bruce had bought for me in New Zealand. The whole process took no more than thirty minutes.

I'm sure Bruce had no idea how difficult it was for a Chinese to get a permit to go overseas. The date on the plane tickets made me panic: it was in one week's time.

People's attitudes at Dragon Pool had changed dramatically. By now everyone in my school as well as in the villages knew I was definitely going overseas. The young ones showed great reverence. The older ones, who had lived in the place all their lives (some had even never been to Licun), couldn't understand why I should leave my job and my mother to go far away. They became cold and indifferent.

My mother would have to stay by herself since Enya had passed the examination to the top high school in Licun and she had to stay at school during the week. I wrote a letter to Superb and Main, telling them I was going to New Zealand for one year. Only a couple of days later, Main and his two daughters arrived at Dragon Pool. My mother was delighted and I was amazed by Main's humble manners. Did the trip to New Zealand mean so much that I was now seen as a different person? They decided to let Bell, their younger daughter, stay in Dragon Pool to do her schooling to keep my mother company. I was very happy with this spin-off from my overseas trip: Mother had got her son back at last.

Foreign currency was tightly controlled by the government and it was no small matter to get even a small amount of foreign dollars. At the Bank of China, the person in charge was a man with a sullen face. He impatiently told me that I needed an official letter from my workplace before I could get any foreign currency. It took me two days to get the required official letter. When I returned to the bank he seemed unhappy and said there were no Hong Kong dollars available at the moment: 'Come and try next Monday.' Two more days passed and I went to the bank again, only to find that he was at a meeting and would not return until the afternoon. At last he came back and I got the money, but time was now very pressing. Later, I realised I should have offered him a bribe and he would have obtained the money for me much more quickly.

I hurried back from the city, packed my travel gear, said goodbye to my mother, went to Licun, said goodbye to Enya at her school and Nini at her kindergarten, and got on the train via Wuhan to Guangzhou.

Only in the train did I have the time to think about what I'd left: my aged mother, our home, two young daughters and an unfulfilled love affair. I was facing a trip to a strange land, a little corner on the map of the world. What was New Zealand like? Could I cope with it? Could my mother and children survive without me?

In Luohu railway station at the border, a young officer checked my luggage in great detail. When he found I had a book of Chinese songs with me, he asked, 'Why do you need this in a foreign country?'

'I can sing my familiar songs when I am homesick,' I said with emotion.

The young soldier frowned and said, 'How could you be homesick for this bloody country?'

To enter Hong Kong from mainland China, every Chinese had to be checked by Customs officers. In a huge hall, I waited in a queue as long as an endless and crooked dragon. Time was flying by and I was desperately worried since my flight was the next day. What if I missed the train to Hong Kong tonight? What if I missed the plane?

The fraught crowd, most of them first-time overseas travellers, kept walking to and fro, asking all sorts of questions. The Hong Kong officers in handsome dark blue uniforms concentrated on their job, ignoring the worried travellers. I saw an old man, sick and weak, who could hardly stand but still had to wait in the long and bustling queue, vomiting yellow liquid frequently onto the ground. I saw women with little crying babies in their arms, strenuously lifting heavy luggage.

The Customs officers of Hong Kong were efficient and all my worries were unnecessary. I was in the Western world in the middle of the afternoon. My half-brother Ming-Chin in Taiwan had booked me a hotel in the centre of Hong Kong; it was shockingly expensive but he paid for me even though the branches of our families hadn't seen each other for forty-six years.

The flight was long and tiring, and the seats were uncomfortable, but I was overseas now. How happy I was! It was December 1985; I was forty-one. Another dream had come true.

As soon as I stepped out of the Auckland airport I heard Bruce calling my name. He looked well, and his face was a healthy pink. I saw the beautiful New Zealand sky, low and impressive, as if within arm's reach; its blue colour was so distinct that it almost looked unreal. The white clouds were like a huge watercolour painting.

Riding in Bruce's Mazda, I felt dizzy and strange in the different South Pacific air. I couldn't understand one word when Bruce tried to tell me the names of places and buildings along the road while we headed for Warren Freer's place. The strange environment and sudden climate change, combined with my tiredness from the trip, had knocked me back and my mind had stopped working.

When our car passed through the city centre of Auckland, I was surprised to see all the shops full of beautiful items, yet so few people inside, as if Auckland was a fairyland built by elves who had then flown away.

Arriving at Warren's place, I was overwhelmed to see all sorts of exotic, beautiful flowers everywhere — on the roadside, in front of the houses, even around the electric power poles along the streets. I saw a young girl walking in the immaculate street with a relaxed smile on her pink-brown face with a little dog in tow. She looked so happy, relaxed and carefree. Suddenly I became emotional. Mixed feelings rose in my heart, tears burst out. I realised that life could be so different. How far away it was from my poor mother's life at Dragon Pool. I thought of my shabby home, my wrinkled mother, my parentless daughters and my hopeless love life. Tears poured out freely.

Warren Freer had the charisma of a long-term politician. He told stories, joked with his sister and laughed infectiously, which made me feel very much at home. But my English was very, very poor, I couldn't even understand the simple words Warren said to me, like, 'It is going to rain.' Mrs Freer was a gracious lady, silver-haired in a colourful dress. She made me nice tea. I was particularly impressed by her bright kitchen, which was as big as our whole house in Dragon Pool.

'What a beautiful kitchen you have!' I burst out.

'You'll have a kitchen like this when you get older,' she said kindly. I was surprised and didn't believe it.

The next morning Bruce and I drove to Okaihau, a small town near Kerikeri. He, his son Andrew and his daughter-in-law Carol lived in a huge, beautiful place called 'Te Rimu'. To my surprise, there was no houseful of people waiting to see me, a Chinese guest from afar; there was no buzz of excitement as there would be if you were expecting guests in any Chinese household; there was no fuss in the kitchen; and I could see absolutely no food in the big lounge that adjoined the dining room and kitchen. This was a big culture shock.

Later I was offered some cold bread and butter for lunch. After lunch Bruce took me to see his garden, a huge 36,000-square-metre area with big, ancient trees around. I started to ponder nervously: Is this big place occupied by only three people? Don't they feel isolated and lonely? There were no human sounds, which was so different from China. I heard a bell ringing; I thought it was a bell from a nearby church. To my disappointment, I soon discovered it was just wind bells ringing underneath the veranda, no church nearby. The nearest neighbour was more than two hundred metres away on the other side of the thick wood.

Night fell. I could not sleep because I was hungry. Without much lunch, I had looked forward a big dinner. To my surprise, dinner was not big. Not as I imagined, anyway. (According to Chinese custom, many dishes would be prepared for the first meal for a faraway guest.) The meal was oriental-style: rice and stir-fried dishes. The problem was, nobody tried to tell me to eat more as we did in China, and I felt extremely embarrassed to pick up dishes without the host's pushing. So I finished my first New Zealand dinner with my tummy only half full, even though there was food left on the table. In China, a guest never finishes their meal to show that the host was generous and had prepared more than enough.

Lying in bed downstairs, I was scared and nervous. The wind was blowing, the trees were making enormously loud sounds, and possums jumping on the roof kept waking me up.

I tried to help the family do some housework but I couldn't handle the New Zealand knives properly and my finger kept getting cut. When I tried to cook some vegetables I put too much oil in the dish. Bruce was nice and he tried to talk to me but I couldn't understand him apart from a few everyday sentences.

I became a lost soul and missed China very much. The weirdest thing was my opinion change. When I was in China I had lots of complaints about the country, but now it seemed as if even its shortcomings became good points and I just couldn't enjoy the beauty of New Zealand. On Christmas Day I hid myself in the toilet and wept bitterly.

Coming from China, a densely populated country, I was keen to see crowds and listen to sounds. I found New Zealand unbearably quiet. The individuality, which I love so much now, was alien to me then and was one of the biggest cultural shocks in those early days. Only when I was sitting in big shopping malls and watching people bustling around did I feel happy.

I was deaf because I could not understand others' English; I was dumb since I could not express myself properly; I was lame and could go nowhere because I didn't drive and there was no easy public transport available.

Not communicating well, I repressed my feelings, which caused depression, confusion, anxiety and loneliness. Weeks passed without much communication between me and others. At first I was not unhappy and celebrated my character change — moving from a talkative person to a quiet person seemed a positive step towards maturity — but soon everything went wrong. I became more and more depressed, I was scared at night and slept badly, and I wept easily over tiny disagreements with others. I had developed the disease of language loss. There was no other way to overcome this psychological problem but to work hard on improving my English. Wherever I went I carried a pen, a notebook, an English–Chinese dictionary and a Chinese–English dictionary. I tried to talk as much as I could to every English speaker I met. I tried my best not to talk to any Mandarin speakers even though I was longing to do so. I constantly interrupted conversations whenever I heard people use a new word and asked them to spell it for me. I would then write it down in my notebook and read it over and over during the night. I toiled into the early hours, even though this gave me headaches and exhausted me.

Bruce took me to Okaihau College to learn English. The day before I started, the whole school was informed by the principal, Les Laurence, that a Chinese 'lady guest' was coming. The next day I went to school in my *qipao*, a tight-fitting long silk robe with shining crimson peonies on a black background. Bruce tried to tell me that it was not appropriate to wear it for school but I was not sensitive enough to the subtle Western way of speaking and I didn't catch his point. So, with my fancy *qipao*, I found myself amongst hundreds of kiwi kids; everyone was trying their best to be polite and not to stare at me, this strange creature wearing an evening dress in the daytime.

Les looked after me very well. He allocated me an office, so before and after lessons I either stayed in the library or in my office to read, recite and write in English. I was not sure whether I was a staff member or a student. I shared morning and afternoon tea with the teachers in the staff lounge every day. Everybody was very nice to me and the teachers, especially the women teachers, looked after me so well. Beautiful Jenny offered me so much with her warm friendship. She liked to take time and talk to me. My

With the Okaihau College staff 1986 (me, second from right, first row)

life in China intrigued her and her family a lot. The first question her family asked when she arrived home would be 'What did Weijun tell you today?'

I was treated kindly and tolerated by all. At the end of the school year I was even selected to be one of the distinguished guests sitting on the stage when the merit students received their awards, but my female teacher friends did tell me beforehand, 'Weijun, before you get on the stage, put on a skirt that matches the colour of your blouse.' I knew nothing about the convention of dressing by colour code and in China nobody had this kind of knowledge.

During the school holidays, helped by Bruce, I travelled to various towns such as Whangarei, Paihia, Auckland and Nelson, where his daughter Joanne lived. As an exotic figure I was a curiosity, causing a sensation in the community. I was invited by the Lions Club, Rotary Club and a Muslim society to give talks. I gave a Chinese cooking demonstration at a church service in Whangarei: two hundred tickets were sold, instead of the sixty predicted, because 'a Mainland Chinese lady is going to perform Chinese cooking'. Unfortunately my English was so limited that I didn't know how to explain how much salt, soy sauce or whatever

I was using, so I used the term 'a pinch' for each, causing roars of laughter from the audience — but they gave me resounding applause, too.

The New Zealand climate, pleasant as it is to me now, was almost unbearable with its cool summer and warm winter. I missed the extremes of Chinese weather — sensational hot summers and exciting snowy winters. I didn't realise that Westerners have a slightly higher body temperature than Asians due to their eating more meat. I tried to put on the same clothes as my New Zealand friends, only to find I was shivering with cold. The bright New Zealand sunshine was a dilemma, too. My eyes watered whenever I was in the sun.

Another culture shock was New Zealanders' habits regarding clothes. New Zealanders wore casual clothes most of the time but dressed well for evening parties. I saw many beautiful clothes for sale in shops and couldn't understand why people in the streets wore T-shirts, wrinkled jackets and torn jeans — not smart at all in my eyes. In China we wore our best clothes in the daytime since we were to be watched, commented on and judged. And we didn't change into evening dress for any events since to do so was considered indecent. A well-known Chinese saying is *wan shang da ban zhao lao ban*, if you make up yourself in the evenings, you are looking for sexual partners.

The biggest culture shock of all was food. Eating habits are established in early life and it is almost impossible to change. The first cup of coffee made me suffer a headache for several hours. Dairy products made me sick. I craved Chinese food, especially north Chinese food, which was not available in those days. Then when I was not well, I found the New Zealand medicine couldn't cure me because our Chinese doctors liked to use strong antibiotics. Even the medicinal toothpaste was too weak for me. Once I developed gum disease and I tried almost all the toothpastes produced in New Zealand, but none of them worked. My gum was swollen and painful and I could eat nothing but soup and other liquid food. Eventually I had to write to my family for help. As soon as the toothpaste arrived, I used it and the next day my gum problem was gone. Nobody in New Zealand had that kind of severe gum disease.

By the time I had been in New Zealand for four months I started to dream in English, that is, people in my dreams talked in English. I was thrilled by this discovery, as it was a clear sign that I was able to think in English — at last! With my improved English I was able to make friends easily, and I made a lot. Bruce and I attended meetings of the China Society of Northland every fortnight and the members were very friendly. I enjoyed political argument with Andrew; I appreciated Carol's sensitive talk. Fay, the manager of the macadamia plantation at Kerikeri where I worked occasionally, offered me a free ride home. Almost all the female teachers from Okaihau College invited me to stay weekends at their homes. I cooked Chinese meals for them and they taught me Western culture.

Apart from my social life, however, most of my time was occupied with the hard mental labour of learning English and my main comfort was from exchanging letters with Enya and Field.

To my great surprise, Field proposed to me. After seven years of uncertainty, he had made up his mind and my long lonely life got its reward. His parents didn't object to our affair any more since I was an overseas Chinese — a higher hierarchy.

I started to plan our future together, which I knew wasn't going to be easy. I didn't want another sad 'marriage in separation'. I wanted to live with my husband, together every day. However, I didn't know how to shift Field's work from Ulumuqi to Dragon Pool or nearby. It didn't matter. I could support him with my wages. Money is like time: it can grow more if you know how to deal with it.

In June, during the school holidays, I went to Auckland to try my luck at earning a bit of money. After much searching I found a job as a factory hand in west Auckland, but the job was exasperating. Lonely and confused in a strange city, the long hours of factory work were too much since I couldn't sleep well. I stayed with the Ross family, who tried their best to look after me, a lonely alien from a different world, but my situation was beyond their comprehension. Not speaking the language well, I talked little and laughed a lot, a false attitude people tend to use when they're not self-confident. Although I felt guilty that I couldn't repay their hospitality, I didn't know I should pay rent to them — in China you never charge money for anybody you invite to stay at your house. The Rosses weren't aware that I didn't know the rule, and they never directly asked me to pay rent. They might have tried, but again I didn't catch the point behind the sophisticated way of conversing. The factory job, which was planned to the minute for the whole eight hours of the day, was a far cry from our way of working in China — after a cup of tea with a newspaper and a lot of chat, you spent the remainder of day working. Chairman Mao was right — the capitalists are bloodsuckers.

The long hours of hard work combined with sleepless nights became murderous to me. My energy was gradually draining. On the Thursday night of the sixth week, I went to bed at nine after taking two sedative pills. I was still wide awake by ten, so I got up and took another pill. At eleven I was still awake and became more and more panicky. The long work day waiting for me only a few hours away was terrifying. How could I get up at six, catch the bus in time and cope with the whole day's physical labour? The more I tried to sleep the further I drove it away. At twelve-thirty, I decided to use my last solution. A few days before, one of my workmates had sneakily presented me with some biscuits made from a marijuana mixture. She told me it was relaxing and maybe it could help me sleep. I had a bite of it. The taste was fine but soon things were going wrong. My heart was pumping madly and I perspired copiously. With a buzzing head and a throat on fire, I tumbled out of the bed, only to find that my legs weren't responding to my brain. I knew I would lose consciousness if I lay motionless, so I struggled to roll along the floor, and then with great difficulty I tried to climb up the stairs for help. Surely I am dying, I thought, but I must let my hosts know what is happening to me. The two flights of stairs were like an endless path and it seemed like hours before I reached their bedroom. My head knocked against the door, waking up Mrs Ross. 'Sarah, I am dying,' I mumbled and collapsed. She rang the doctor, who said that he would come soon, and instructed them not to let me take any food or drink before then. I was extremely impressed by the Doctor's efficient response. Somehow the fact that a doctor was coming to see me at two in the morning stimulated my nerves and I was able to move a bit. I scrambled up, grabbed a glass and moved to the water tap. The Rosses jumped and tried to take the glass from me. I didn't give up. I gripped the glass and ran some water and poured it into my burning throat. The Rosses were so frustrated. Mr Ross held my head from the left and his wife clutched my shoulder from the right. I was sandwiched in between, unable to move until the doctor arrived ten minutes later. A man in his thirties, with a soft voice and sincere manner,

With Warren Freer and Mr Zhu, the mayor of Qingdao, 1992
(I was their interpreter)

he laid me down on the floor and checked me. And then he shook his head, puzzled.

'Doctor, I can tell you what has happened to me but you have to keep the secret for me. Can you promise?' I mumbled.

'I promise,' he said.

'I have taken some marijuana together with some sleeping pills.'

The doctor relaxed immediately. He gave me an injection and then my whole body started to shiver. Before he left, the doctor told the Rosses, 'She is not happy.' Mrs Ross said, 'She *is* happy.' I said, 'No, I am not happy. The doctor is right.' The Rosses looked at each other. They could not understand my feelings.

My endeavours to make money in Auckland came to a sudden halt. That afternoon I took a bus and went back to Bruce's place. For the rest of the year I put more effort into improving my English.

In October 1986, with Warren Freer's help, I obtained a visa for a further year. However, once I got the permission to extend my stay, conflict raged in my mind. I knew I would have a better life in New Zealand, but on the other hand I was responsible for my children and my aged mother. I missed my teaching career; and above all I wanted to marry Field.

In China, men had young girls as their wives but for a woman to marry a man nineteen years her junior was unheard of. I believed it was unfair to women. I hadn't heard of feminism at the time but sex prejudice was common in China. Curiosity and adventure were in my blood. To swim against the tide was my nature and I didn't play by the rules. I never believed in Chinese sayings such as 'women have long hair and short eyesight' and 'women and men would never be equal even in two thousand years' time'. Let me have a go and find out the response. It would be risky and difficult but exciting!

It was very difficult to make a final decision. Should I stay or leave? People would laugh at me after spending merely one year in New Zealand. Traditionally, overseas Chinese never returned home unless they became rich: *yi jin huan xiang*, back home wearing silk and satin, was the way.

Enya offered me wise counsel. In her letter she wrote: 'Mum, when making a decision, the most difficult one is the right one.' So the decision was made. I would leave for China on December 20, 1986.

The rest of my time in New Zealand became very tedious and I counted the days until the end of the year when I could leave and go back home.

CHAPTER EIGHTEEN

I was in a desperate situation after I got off the train at Guangzhou railway station. I had six pieces of luggage. There were two cases full of the clothes and presents my friends had given me, there were many packages of chocolate and cigarettes as presents for my neighbours, there was a duty-free colour television set and an electric keyboard I had bought in Hong Kong. No trolley was available at the railway station, or porters to turn to. I stood at the platform, watching the crowds bustling along, and nobody even cast a glance at me. Helplessly, I stood beside my mountain of luggage and looked around in despair. Suddenly I saw Field running to me.

No platform ticket was sold here lest people use them to smuggle themselves into Hong Kong. How had Field got in? He gave me a cunning smile: 'Nothing could stop me seeing you,' he said. He was wearing a dark green suit and on his right arm was a red spade-shaped sign that read: CONDUCTOR. 'When did you become a conductor?' 'Shhh,' he whispered in my ear, 'I bought them in the black market. Listen, I want you to fake being ill.'

We were walking towards the exit. I was very nervous. Two gatemen were there to check tickets. I bent my back, frowned, moaned and clutched my hands to my belly, and wobbled to the exit. Field smiled to the gatemen and said in a confident voice, 'A patient from my carriage. I believe she's got appendicitis and needs an operation at once.' The gatemen let us through.

We went to a small hotel where Field had stayed the night before. Holding me in his arms, he made a long speech, which surprised me a lot. I was not aware he could be so eloquent. However I was happy he was with me again after so many years of waiting in solitude.

The next day we set off on the train journey from Guangzhou to Qingdao. When we changed trains in Wuhan we checked into a small hotel near the railway station. At midnight I was woken up by a rustling noise outside the door. Before I had time to get dressed, the door was kicked open and a crowd came in. A man in police uniform said, 'Are you husband and wife since you stay in the same room? Show us your marriage certificate!' His followers were bustling around and jingling their handcuffs. I calmed myself, showed him my passport and spoke as quietly as I could, 'I am an overseas Chinese just back from New Zealand; he is my nephew who has come to meet me.' As soon as the man heard the word 'passport', his expression changed from hard to soft, from an officious frown to a flattering smile. He glanced at Field, who was sitting on another single bed looking dumb and innocent. 'I am sorry. Please go back to sleep.' He turned to his men and yelled, 'Get out, quickly!'

After the steps faded away, I lamented, 'How could they intrude on our privacy like this?'

'Do you think you are still in New Zealand?' Field said and shook his head.

On 23 December 1986, buffeted by a high wind, Field and I arrived at Dragon Pool in the evening, together with Enya who had met us at Qingdao station. It was supper-cooking time and a foggy smoke was blowing over the green wheat fields. An aroma from grass burning floated in the mountain air, so familiar and homely. Tears welled up in my eyes.

My old mother struggled up from her bed and touched my face with her thin, dried hands. 'I thought I would not see you again,' she said in a trembling voice. Our small home had become shabbier. The only food available in the household was a couple of steamed buns and a few cabbage leaves. There was a power cut. I was knocked by a reverse culture shock. After a year of living in an affluent country, the material scarcity was difficult for me to handle. However, I did not regret going back. The day after I arrived, Mother's backache was relieved and for the first time in a few weeks, she could get up and walk freely. What better reward could I have? The small stove I had made years ago was no longer practical since we had Field, a man with a bigger stomach, now. We made a hole in the

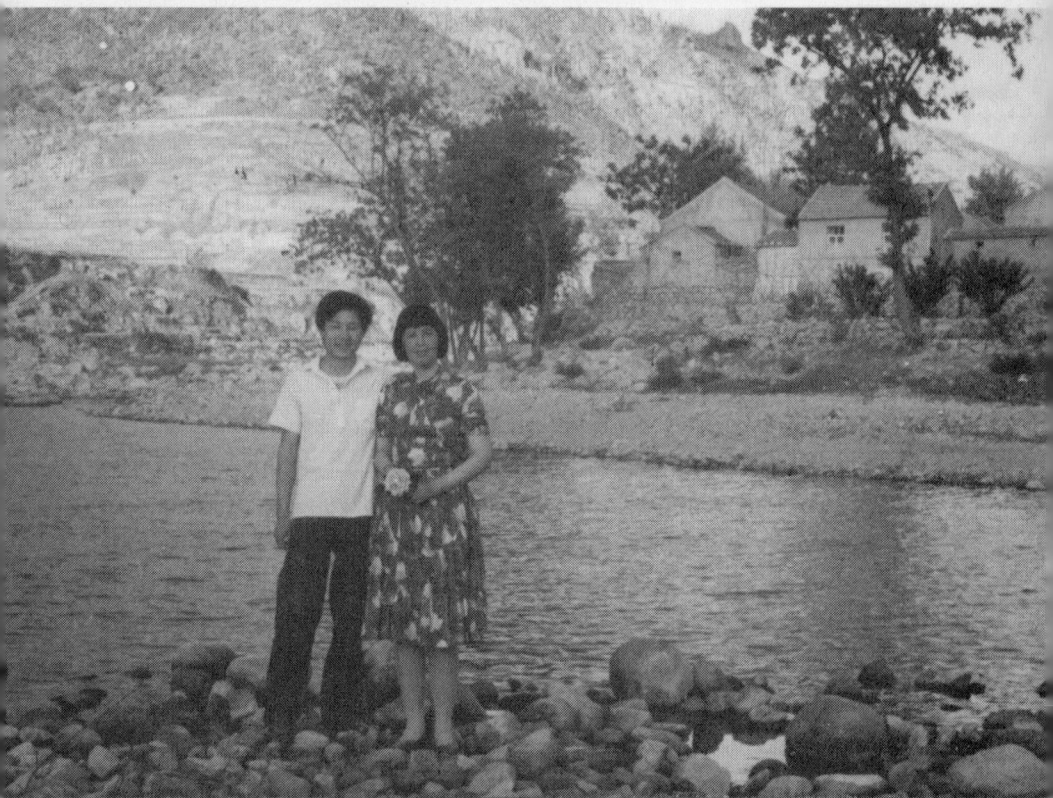

*With Field at Dragon Pool, 1987; one of the huts in the background
was our home*

roof and built a chimney. At the doorway we built a concrete stove and
fixed a wok in it. It was as big as a round bath tub and it would use a
minimal amount of dried grass, sticks or powered coal.

Field and I started our wedding preparations. With my wages saved up
— about 500 *yuan*, a considerable amount at that time — we bought meat,
chicken, seafood, vegetables, ten kilograms of sweets, dozens of bottles of
beer and spirits and a hundred packets of cigarettes. We borrowed an empty
house nearby and it took us three days to clean it to make it decent for a
wedding venue. We went shopping in Qingdao, trying to spend as little as
possible on my wedding garments.

On January 22, 1987, when I was forty-two years old, I married my
long-lost lover. Another sweet dream came true. After we had our official
ceremony in the government house in Beijai, Field and I had our wedding

feast for fifty people. We hired a chef to cook the twenty-four kinds of dishes at my place. Enya and a couple of my students acted as waitresses. My mother, now eighty-one, lay in bed to save room for the wedding activities. As well as being the bride, I was the general director of the banquet to make sure everything was all right: to watch the time; to welcome every guest; to arrange the fireworks; to make sure there were enough glasses, chopsticks, plates, chairs and tables; to help in the kitchen; and then to get myself ready.

Guests started to arrive at ten in the morning. I stood on the road, greeted everyone, led them to the wedding house and offered sweets and cigarettes. In between I ran back to my house to make sure the cooking process was all right and the chef was satisfied. All the time Field was standing in front of a mirror worrying about his jacket, which he had made himself. He looked fine to me but somehow he was not satisfied with it. He was upset that the flare at the back was not perfect, and he caressed it again and again, like a dog running after his tail. At last I persuaded him it was okay and arm in arm we appeared in the wedding room. The guests had already started smoking and drinking. As the public basically diapproved of our marriage, nobody took the wedding seriously. It was a funny, chaotic, anarchic wedding, and it didn't finish till midnight. At ten o'clock I was still heating dishes on a gas stove in the wedding house for some remaining guests. I was empty-bellied and my new wedding clothes were dirty with grease stains.

The news spread far and wide about our marriage. In conformist China our marriage broke virtually all the social codes. For months Field and I were the subject of hot gossip. Once in a bus station I heard a group of women chattering about Field and me. Some of them were anxious to meet me, the woman of bold behaviour, so I said to them, 'Don't bother to search, I am the one you are talking about.'

I regarded my marriage to Field as a triumph, since I had never had a proper wedding and I had never expected it to happen. I loved Field so much and I wished he could have a job at Sunjia School so that I could see him day and night.

In April 1987, Field and I had a little house built for Bruce in our courtyard. The construction was extremely difficult. It took us a couple of months to prepare all the material needed — the sand, cement, bricks, window frames, door, rafters, roof beams and tiles. In a remote place like Dragon Pool, to bring every item home was a struggle. As we could not afford to buy enough bricks, we picked up old bricks from derelict building sites. Field and I made many trips, pushing a wheelbarrow, to transfer the old bricks to our courtyard. The ones we collected were only enough for the upper half of the walls; for the lower half we used stones from the river bed. For the door and window frames, we bought second-hand timber in a town thirty miles away to save us forty-odd *yuan*. It was a hard job to find transport. I went to various houses in both Lying Dragon and Sunjia Village, offering cigarettes, being humble, begging help from the tractor drivers.

I organised sixteen peasants to build the house. Field and most of the workers carried water from the river and mixed cement with sand and water; carried stones from the river and cut them with hammers into the desired shapes. Our village friend Outstanding, who lived at the other end of the bridge, took on the major job of building the four walls. It was very hard for him since he had to cut the stones into the exact shape to fit each other before he could place them in the wall.

My job was to offer the workers tea and cigarettes as well as lunch and dinner. It was the custom that when you built a house, you got help from neighbours and offered them meals as thanks, since nobody was rich enough to pay in money. However, it was not acceptable to offer everyday meals. You must offer exquisite dishes of meat, poultry and seafood, and the main filling food, the steamed buns, were white fine ones. This job was lighter but more complicated, leaving me virtually no break. I wore my working clothes and took the bus to Licun again and again to buy everything I needed for cooking. The day when the roof was put up, we had four more workers and I had to buy sixty steamed buns and carry them home.

I rode in the bus for one hour, walked to the market and bought the sixty buns; each one weighing half a pound. Carrying the huge bundle, I walked to the bus station, bustled in the crowd and got back on the bus. I ran and shoved amongst the crowd of young men with all the strength I could summon. I was excited at seeing one empty seat in the back row and I pushed myself into the seat and put my heavy bundle on it. A man sitting in front of me jumped up and yelled, 'That seat was reserved for my friend!' He pulled me out of the seat and threw my bundle on the floor. I carried it on my shoulder, standing in the crowded bus for an hour and trudged uphill for more than half an hour before finally I arrived home — just in time to cook lunch and dinner for all the workers.

Bruce liked the little house very much and called it 'Bruce's Guest House'. To keep it clean and neat, it was locked until Bruce arrived. He came to China every year and stayed with us for one to three months. We offered him free beer, free accommodation and I was his interpreter. I was happy I could repay his kindness at last.

One year later at the beginning of 1988 I took on another challenge — trying to enter the holy place of my heart, the university campus. I had dreamed of going to university ever since I was rejected from it when I was 18, and for decades I had never given up the dream. A friend intro-duced me to Mr Qiu, the head of the English Department at Qingdao Educational Institute, which later became the Educational College of the University of Qingdao. I passed the oral English test in the interview and the next step, Mr Qiu suggested, was for me to give some trial lessons to the students. Still working at Sunjia School, I prepared my lessons for the university at night. Once a week for four weeks I took one day off when I didn't have lessons in Sunjia School and went to Qingdao to give the university lessons in secret.

Carrying a heavy bag with books, notebooks and student's homework, I walked in the rain, in the wind, in the heat. One of the bridges on the way to Licun was broken by a storm and I had to walk half the distance. The whole trip took me two and half hours before I arrived on the seventh floor of the teaching building. I gave a one-hour lesson to the class of thirty-eight students. Sometimes professors in the department and directors of the university would listen to my trial lectures. It was a hard and stressful time, especially as I couldn't let anybody from Sunjia School know what I was doing. People would be jealous and make obstacles if they knew I was trying to promote myself. When my tired body wanted to give up, my willpower would carry me on. I believed that life was fair and God would see my endeavour and I would be rewarded.

The first four trial lessons were not successful, but fortunately the spring holiday came at Sunjia School and I used the two weeks to prepare my lectures at the university. I stayed up late to record my lecture, listen to it and correct it again and again.

The whole process took me more than half a year. There were times when my self-confidence ran out and I was overcome by melancholy. Other times I encouraged myself and thought optimistically. But I failed at the last step.

Standing in front of Mr Qiu in his house, I could not hold back my tears. He was telling me why I'd failed in my quest. The officials of the educational bureau I belonged to had informed Ms Dung, the personnel officer of the university, about my marriage. She said to Mr Qiu: 'This woman would have a bad influence on our students.'

'Why?' asked Mr Qiu.

'She has married a younger man.'

'Does the law limit the age difference for marriage?' asked Mr Qiu angrily.

'The university has made the decision not to accept her to our staff,' answered Ms Dung.

It was a bad knock, but I was not going to give up easily. I took advantage of the regulations: as a permanent teacher at Sunjia School I was allowed to take long-term sick leave and still receive eighty percent of my wages.

I needed money and time to take action again.

CHAPTER NINETEEN

'Success is the side product of perseverance.'

One day in October 1988, Field was driving our three-wheeled motorcycle, with me riding on the trailer. We were going to meet Bruce at the Qingdao railway station.

After much frustration trying to find a job for Field that he fancied, at last we decided to borrow some money and buy him the three-wheeler to take people places, a sort of taxi job. The motorcycle had a trailer so it was useful for passengers who wanted to carry goods. It turned out to be quite successful and within one year he had earned enough money to repay the debt. But it was a tough job and we had to fight for business against other three-wheeler drivers. I was sad and depressed that I, from an intellectual background, had become like a street vendor, crude and rustic, having to argue over small amounts of money. How far it was from my academic dream.

Field and I joined the crowd and waited for the train from Beijing. To our disappointment, Bruce was not amongst the passengers even though we stayed there till the last passenger was gone. I then looked at the telegraph Bruce sent me and found I had misunderstood the date.

By the time all the passengers were gone, the big station square was empty. It was at this time that I saw a couple of foreigners at the exit gate looking around anxiously, a middle-aged Western woman, fair-skinned with an elegant hairdo, and standing beside her, obviously her husband, a dark-skinned man, tall and strong, with an air of arrogance. Observing them for a few minutes, it aroused my natural desire to help others. I walked over to the woman and asked her in English, 'Can I help you?'

'Oh, you speak English!' she exclaimed with evident relief. 'We come from Canada. We were told somebody would meet us but they didn't come.'

'Do you have their address or telephone number?'

'Yes, I have.' She took out a small notebook and there in her handwriting was the telephone number of the No. 2 Asbestos Factory of Qingdao. I looked at the address and knew it was far away from the railway station. I said, 'My name is Weijun. This is my husband, Field. We have the three-wheeled motorcycle over there. If you could trust us, we would like to take you to a hotel and from there I could help you to ring the factory.'

'Hi, Weijun,' she said, 'my name is Doris. This is my husband Mukajee.' They shook hands with Field and me. I told Field to pull the three-wheeler up to the square while I conversed with Doris and Mukajee.

I was told that Mukajee was involved in a co-operative project between the Chinese and Canadian governments. This was their first trip to China and Doris planned to enjoy a holiday while her husband did the consultancy work. 'It seemed they did not know we were coming today and we were really worried before you came to rescue us. Without you we would have been absolutely lost in this strange place without being able to speak the language.'

Field's three-wheeler pulled up and as we started to put their luggage onto the trailer, a security guard in railway uniform came over. 'No private vehicle is allowed in the railway station square!' he yelled at Field. 'Show me your driving licence!' Field dared not show his driving licence, for it would be confiscated. The enraged guard then growled, 'Without your driving licence and you dare to drive? Leave your vehicle here and go home to get your licence!' He got onto the driver's seat and started the engine. He was going to drive the vehicle away. Field and I were vexed. Leaving our vehicle with the security guard would mean a fine and a loss of many days' business, and probably the vehicle would be damaged by rough treatment. Traffic guards were just as tough as policemen and they were every driver's nightmare. At this crucial moment I heard Mukajee say to me, 'I want to have a word with him. Could you translate for me?' I was not sure if it would work, still, there was no harm in trying. I nodded.

With a serious face, Mukajee looked into the guard's eyes and said, 'We have been sent by both of the Chinese and Canadian governments to work for Qingdao. These people are trying to help us and you are stopping them from doing so. We will report you to your mayor if you don't let them go.' I translated his words one by one, happy to see that the security guard was impressed by my language skill and vexed by the words. He got off the driving seat silently but tried hard to maintain an appearance of authority. 'Okay, I will let you go this time. Next time don't let me see you in this place!' he admonished and walked away with the pretence of haughtiness. Field started the engine again. A few minutes later, we arrived at the Pier Hotel which fronted onto the beach of Qingdao. I helped them check in and found a room facing the sea. Flocks of seagulls were flying in the sky, snowy waves beat the red rocks. Doris and Mukajee were happy with it. I picked up the telephone in the room and rang the asbestos factory. The response from the other end of the telephone was amazement: 'We will arrive at the hotel as soon as possible!'

Less than twenty minutes later, a team of six officials arrived: the representative of the mayor, the head of Science Bureau of Qingdao, the head of the factory Party committee, the head of the factory administration, the public liaison director of the Cultural Bureau, and a young man as the interpreter. They shook hands with the four of us one by one. They bowed again and again at least five times to apologise for not coming to the station to meet the guests due to a communication breakdown, and thanked me the same number of times for rescuing their guests. It would be a serious error to fail to meet government-arranged foreign guests. If anything bad had happened to the guests, the officials might lose their positions out of shame.

The four of us had our brunch in the hotel after the factory team left, and exchanged personal information. Doris came from England but Mukajee was from India. They lived in Vancouver, where Mukajee worked as an engineering consultant after retiring from a big company. Hearing that they did the job for China not for the money but to help, I was very impressed. I was also surprised that they were retired since they looked too young for that.

'Oh, we are not as young as you think. I am sixty-four and my husband is sixty-six,' Doris smiled.

Looking at their healthy, energetic figures, I was truly surprised. 'How could you keep so young?' I asked curiously.

'Well, we look after ourselves. We don't do stupid things,' Mukajee said.

Who would imagine he would die two days later? Who would know it would change my life?

'Dear Weijun, you are our rescuer. We would be absolutely lost if you hadn't come over.' Doris and I were drinking tea in the café in the hotel the next day when I came to visit her again. She was a very nice woman and I freely told her about my life's tragedy. She supported my love for Field and admired my bravery in marrying him, even though she could see I was badly hurt by society's reaction. She told me that thirty-five years ago when she married Mukajee in England she had faced the same prejudice. 'Be yourself and do what you want,' she said. 'I wish I could help you.'

She told me she liked sweet potatoes but the hotel kitchen didn't cook them as they were considered poor food, and were never available in hotels. Two days later, with a bag of new season's sweet potatoes in my hand, I caught the bus and arrived at the hotel by late morning. When I opened the door, I sensed something unusual in the air and Doris looked very sad. 'Oh, Weijun, I am glad you came,' she greeted me in a cracking voice. The interpreter, sitting in the chair opposite Doris, was surprised I had come so quickly. He asked me, 'Which vehicle did you take, the car or the jeep?'

'Neither. I came by public bus.'

'So you don't know what has happened? Come outside and I will tell you.'

Outside the room, he told me in a serious voice, 'Something very bad has happened. Mukajee has died.'

I rushed back to the room and cuddled Doris. 'I am so sorry!' Doris wept on my shoulder and said, 'I told them you are my only friend in Qingdao and I need you.' She then told me what had happened.

Two nights before, Mukajee woke up at midnight having difficulty breathing. He took a couple of his vitamin pills, felt better, and went to sleep again. He got up at the normal time and went to work in spite of Doris's suggestion that he should see a doctor — which could have saved his life since his uncomfortable feeling was actually a minor heart attack. At about eleven in the morning he fell to the ground with little sign of life. He was suffering a second heart attack, which in most cases is fatal.

The mayor of Qingdao organised a medical team of fourteen cardiologists to try to save his life, but eleven hours later he died.

Doris didn't attend Mukajee's funeral. 'I don't want it ruin my good memories of him from the past. Could you represent me at the funeral?' she asked, and I agreed.

The mayor of Qingdao, Mr Zhu, was the head of the funeral committee. At the funeral, I presented a bunch of fresh flowers Doris had picked in the hotel garden, and I gave a eulogy for Mukajee in fluent English. The death struck me hard and I wept for a long while. All the bad feelings that had piled up in my chest poured out with my tears. After I arrived at the hotel, I saw Mayor Wu in the hall. He came up to me and admired my English. 'Where are you working now?' he asked. I told him of my failed job application. Mayor Wu said, 'English is very useful. I can help you. Tomorrow you and Mr Qiu are welcome to come to my banquet in the hotel.'

At the banquet Mayor Wu delivered his condolences to Doris. He told her she could ask for compensation from the government of Qingdao and the mayor tried his best to console her for her loss. Doris said, 'During my stay in Qingdao, I received a lot of help and support from Weijun. She sets a good example for Qingdao people: caring, kind and understanding. She is an excellent ambassador for Chinese people.'

After the banquet, Mayor Zhu talked to Mr Qiu in private. Three days later I received a letter from Mr Qiu, the head of the English Department of the Educational Institute, informing me that I had been hired by the university as a lecturer. One more of my dreams was fulfilled as a result of my helping others.

It was seven in the morning of my first day at the university. I was lying in my single bed in the guest house of the campus, thinking hard. It was my way of preparing my lessons. To make my lectures active and natural, I didn't give lessons by reading my notes. Instead, I did full-scale mental preparation.

The bell rang and I sprang up and walked across the lovely garden, enjoying the fragrance of roses, wisteria and gardenias. I walked happily towards the lecture hall, where more than fifty girls and boys were waiting for me.

In those days Chinese high-school students rarely went to a teachers' college by choice since teachers were low in the social hierarchy. A common saying was: 'The ninth class is teachers who have never tried lobsters'; if one tried to describe poverty, a common simile was 'as poor as a professor'. Most of my students came to this college not because they liked it but for one of two reasons: they had failed to gain entry to their university of choice, or their parents were too poor to support them for the full schooling fee. Teachers' colleges were the only kind of educational institutions that offered the students free meals as well as free schooling. So at first the students were in low spirits and my job was to change that.

Standing at the rostrum facing fifty young faces, I was full of enthusiasm. For the following fifty minutes I gave an inspiring speech. I believed that once the students were inspired, they would become the best students they could be and would study spontaneously and conscientiously. As always, as soon as I faced the students, I was able to project confidence, intelligence and inspiration. I delivered my ideas with a lively and restorative spirit. I presented stories, doctrines and quotations from great minds. I talked of my personal experiences and told stories of influence and encouragement. When the bell rang and the class finished, the classroom vibrated with applause. Dozens rushed up to me, expressing their delight with my lecture. A chubby girl said to me, 'Ms Liu, I have been sad being a student of this college. Your lecture has changed my views and I want to be a teacher now!' Many voices joined her in agreement. At the end of the term I was known as a 'teacher of erudition'.

One rainy evening I heard a quiet knock at the door while I was preparing lessons in my office. I answered and in came a male student. He seated himself straight away and said, 'Ms Liu, I am lovelorn.' Tears ran down his cheeks. I put aside my work. After he finished telling me his woes, I talked to him, encouraging him to face life with bravery and positive thinking. Two hours passed, and when he left my room he was smiling. The next day when I stepped into the classroom he was leading a chorus in his class (it was a tradition that students would sing a chorus before class); he was no more the miserable lad.

My family at Enya's wedding, May 2001, from left: Ian, Enya, Kerry, me, Nini

Once there was a letter included with a boy's homework: 'Dear Ms Liu, I have fallen in love with a girl in the class but I dare not to tell her about my feelings in case I am rejected. On the other hand I do want to know whether or not she is fond of me. I have not told anybody about this but I want your advice.'

I wrote him a letter which I delivered in person. I encouraged him in his quest and I suggested that he talk to the girl no matter how shy he was. 'If you are brave, you will win,' I wrote. A few weeks later another letter appeared in his homework telling me that the girl had become his sweetheart.

In the summer of 1989, just before Enya graduated from university, her teacher informed her that she must do something about her future, since the officials from the educational bureau of Laoshan made nasty remarks when they learned that Enya was my daughter. I had offended them by taking sick leave and later by working in the university. According to government regulations, Enya was to work in no other school but Sunjia School since her residence was in the Beijai area. (By regulation, children's residence followed that of their mother's.) And because I had offended the authorities by trying to shift my job to the university, they were not going to be nice to Enya and her future looked bleak.

Enya, cultivated by my mother and influenced by me, had a courageous and adventurous personality. She decided to fight to free herself from the unfairness she faced from the bureau.

Ever since Enya began to live with me when she was nine, we had become best friends. There was no conflict, but only mutual love and support. She loved me with an unusual passion, regarding me as her mother, teacher, mentor and best friend. We always did things together — watering the vegetable garden, picking up the firewood, washing clothes in the river or reading, singing and playing games in the evenings. We would talk while doing these things. They were long, deep, sincere talks, like adult conversations. During her teenage years, she had inevitable emotional troubles but she always told me the truth. I didn't scold her or give her boring and superficial lectures. Rather, I tried my best to comfort as well as guide her. I believe it was the heart to heart talks that secured our relationship. She was never rebellious to me and I always enjoyed her trust, friendship and closeness. Of all the activities we did together, the one we enjoyed the most was walking up the mountains into Beijiushui. Enya's character was formed by the beauty of nature and trained by the hard work of everyday life. She was sensitive, mature and strong-willed.

A new school term started in September 1989 and every graduate had started work except Enya. She had refused the position the educational bureau offered her, the teaching job at Sunjia School. She took trips from Dragon Pool to Licun, to Qingdao, to meet officials. When she finally succeeded at the end of the eight-month battle, she had talked to countless strangers, many of them holding important positions, but she was not afraid. She had been rejected, scolded, laughed at and criticised but she emerged the winner. Her bravery and determination touched Mr Wu, the head of the City Economy Planning Council, a very powerful man. With

COMMUNITY MINDED: Enya Chadderton.

Enya interviewed as an 'emerging leader' in the newspaper

his help, she got a job in the centre of Qingdao as an interpreter for a joint-venture company and, with this position, she was allocated a city apartment, which was most unusual.

In 1991, with $US100 in her pocket, she went to New Zealand. She never asked me to send her money. Instead, I received American or Kiwi notes every now and then with her letters. She was extremely hard-working, doing heavy physical jobs to support herself and to help me. Four years later she obtained her degree from the University of Auckland and became an accountant. In 2003, she was selected as an 'emerging leader' of New Zealand.

When she applied for her visa to New Zealand, the timing was bad. It was after the disastrous Tienanmen Square massacre and the embassy wouldn't issue any more visas to Chinese nationals since they had accepted so many refugee students. I wrote to Warren Freer, boldly criticising the New Zealand government for being hypocritical: 'Your brother-in-law

246

Bruce comes to China every year and we treat him as a friend yet you refuse to accept Enya to your country. It is said yours is a free and democratic country but I can't see how democratic and free you are . . .' Warren replied promptly: 'Your letter is very touching. I am just meeting the Minister of Immigration and I will try to help your daughter obtain a visa.' I was very impressed by Warren's tolerance.

Life with Field was not as smooth as I had imagined. When we got married, I was passionately in love with him, but one and half years later I found out he was having an affair with another woman. Our educational levels were very different and he didn't share my zeal for learning and reading. As a young man he wanted to be a wordly adventurer but I wanted a stable domestic life. Newly out from under his parents' wings, he hadn't developed the habit of doing any housework. I had to cook, do the washing and the shopping, as well as be the main breadwinner. Tired of the job with the three-wheeler, he hardly went out for business and earned almost no money for the family.

Love alone is not enough for a good marriage. Marrying Field out of mere romantic love was a mistake. Long relationships need both parties to mature; responsibility and shared perceptions take time to develop.

My younger daughter Nini was in a difficult situation. I worried about her day and night. She was six now and had started primary school in Licun. When I visited her, I brought her snacks and books. For half an hour we would sit against a back wall on the ground, side by side. I would talk and she would listen in silence, always in silence. Seeing her thin face and subdued expression, I was heartbroken.

Her school courtyard was not as private as the kindergarten had been and soon the news that I was visiting Nini reached her father. Rich threw a tantrum to the teachers of the school and told them not to let me see Nini. He then told them about my scandalous marriage to a younger man so my name in their eyes was ruined and they took Rich's side. The headmistress gave orders that I was not allowed to visit Nini at her school.

Rich and his second wife Sesame didn't have other children. At first I thought Nini would be loved by both of them so I was happy for her. After she had lived with them for a couple of years she was sent away to live with her father's relatives. Rich's older brother and his wife Nice had three children, and each one had a young child for Nice to look after. Everybody was too busy for Nini and she was neglected most of the time. She was growing very lonely and she hardly talked. I wanted to offer my love to her but how much opposition I faced! Almost nobody was on my side and nobody was concerned about Nini's emotional needs. Everyone believed that I had no right to contact her since her father provided her with money and even the people from the Women's Affairs Council took Rich's side. They told me, 'We have investigated Rich; he does well in his job. We cannot help you since he is a good worker.' Numerous times I went to Licun and talked to as many authorities as I could to win the right to see my daughter.

I went to Nice's house trying to see Nini but they rudely sent me away. I went to the workplaces of Rich's nieces and pleaded with them to help me but they didn't think I had any right to see my daughter. I kept on writing pleading letters. I wrote to Rich as well as to every one of his relatives — his brother, his sister-in-law, his nephew and his two nieces, but nobody ever answered me but his wife. Sesame wrote, 'You have no right to see Nini since you abandoned her in the first place. Moreover, we think you are a bad influence on her, being shameless with men.'

I decided to go to court to try to get justice but the judge didn't accept the case. He said, 'Whether you see your daughter or not is your domestic affair. You should solve it by yourselves. The court doesn't want to interfere in your personal business.'

'By law, I am still Nini's mother and I have a right to see her, even though her father has custody,' I argued.

'Then you should discuss it with her father not us,' said the judge.

With a triumphant expression on his face, Rich walked out of the courtroom. I followed him and begged him allow me to see Nini. He said, 'All the town knows how shameful you are — you married a young man. Don't imagine that anybody will take your side.'

I wouldn't give up easily. I kept on talking to everyone who might offer some good ideas; I took my chances to meet Nini, on her way home from school, at the door of her classroom, at the school playground when she had physical education lessons . . . And to help her, I put books into her bag. I wanted her to get an education from reading which I personally could not give her. Books had already helped her tremendously in her parenting-deprived life — she had formed a strong hobby of reading and her mind had developed well.

When Nini turned eight, I managed to take her to Dragon Pool for an overnight stay. When she was nine, she would run out of her aunt's house and take the trip by herself to Dragon Pool.

Nini was warmly welcomed by everyone in Dragon Pool. Granny gave her big cuddles; Field took her to the river for fishing; Enya and I cooked her favourite dishes. However, each time she was with me, a nasty encounter would occur. One time at midnight Nice and her son-in-law came and took Nini from me by force, even though I had left a note informing them of her whereabouts. Another time I picked up Nini on her way home from school and the next morning Rich came and had a fight with me. It happened on the stone bridge beside my home. I was faced with Rich suddenly as I rode my bike towards Da Lao bus-stop. Field, with Nini on the back seat, had ridden on ahead. Seeing Rich, I stopped and greeted him. Ignoring my greeting, he yelled at me, 'I fuck your mother. You are a child-thief!' I told him Nini was on the way home with Field. He shouted, 'Don't you dare lie! Return the child!' As if magic, the empty place was filled with spectators in no time. People ran from the road, the mountains, the houses and the river bank, calling out excitedly, 'Fighting! Fighting! Hurry up!' Soon Rich and I were circled by a big crowd. Rich was pushing me and kicking me. I kept on watching the far end of the road, waiting for Field. The mob, their eyes opened wide and excited, patiently waited for a good fight. Rich roared, 'I am going to give you a good lesson today! You will never dare to steal the child again!' Suddenly I relaxed as I saw Field at the high point of the road. Like a flying arrow, he shot down to the crowd, which parted for him to enter the centre of the circle. The eyes of the watchers glittered in anticipation of action. Rich said to Field, 'It's none of your business. You stand aside. I am going to give the bitch a good lesson!'

'If you touch her, I will attack you,' said Field.

'Shut up! It's none of you business!' Rich said, and he struck me again.

'Stop touching her or I will beat you up!' warned Field. He started to counter-attack when Rich hit me again. Rich threw himself on Field and the two men struggled together, howling and biting. At this crucial moment my friend Outstanding came over and whispered in my ear,

'Catch his hair.' I gripped Rich's hair and he couldn't move his head. Field seized the moment and got in a few good hits. Soon Rich freed himself from my grip and the two men started a fervent fight. Field was younger and fitter and kicked his rival hard. Rich fell down to the ground. Field, on top of Rich's body, got in some good blows. Rich rolled over and managed to stand up. They started fighting again. Nini was crying fearfully behind me. I called to the crowd, 'Please, help! Please stop them!' Everybody moved a step back at my words and their eyes opened even wider with excitement. Nobody bothered to stop the fighting. Nini's tiny body was shaking: 'I want to go home!' Clearly she meant to my place but I felt my home was not legally her home. I turned to the two men and shouted at them, 'Stop! Stop now!' Both dropped their fists. The crowd slipped away immediately, disappointed. Picking up his bicycle, Rich turned his head to Field, and yelled, 'You wait, when you go to Licun I'll let you know I am not alone!' His big eyes were red and had a wild expression. He then turned to me and roared, 'Next time I catch you with Nini, I will break your legs!'

I believed him. He was a man of fierce temper. If he said he would break my legs, he would. Even if he didn't do it himself, it was easy to pay somebody do it. The market price for breaking an arm was five hundred *yuan*, and a thousand for a leg. I was in great danger if I went again to see my daughter. On the other hand, it was better to lose a leg than to let my daughter lose her mother. I gathered all my courage and kept going to see Nini.

One day after I took Nini to Dragon Pool again, Rich's sister-in-law, his niece and her husband came to my place at night. Their severe voices stirred the quiet village. Neighbours sat on the wall and watched. Many were on Rich's side, commenting loudly: 'Weijun doesn't have the right to see the little girl. She doesn't have custody.'

Another time, Rich arrived at Dragon Pool after midnight. Using a big stone, he hit the metal door of our courtyard and yelled out, 'Return the child!' I answered through an open window, 'She is my daughter too!' All the neighbours were up. With trembling voices, they talked to me over the wall between my house and theirs: 'Please, Teacher Liu, give the child back to her father. Otherwise he might kill.' Bang! Bang! Bang! the attack on the door continued. Nini was shivering; Field pulled her up to the

My younger daughter Nini and Bruce, 1991; soon after, she moved in with me after years' battle with her father and his relatives

window sill on the back wall and they jumped out. Holding Nini in his arms he fled along the river bank to Laughing Lady's house in Lying Dragon Village and left Nini in her kind care. Then Field came to the front of the house where Rich was still hitting the door. There were many dents on its surface now. Field said, 'I didn't know the door was so hit-proof.' Rich was so startled by words coming from behind him in the dark that in shock he threw the stone down and ran away.

Time moved on and Nini's well-being worried me more and more. Even though I could manage to take Nini to Dragon Pool more often, it still didn't mean she had a better life in her aunt's place. I needed her to stay with me permanently, but how? Rich had custody and Nini was still too young to decide her own life. At last, life itself helped us: Rich's wife Sesame committed suicide.

One day in November 1990, I wrote another letter to Sesame, trying to gain her sympathy. Weeks passed and there was no answer from her. I decided to go to her workplace and talk to her in person. In the office, her deputy director met me and told me the story: one day when Rich went home for lunch he found Sesame standing underneath one of the interior doors, not moving. He was angry and asked, 'Why do you stand there?' She didn't move or speak. He came up to her and saw her tongue was out, her body cold.

Immediately after I heard the news, Field and I developed a plan together with Nini.

One early morning in the spring of 1991, Field drove the three-wheeler to Licun where in one of the streets, Nini was standing in the empty street in front of her school in her thin dress, her schoolbag on her shoulder and holding a transistor radio, a present from me for her eighth birthday, in her little hand. The three-wheeler stopped, the door of the trailer opened, both my hands and the hands of my friend River stretched out and pulled Nini in. As soon as she was on board, the three-wheeler shot away like a whirlwind. I sent a letter to inform Rich where Nini was, and River undertook the difficult task of seeing him in person. Rich threw a huge tantrum, but River was younger and very tall. Verbal abuse was all Rich dared to do to River.

The next day, Rich came to Dragon Pool and asked Nini to come back but she said, 'No'. I talked him through everything and eventually he saw the logic, that Nini would be better off living with me than with her aunt. Now he was a widower and he needed time to find himself another wife. He dropped the custody battle. Together with my daughter, I had won the five-year battle. Nini moved to Dragon Pool where she had the best time in her life so far.

CHAPTER TWENTY

In 1992, the paramount leader of China, Deng Xiaoping, did a countrywide tour, telling business people that, to promote economic development, every company should try their best to attract foreign funds. In no time there was a widespread trend of attracting foreign investment. Seeing I had a foreign guest, groups of business people, one after another, came to us and tried to talk Bruce into investing his money in their businesses.

After much resistance, an especially clever negotiating group finally trapped Bruce. This group, headed by a Mr Tan, was from the Star & Fire Company of Huangdao. Mr Tan was the vice general manager of the company which involved several projects, including a textile factory, a chemical factory and a dairy farm.

The Star & Fire Company was located in a small town called Jaonan outside Qingdao, about eighty miles away on the other side of the Bohai Sea. The idea was introduced to us by a respectable member of the Political Consultation Council of Qingdao and immediately Bruce was obsessed by the proposition. The suggested product of the future joint venture was an electric device for heating water. Households in China had no running hot water from the tap, which was a pain in winter. If this device worked, water would be heated before it ran out of the tap, which would be a great convenience for every household and Bruce could see it would have a good market.

The next day, the negotiating group took Bruce and me to visit Mr Wang, the engineer who had invented the device. In a workshop in his home, Mr Wang showed us the electric heater which was attached to the tap. When the button was switched on, the water became hot in a few seconds.

After the visit, Bruce and I were offered a big banquet, hosted by the general manager, Mr Kun. He was a famous figure as a private business-man in Shandong province, and he seemed honest and amiable. Around the big round table, eight people sat with Bruce and me, showing us great hospitality. Two pretty young waitresses provided attentive service. Good liquor was poured constantly, delicious food was piled on our plates; humorous talk made Bruce laugh heartily.

Bruce was very touched by the friendly approach and he was happy to discuss the joint venture. They asked him to invest $US40,000 which was a smaller amount of money compared with the other proposals; and Bruce was happy and willing to do so.

On the third day, Bruce and I were taken to another posh restaurant for a big banquet and enjoyed the warm hospitality again. Bruce's heart was further moved. During the lunch with twenty-four dishes served in the bright, beautiful and immaculate banquet hall, he said to Mr Tan, 'I am old and I cannot stay in China to look after the joint venture. The business will depend on you people. What if the project fails? I need security for my money before I consider investing.' Mr Tan immediately offered Bruce a deal. He said that they would repay Bruce the $US40,000 no matter what happened to the joint venture in five years' time. 'We can always take money out of our other projects and repay your money in full,' he said, 'and we will write a guarantee letter for you, Mr Bruce. It is no problem, no problem at all.'

After more banquets over the following three days, the negotiating group took Bruce and me to their company in Jaonan and showed us around their various workshops and premises. In their big, bright office, Mr Kun and Bruce signed the contract: I was to be Bruce's representative when he was not in China. They decided that Mr Tan would be the general manager and I would be the vice general manager of the joint venture. As soon as the contract was signed, Bruce asked for the bank account number of the Star & Fire Company. I was astonished and tried to stop him: 'Don't deposit money in their account just yet, Bruce.'

'They are very friendly, don't try to cause trouble,' Bruce said to me in an authoritative manner and I became silent. How much I regretted not standing my ground.

A few days later Mr Tan and a couple of his young assistants came to the city apartment that Enya left me and informed Bruce that they had received an electronic bank draft for $US40,000. Bruce mentioned the guarantee letter and Mr Tan tore off a piece of paper from a notebook on my desk and wrote, 'We, the Star & Fire Company, promise to our joint-venture partner Mr Bruce Renton that if the project fails to make a profit in five years' time, we will arrange to return to him the $US40,000 in full.' After he handed the letter to Bruce, I asked, 'Mr Tan, could I have a copy of the letter too?' Mr Tan frowned but he tore off another piece of paper from my notebook and wrote another letter for me, its content the same as the one he gave Bruce. As Bruce casually put the guarantee letter in his travel bag that was lying on the floor, Mr Tan watched attentively. I felt a chill down my spine but I could not figure out why.

A few days later, Bruce took a trip to travel in Inner Mongolia. A few weeks later, he came back to Dragon Pool and stayed with us for another week, then flew back to New Zealand.

After Bruce was gone, I felt the heavy responsibility of being the vice general manager in the joint venture. At this time, I had been appointed lecturer at the English Department. My new job in the university was challenging as it involved lots of reading, and it was time-consuming to prepare the lessons, but I enjoyed it a lot. However the big hat of 'vice general manager of the joint venture' was a constant burden and the role was actually too big for me.

Fortunately, university staff in China don't have to stay in the office. As a matter of fact, there was only one office no bigger than twenty square metres for the whole department of thirty-odd staff. We went to the office only for a short while between our classes. For the rest of the time everybody stayed at home to prepare lessons. Still, my time was tied up with the two jobs of the joint venture and the university. The two jobs took a lot of time and I often had to stay at the city apartment and could not go back to Dragon Pool to be with my family.

Field went to Ulumuqi to seek business opportunities. It was a Chinese tradition that a promising man should be away from home and 'walk in four directions'. He didn't make any money in Ulumuqi but brought back a young girl, his stepniece named Orchid. He was going to present Orchid as a maid and mistress to one of our connections, Mr Kai, a member of the Party Committee of Laoshan County, a position with solid power.

It was a new fashion to present young girls to your high-positioned connections. Field was clever enough to find the social pulse, but I was much dumber. Field often complained that I only knew how to work as hard as a donkey. When dealing with people, he ridiculed, 'you only know how to speak the truth'.

As China moved further and further towards being a money-oriented nation, I found myself unsuited to the new society. I couldn't bring myself to tell lies to make money, and I tended to believe lies easily. Everybody around me was becoming devious and secretive, leaving me feeling dull and idiotic.

Mr Kai was an eminent man with great talent. He was a profound writer, a poet, a Chinese painter and an artistic stone carver. He was understanding, prudent and full of sympathy. He refused to accept Orchid.

Orchid did not want to go back to her home village in the Gansu province where the living standard was very low. I understood her position and arranged for her to enrol at Sunjia School as a secondary student, and I paid for her living and schooling. She was so appreciative that she helped me to look after my mother and do the housework. She was good company for Nini, too.

At one stage, Mr Tan and his colleagues often came to my city apartment and chatted away the time. The city apartment was a big single-room flat, its toilet and the kitchen separated by a corridor. When I made tea in the kitchen my guests could help themselves to anything they fancied in the room.

Suddenly, Mr Tan and his fellows stopped visiting. When I rang them, I could not reach Mr Tan or anyone who could give me useful information about the joint venture, which made me feel uneasy. I went to the post office to send a fax to Bruce, but he wasn't worried.

Three months had passed since Bruce had signed the contract but nothing had happened in terms of production. I rang Mr Tan many times and there was just no answer. I sent faxes to Bruce again and again, and eventually he became irritated. He asked me to go and talk to the Star & Fire Company to find out what was going on.

I regarded Bruce as my benefactor and I would not let his money be lost. I would do anything and everything to protect his money.

I had to travel through the city to the seaport, waiting in the cold hall for the ferry, eating lunch on board. After the ferry ride, I waited at the bus-stop before I could get the bus to Star & Fire. After several trips, I eventually found Mr Tan, who told me that they had rented premises for the joint venture. He showed me the lease contract and I thought the price was astonishingly high. They told me they would pay the rent with Bruce's money, which was a change from what they had said in the contract — that they would offer the factory building as their investment in the joint venture. I was now alert to the possibility that Bruce's money was in real danger. In despair, I went to the post office again and sent another fax to Bruce. In reply he asked me to get the $40,000 back from Star & Fire. An almost impossible job fell on my shoulders.

With great sorrow, I gave up my job in the university so that I could spend all of my time and energy on finding out what was going on with Bruce's investment. To make a living for my family, I taught a few classes at a night school. My life became hectic and problematic. I had sleepless nights trying to think about how to deal with Star & Fire, or rather, how to protect Bruce's money. My health deteriorated tremendously. Day and night I suffered not only severe insomnia but also anxiety, which triggered bad headaches that felt as though thousands of needles were probing my scalp. Many questions were spinning in my mind. Where was the money now? What were the channels to get the money back? It seemed that Star & Fire was quite happy to hold Bruce's money and do nothing. They had already attracted foreign funds and didn't bother to do anything else.

My first thought was the guarantee letters. They might help me get the money back, and also they could become evidence if I had to sue Star & Fire. To my dismay, my copy of the guarantee letter, which was previously in one of the drawers of my desk in the apartment, was gone. I thought hard and realised what had happened to it. Now I understood why Mr Tan and his colleagues came to my apartment frequently at one stage, but then stopped abruptly. I sent a fax to Bruce asking him to send his copy of the guarantee letter over to me. In his return fax, Bruce told me that his copy had got lost too. Actually he had never seen the letter after he put it into his travelling bag so carelessly. The strange coincidence of the two missing guarantee letters made me panic even more.

'How could you ever think about asking for money back from a Chinese company for a foreigner? It is against the tide!' everybody said to me. 'The government orders us to attract foreign funds and everybody is trying their best to grab foreign funds. Once they get the funds, they hold on to them tightly. You will never get the money back.'

Some foreign partners of the failed joint ventures had sued their Chinese partners and won their cases in the Chinese courts but there was no way they could get their money back. The money they invested was taken by the company and nobody could tell exactly where it had gone. Warren Freer had a joint venture to farm prawns in Auckland but within two years, the prawns were dead, his money was gone and the Chinese government gave an apology: 'Sorry, we sent the wrong people to New Zealand.' The money lost on the Chinese side belonged to China but to nobody specific.

I talked to everyone that I could think of to get ideas. Somebody suggested that I get help from the black market. I decided to try it. One day, I snaked my way deep into a narrow lane in the old part of Qingdao. The broken pitch road was dirty and narrow. Shabby houses crowded together on both sides of the lane. Women were busy cooking on a small coal-burning stove in the footpath. They squatted on the kerb washing rice and poured the dirty water onto the street. Men squatted at the side of the road, brushing their teeth. Walking in the slush, I couldn't help but feel very depressed. I wanted to leave but I couldn't. What about Bruce's $40,000? Could I give up trying and just tell him the money was lost? No, never!

Finally I saw the number at the top of an old, blood-coloured shabby door. A thin dark man answered my knock. The room was small, smelly and unkempt. A baby crawled naked on the dirty earth floor. His mother, sitting on a low wooden stool, was washing clothes in a tub, immersing her hands in sludge. I couldn't believe this was the home of a member of the black market, the Nine-Headed Birds. Probably he was ruthlessly exploited by his head. These people had a reputation for violence and cruelty. I remembered the ancient legend that said that nine-headed birds were vicious and dropped blood wherever they flew. Anybody who was touched by blood from a nine-headed bird would die immediately. Sitting on a greasy chair, facing one of the members of the Nine-Headed Birds, I felt my body tense and my blood congeal. Luckily his family was here, which made me relax a bit. I would not want to be alone with this man for any price. He spoke gruffly to his wife: 'Go out and take the baby with you.' She wiped her hand on her hip, picked up the baby and was gone. My breath stopped after the door closed. What was the man going to do? Was he going to rape before talking or talk before raping? How could I engage with such people?

He lit a cigarette. The smell from the cheap tobacco made me cough. How stupid I was to believe such a man could help me. He said, 'Do you want us to help you collect debts? We could do the job for you but you have to agree to share the money with us half and half.' I was demure, as if I was thinking. The man smoked and waited. I could hear a clock ticking. Suddenly I jumped up and ran out of the house into crowd.

I couldn't offer them what they wanted, $US20,000.

Another day, wandering amongst the tortuous streets of Qingdao, I tried to find the roads and the often-unnumbered houses of anyone I knew who might be able to help me get an introduction to a lawyer. In China, to succeed in anything, you had to use connections. To deal with strangers just didn't work, no matter how promising your case was. After days of physical drudgery and spiritual exhaustion, eventually I found a friend who knew a competent lawyer but would not easily introduce him to me. This was the common convention. A connection is an asset and you do not give it away for free. So, my friend gave me a long, tedious lecture to let me know, without frightening me off and him losing face, that I could meet the lawyer only through him.

I arranged big banquets in a posh restaurant for the friend and the lawyer. With cautious words and a deliberate smile, I put forward my problems. Every Chinese knew the most difficult and heart-wrenching task was trying to plead with a powerful person to do things for you. You had to humble yourself to begging and pleading. Holding my glass of Maotai spirit, the most expensive Chinese liquor, I extended the honour to my friend who had introduced us, a vitally important role in every corner of society. I mumbled all sorts of flattering words and tried hard to please the lawyer. Red-faced from the drinking, full-bellied from the rich food, the lawyer said arrogantly, 'Yes, I could do the job for you, but you must hire a new luxury taxi for me. I would not be accepted arriving at the court in an old taxi and wouldn't even think of riding in a bus. Plus, you need to offer me two meals in decent restaurants every day. As for breakfast, I can save it for you. Also, you must know, there is no guarantee that you will win even though you have me to deal with the case. Only one with strong connections could guarantee a win.' The lawyer then told me the stories from the law court. A man who had a death sentence was bailed out on grounds of sickness because the judge was 'properly bribed', since the father of the convict was a millionaire. Another criminal was set free because he was the judge's nephew. A serial rapist got parole after a month in jail because he bribed the head of the prison 'properly'.

I did not see the lawyer again since I could not afford the expense.

'Maybe you should try to commit suicide to force the Star & Fire Company to return the money,' Field said. I didn't know whether he was serious or just joking. However, as casual as his words sounded, it inspired me. Yes, maybe the only thing I could do was to take action that was free from ordinary thinking. Yes, I would do something radical and different, something that would surprise everyone.

I decided to go on a hunger strike.

One very cold morning, I woke up in the apartment and found myself in a desperate situation. The job at hand, to retrieve the money, was far from finished. There was no sign that Star & Fire would give me the money back. Would a hunger strike work? I was not confident, although I wanted to do it anyway. To relieve my conscience, I had to take the risk.

I prepared a travel bag, placed a hot water bottle and a few sleeping pills in it and tumbled out at seven. Coming out of Liaochen Road, I turned to the left and arrived at Jiaozhou Road, the busy commercial street of Qingdao. In front of the closed doors of Hua Long department store, musicians in red and white uniform were playing silver drums and gold trumpets. This was a new trick to attract customers. Huge crowds were attracted by the strong and vigorous military music. Some were waiting for shopping but most were just passers-by. I was in no mood to listen to the military music. Turning to a narrow lane off the street, I dived into the bustling stream of human beings. What were these people doing?

Where were they going? Would I see these faces again one week later or would I already be dead from hunger? Seeing a food stall on the roadside, I seated myself on the low bench and filled myself with some spicy tofu soup. I spied a book stall. Anything to do with books never failed to catch my attention. On a big piece of canvas, all sorts of books were randomly scattered on the ground. Squatting down, I picked up one book after another. Suddenly I saw an interesting title, thin, black-bound and translated from Japanese, *Tactics of Persuasion*. Without hesitation, I bought it.

The cold wind buffeted me as I stood on the deck of the ferry crossing the Bohai Sea. I had made up my mind that this trip was the final one. I should not be afraid of the hunger strike. All I needed to do was lie on the floor with no food, no drink. I was not afraid of the result, either. With a body that had come through all sorts of adversity, I could withstand one more peril. A week's starvation wouldn't kill me. Very possibly I would develop a stomach problem, but I was not afraid of that since I had experienced stomach ache for several years in the past and eventually I recovered. I would be all right this time, too.

When I arrived at the Star & Fire Company in the evening I received a cold greeting from Mr Tan. After a poor dinner provided by his secretary, he led me to their guest quarters. It was a huge four-storey building with many rooms but I was the only guest in it.

It seemed the company was once prosperous, but was not so now. Like all the small businesses run by villagers in the countryside, it did not get any support from the government; rather, it had to pay huge taxes to help the state-owned businesses. The government officials who looked after the state-owned businesses did not own them but had the full power to have a say in all matters. As a result, the businesses failed and the bosses became rich. When a state-owned business went bankrupt, the boss would be shifted to another business and he would grab more money for himself from the new position. The only loser was the state, that is, the public. This weird system was the reason that companies like Star & Fire deteriorated more and more.

My heart became heavier and heavier as I pondered Star & Fire's situation. They would surely hold on tightly to the $40,000 since they were in such a poor condition. Was I in a lose–lose situation — sacrifice my health and still lose the money? Was there any better way to solve the problem? This must have been the thousandth time I contemplated the problem of Bruce's money. Before I went to bed, I drafted a letter to Field and my mother, informing them that I was on a hunger strike at Star & Fire. I assured them not to worry about me and that I would be back one week later. I then started reading *Tactics of Persuasion*. As always when I was reading, I was inspired after I had finished the book and I felt more confident. At eleven I was ready for sleep.

Snarling wind was blowing through a gap in the windows and I felt frozen with cold. I filled the hot water bottle and unfolded the quilt. It was square-shaped and too short to cover me. I used three of them, one after another, like Spanish skirts. But sleep refused to come. I took two sleeping pills and lectured myself, 'Do the generals in war sleep when they face a battle the next day?' 'They would,' I told myself. 'You should take them as an example, then.' The next thing I knew, it was five-thirty in the morning and my mind felt well refreshed. I got up, skipped breakfast and strolled about in the little town.

At seven I entered the Star & Fire office. The gold-plated board on the door, shining in the morning sun, read: 'Star & Fire Company — provincial model company.'

I climbed up the stairs and saw the meeting room, bright and clean, many upholstered chairs around a long table, dark red velvet curtains draping down. I would use this room for my hunger strike, I told myself. I walked on and met Mr Tan at the door of his office. 'Aha, Ms Liu, you are early. Have you had your breakfast?'

'No, I haven't.' I answered in a solemn tone. He frowned and pretended he hadn't heard my words. He must have though I was asking for breakfast from them. I said, 'Where is the general manager, Mr Kun? I must see him today.' Time and time again I had been in this building but was never allowed to meet Mr Kun.

'Wait here, I will go to his office to see if he is here,' said Mr Tan as usual and he left me, but I already knew the answer. A few minutes later he came back and said, 'Mr Kun has gone to Qingdao for a meeting and will not come back till late afternoon.' This was the standard answer I got every time. I straightened my back, looked into his eyes and exclaimed, 'Look, Mr Tan, I have been here many times for Bruce's money. Now I have given up hope of getting the money back, but I want to protest your wrongdoing. I have decided to go on a hunger strike in your meeting room.' With these words, I walked quickly towards the door of his office. Mr Tan jumped to his feet, gripped one of my arms and said intently, 'Come back, come back! Don't be silly. Here, here, please eat something.' With one hand grabbing me, he pulled out snacks from a cabinet behind his desk. Apples, sweets, dried-beef slices and instant noodles were piled on the desk. 'Help yourself, please. No wonder you said you didn't eat breakfast. "Health is the capital for revolutionary work." You must eat.'

'No, I will not eat or drink if Mr Kun refuses to see me today.'

'Okay, okay! I will go and look for him.'

'I'll wait here for no more than ten minutes and then I will start my hunger strike.'

Five minutes later, Mr Tan came back followed by a red-faced Mr Kun. Mr Kun started to talk.

China has got a name as a 'country of language'. A skilled talker is always highly admired. Textbooks adopt articles from the Han Dynasty, 206 BC, to teach school children how to learn fancy talking from a superior arguer, Yan-ying, an ambassador who won his warlord status through clever talk. So, as a successful businessman, it was inevitable that Mr Kun was a good talker.

Sitting opposite me, face to face, breathing deeply, Mr Kun prepared for a fluent, roundabout and hard-to-interrupt lecture to win over my mind. What should I do? If I listened to his non-stop lecture, I would never get what I wanted. I used the first tactic learned from the black-covered book. Looking out of the window, scratching my head, shaking my legs, playing with my hands, looking up the ceiling, I did anything but look at Mr Kun. *Tactics of Persuasion* told me that I mustn't listen to him attentively. If I did, I would make myself like a student listening to a teacher, and a student has little chance to persuade his teacher. Within ten minutes, Mr Kun became frustrated by my distraction and his lecture became less and less fluent. Before long he lost the thread of his argument. Seeing that the strategy worked, I became confident. I said to him, 'You see, Mr Kun, I know your company will not give the money back to Bruce but that is wrong. The money is his and now he wants it back. You have no reason to refuse to give back to somebody his own money.'

'We have agreed to establish the joint venture and since the money belongs to the joint venture, Bruce has no right to ask for the money back.'

'But you haven't even put anything into the joint venture. You don't even have a workshop.'

'Yes, we do. Don't we, Tan?' Mr Kun looked at his deputy. Mr Tan looked nervous. 'Oh yes, we do,' said Tan.

'I have been to the factory you were supposed to lease, and I have found that another company is using it.'

This must have been a big blow for Mr Tan since he wouldn't imagine that I, an intellectual-looking woman, would be that adventurous and go to such a hard-to-reach place, the so-called leased premises, to investigate. Mr Kun stared at Tan unpleasantly. Obviously, Tan had not told all the facts to Mr Kun, his boss. It was apparent that he was in no hurry to do any work since the foreign funds were in their hands. I realised again that often honesty didn't necessary win honesty in return.

I arranged my thoughts and I used my second strategy, putting myself in their shoes and thinking for them. 'Well, Mr Kun, yours is a big company and I noticed at the gate of your company, on the gold-plated board, that you are a provincial model company. I don't think you want to ruin its name.' I opened my business card album and showed him the cards that I had carefully arranged in the order of hierarchy: director of the Foreign Economic and Trade Council of Qingdao; director of the Political Consultant Committee; journalists of the *Qingdao Daily*; journalists of TV Qingdao . . . 'I will go to the post office to send faxes and make telephone calls and let these people know that I am having a hunger strike in your meeting room. Just think about it, a big, well-named, good-willed company like yours, for $US40,000, you let a woman lie in your office dying. Crowds of journalists from newspapers, radio and television will come for the story. Is it worthwhile?' Mr Kun looked stressed. I was now ready to use the third strategy I had learned from the book: ask a question to get what you want. After a deep breath, making my question sound as casual as I could, I asked, 'Mr Kun, will you transfer the money to my account or Bruce's?'

'It is up to you,' Mr Kun said, and immediately he realised his mistake and looked very flustered, but it was too late. I didn't give him any chance to change direction. I said, 'Please Mr Kun, make a call to the accountant and transfer the money back to Bruce's account.' Seeing his boss was picking up the telephone receiver, Tan was so tense that he jumped up and looked as if he would grab it back from Mr Kun's hand, but he dared not. Sitting back in his seat, he looked like a naughty dog, thoroughly submissive.

Once seated on the bus back home, I reached into my pocket, got out the letter to my family about my hunger strike and tore it up into many small pieces and threw them into the Bohai Sea. I watched tens of white butterflies dance lively in the cool evening breeze.

It took another month's perseverance for me to transfer the money out of the Star & Fire Company's account into Bruce's account at the Bank of China, since foreign exchange was still tightly controlled by regulations and it was very difficult to do any transfers. During that whole month, I went to the bank, to all sorts of offices, to many of my connections. I talked, pleaded and argued, even threatened. At the last stage, I used the golden doctrine, 'Officials fear foreigners.' I shouted at the director of Foreign Currency Administration in Qingdao, 'Do you know there are nine joint ventures between New Zealand and China and eight of them have failed? The last one is half-dying. Now, if you want to keep the funds from Bruce, can you shoulder the responsibility of ruining the international reputation of China?'

CHAPTER TWENTY-ONE

Bruce took a flight to Qingdao as soon as he heard the news. He was very happy when I handed him the cheque for the full amount of $US40,000. Although he had no idea how difficult it had been to get the money back, he kindly left some money for me since I had lost my job at the university for the sake of collecting his debt. Field and I decided to buy three *mu* (about two thousand square metres) in Lying Dragon Village and set up a flower business. Bruce was happy about this and he told me he was going to rewrite his will and leave the business to me after he died.

The business turned out to be very difficult, not only because of the hard physical labour but also the invisible obstacles of corruption. Everybody who wanted to achieve anything in China had to face the reality — corruption was the character of the system and nobody could avoid it. You needed *guan xi*, connections, with all the people you were doing business with.

First of all, I visited the authority of Beijai District Government to ask for permission to buy the land, even though it had originally belonged to the residents of Lying Dragon Village.

After the Communists grabbed power in 1949, they had distributed the land that they had confiscated from the land owners to all the countryside residents evenly. Mao Zedong knew that he had won his revolution victory with the help and support of the peasants, and he had made pretty promises to them before he won the civil war. The peasants did get some land for a couple of years, but that was about all that Mao kept of his promise. He knew that the poor and low-educated country residents were

266

easily controlled and intimidated. Within a couple of years Mao devised a way to take the land away from the peasants. In 1952, he initiated land reform to establish 'the junior co-operation groups'. The villagers were asked to join into a co-operative group and bring their land, beasts and productive tools into the group. Thus the assets were owned by the group, not by individuals. This was the first step; and then in 1955 all the groups in a village joined together into one big group, 'the senior co-operation group', and the individual lost even more say in such a big organisation. Finally, in 1958, Mao gave orders to establish 'communes' in the rural areas. All the members of senior co-operation groups joined together and became a commune. Administration of the commune was conducted by officials sent by the high layer of government, who were not members of the local villages. The officials had the power to decide how to use the land, what to grow, what percentage of the harvest should go to the government, how much personal tax the villagers had to pay, and so on. Later their power expanded, so that they could determine when you should get married, which year you could give birth to your child, where you could build your house. Thus Mao's philosophy of land reform led to the countryside residents losing their land and freedom officially and totally. After 1958, there was not one piece of land in China that was privately owned. The state, Mao's kingdom, owned all the land. For the first time in history, peasants who had relied for their living on the land had no say about the land but had to pay land tax, birth tax, personal tax and all sorts of other taxes to the central government as well as to the local government. The countryside, eighty-five percent of the country, was vast, remote and poor, and hardly any foreigners would go and visit it. Mao Zedong feared not his citizens but foreigners. So long as foreign visitors were happy with what they saw, he was content. Few foreigners had ever thought about travelling to the real, poor, remote countryside, partly because it was so uninhabitable that few overseas visitors had any desire to go; but mainly because the government stopped potential visitors lest these backward places made China lose face.

I was destined to face perils with the land purchase. I had to deal with a Mr Yin, a man with solid power, who was in charge of land sales in the Beijai area. I could not do it in his office, in the eyes of the public, but at his home, which was how the game worked. I spent much time and energy shopping to choose appropriate presents for him. It was a complicated and sophisticated task. If the present was too cheap, it wouldn't work; if the present was too expensive, I could not afford it; if the present was too big, it would be seen by neighbors which would be dangerous. Officials were very discreet about accepting presents in case they were accused of corruption. Corruption was severely condemned by the Communist Party and there was a Rules and Principles Investigation Committee to prosecute the corrupt officials. They tried very hard to avoid being accused of corruption, although everybody was either bribing or being bribed.

On a cold, moonless night, carrying the present that I carefully chosen, I walked along a dark street. When I crossed the street near Mr Yin's home, a motorcycle suddenly appeared at the corner of the street and I was knocked down. I had to stay in bed for many days to recover. My chest was hit by the handle of the motorcycle and two of my ribs were broken. That was only the first price I had to pay as I tried to become an owner of a little piece of land in China.

Weeks later, on another dark night, I went to see Mr Yin again. Finding the right apartment amongst the forest of modern buildings in the crowed town was not fun and often the person you wanted to see was not home. You had to try your luck by going again and again. There was no way you could make an appointment by telephone. You wouldn't get any answer. Even if you did, it was always the official's wife or child who answered, and they never knew when the master would come home. Every one who wanted to keep their position as a government official had to spend most of their spare time building up connections with their superiors. Otherwise the position would be taken by somebody who did a better job at making connections. However, Mr Yin was at home and I was so pleased by my good luck that I failed to think properly about what this meant. Why was he at home when he should be connecting with his superior? Had he lost favour with his boss? Was he still the right person for me to rely on? I tried to drive these gloomy thoughts from my mind and concentrate on my task.

I smiled at Mr Yin and took out the presents — a bag of fruit as a cover and two hundred American dollars. American currency was always welcome with anybody in China. He smiled when he saw the green notes but he said no several times. I argued for the same number of times until he accepted them. It was part of the game that he would not promise anything the first time. I needed to make more effort to build a solid connection with him and only then he would say yes to my request. Over the next two months I visited him again and again, and each time I presented proper gifts and each time he promised more to me, which decreased my doubt about his power. Apart from presenting him with gifts, I also took him to expensive restaurants for exquisite dinners. I invited several friends who helped me to make Mr Yin happy. Some of them took on the job of admiring Mr Yin to boost his ego, while others who could drink a lot took the job of drinking with Mr Yin. It was vital to make him happy. The whole business could be blown apart if something upset him, even if I had paid several thousand *yuan* for the meal. At last, after the marathon process, Mr Yin said yes to me. I was very happy. You didn't always get a yes, despite all the money, energy, intelligence and time you had invested. However, Mr Yin told me that it would take several months to get permission to finalise the land purchase since the business would involve three layers of government — the Licun township government, the Qingdao city government and the Shandong provincial government. 'I will deliver the application as soon as possible and you will have to wait,' he said. I was surprised about the long process to buy a small piece of land. 'Couldn't you issue the papers for me?' I asked hopefully.

'I used to be able to, but recently a new policy was issued and the provincial government has to approve any land purchase.'

'How long will it take?'

'It is difficult to say. It cannot be quick since it is to do with provincial government. Maybe it will take three to six months.'

I was vexed.

'You could use the land while you are waiting for the paper,' Mr Yin suggested. It sounded like a good idea. I could lease the land to catch the growing season while waiting for the purchase to go through.

I regarded Mr Yin as a friend now, since I had invested heavily to build up my connection with him and I had to trust him and do what he told me. I signed a lease contract with the head of Lying Dragon Village and rented three *mu* so that Field and I could start the flower business.

By now Field and I hardly ever stayed together. If I stayed at Dragon

Pool, he would stay at the city apartment. And if I was at the city apartment, he might stay at a rented place in Licun. He insisted it was useful to have a place in Licun for his business. I didn't realise it was for his mistress. During the past couple of years he had been involved in all sorts of weird business but had never brought any money home. As for everyday life, he was a procrastinator. I was driven mad by his indolence. Our relationship had been going downhill and we were no longer compatible, not only because of the age difference but also for more fundamental reasons. He was talkative and practical, and didn't share my zeal for thinking and learning. I was a bumpkin and a square peg in Chinese society. He wanted me to take him to New Zealand and pestered me all the time. I urged him to learn English and was frustrated by his procrastinating. He enjoyed playing cards until midnight and our neighbors laughed at me when I yelled at him, asking him to come home. I was considering getting a divorce but he didn't accept it. Often after a quarrel he would pack his luggage, carry it to the door of the courtyard and say, 'I am leaving!' But he would stay at the door, waiting for me run after him and beg him to come back. And if I didn't, he would wait until somebody came. Our place never lacked for visitors, and when the visitor came he would repeat, 'I'm leaving! We will divorce.' The visitor would grab his luggage from his hand. It was the social convention that one should help couples reconcile. Although Field refused a divorce, he was growing more and more distant and secretive.

Things weren't going well with the land. The villagers who previously used it refused to vacate the land even though we had paid the rent as well as the cost of the plants. I was not allowed to build a house on the land. I asked the head of the village and his five assistants to a banquet. They accepted my invitation willingly but refused to co-operate with me. They looked sullen during the meal even though I tried hard to please them. I then visited the head's home several times, telling him about my difficulties and asking him for help, and each time I left him some presents as well as American dollars. But the land was still partially occupied by the peasants and Field and I still could not plan our scheme on the land. When I was feeling close to a nervous breakdown, Enya returned from New Zealand for a holiday and immediately dedicated herself to helping me. She had a special talent for public relations and within a few weeks she had successfully won support from Mr Chu, the party secretary of the Beijai government. Of course, the four hundred dollars played a critical role too.

Mr Chu investigated the land dispute and he gave orders to take the position away from the head of Lying Dragon Village. A new head was appointed and my land was cleared within a few days.

Helped by villagers, I built a house on the land of about thirty square metres, divided by a brick wall into two rooms. The big one was used as a storeroom to hold tools, seeds, flower roots and other productive necessities for a flower business. As for the smaller room, we offered it to East, the poorest man in Sunjia Village.

East had become a tramp now. He begged for food from door to door, and collected empty beer bottles to sell. His land had become wild. The land, to use not to own, was distributed to him in 1982 under Deng's policy, but he was too lazy to work on it. He used to be a member of the commune in Mao's time and got the same food as anyone else, but didn't bother to bend his back and pick up a tool. Now that everybody took responsibility for their own lives, East was left behind. On a snowy winter day, Field and I picked up East in the street. Like a frozen fish, he was lying on the bare ground in a thin shirt and a pair of short pants. We carried him to his home and were shocked by his impoverished condition. High weeds grew in the courtyard, the walls had collapsed and a tall parasol tree was growing in the middle of the kitchen. Its straight trunk grew out of the broken roof and the blue sky was visible from inside. A pumpkin plant was crawling all around. In his bedroom, two narrow boards stood on mud bricks. I saw something like a pile of rotten matting, which was his only bedding, an old quilt he had inherited from his late mother's dowry. He lived at the edge of death. When the house in the garden was built, East moved in and his life was saved.

To buy rose plants, I took the bus to Han Village, about forty miles away, which was well-known for growing roses. I was introduced there to a man called Steel. My acquaintance said, 'Steel's rose plants are especially good and he is a nice person. You'll never have any problem with him.'

Steel and his wife were only too happy to see me. They offered me the best green tea, and smiled at me while offering excessive compliments. I told them we wanted to run a cut-flower business and wanted to buy rose plants for that purpose. 'There is no problem. We will supply you with good roses for cut flowers,' they said. And then they agreed with my price without even bargaining, which made me suspicious. Was there a catch? Were his plants weak or diseased? I went with him to the garden and checked the plants, but I could not find anything wrong with them.

The next day, Steel arrived at Dragon Pool with two thousand rose plants on a truck. To catch the early spring season, Field and I planted them immediately. With the help of a couple of friends, we stooped and unstooped to the earth and planted all two thousand plants in three days. I suffered severe back pain for months afterwards.

A couple of months later, the roses were in bloom and they were very beautiful. I excitedly picked dozens of them and took the bus to town. I visited all the florists in Licun and Qingdao but it was a waste of time. Nobody accepted my roses. They told me my roses were 'wrong': 'They are not for cut flowers but for growing in gardens. Their stems are too short and the flowers will wither in a short time.'

Holding my roses, withered already, I went back to Dragon Pool and told Field the bad news. Both of us felt thoroughly beaten. What could we do with them if we could not sell them? How could I make a living if I could not sell the flowers? Sleepless nights were followed by hard-working days since we couldn't neglect the growing plants even though they were 'wrong'.

After a series of failed experiments, I decided to copy what I had seen in New Zealand in 1986, which nobody had ever done in China: to sell my flowers straight to customers in restaurants, night clubs and hotels. Field was not happy about it. 'People will look down upon you for doing such an abject thing,' he argued. And my neighbors warned me, 'Nobody will buy a bunch of roses if they can buy a roasted chicken with the same amount of money.' But I was adamant, and the novel way of selling flowers turned out to be successful since I had a monopoly on the evening flower market in Qingdao, a city of seven million. The sales were so strong that the flowers from our garden were not enough and we had to buy flowers from market stalls or from florists. Many more florists opened in Qingdao as a consequence, and the flower growing business was booming.

Once a week I gave a business lecture in a classroom that I rented from the university. My audience was made up of the students who answered my advertisement for flower sellers. Many university students in China were from rural areas and their parents were too poor to pay the education fees, which had become higher and higher. My business lecture was popular amongst those who wanted to earn a few notes in their spare time. I started my lecture by talking about famous people's lives, normally those who were from a poor background and who became successful by working hard. These true stories became a catalyst to increase the young people's confidence. When my lecture finished there was always a dozen excited boys and girls willing to go to the streets to sell flowers. Along the beach, in the busy streets, with willow baskets full of fresh roses, my sales agents worked for me.

Some evenings I took a basket along to the street too. Wearing a black silk dress with a red rose pattern, I walked fast, the long panel of my dress floating in the cool breeze. My face gleamed with beads of sweat and my hair danced. Passers-by admired my flowers and I was intoxicated by the subtle perfume of roses and the rich fragrance of lilies, tuberoses and gardenias. I felt confident and bold. The buildings were flooded with light, sweethearts were walking hand in hand, happy sounds came from restaurants. Many restaurants didn't like flower selling in their premises and I was treated rudely. I had to be very brave to overcome their rejections. However, I did meet some beautiful people. Once on a Saturday evening I stepped into the restaurant attached to the Guohuo Department Store of Qingdao. I came up to one of the tables where four men were sitting. At the end of the table was a young man in his early thirties. His thin face looked amiable and his dark eyes were the sort that you would trust immediately. He asked me, 'How much for a rose?'

'Ten *yuan* each.'

'How many roses do you have in your basket?'

'Thirty altogether,' I answered.

He reached into his pocket and took out three hundred *yuan*. He handed them to me and he scooped the flowers up and placed them on the table. He turned to me and said, 'Go home and have a good time with your family.'

In the beginning of 1995 Mr Yin lost his position. My land purchase failed. It was only later that I learned that my way of doing land business was wrong by Chinese standards.

The real-estate business started booming in 1993. Ten years later ninety percent of the wealthiest men in China were real-estate dealers. They had a typical strategy to make big money quickly. First of all, they would buy a piece of land from the rural government, which was always short of money and the price was normally ridiculously cheap. They then used their official connections, who had been amply bribed, to value the land up to a hundred times higher that it's worth, or even more. Using this valuation they would get the relevant amount of loan from the bank and use that to fund their buildings. And by selling the buildings they became multi-millionaires.

After living in poverty for decades, the Chinese were fanatically devoted to moneymaking. New Man, Field's brother-in-law, had his own business established even though he had absolutely no capital. He had a theory: 'If I was the president of the state, I would only choose men who were liars. The ones who don't know how to lie are useless.' Using this theory, he had successfully collected his first bucket of gold. He bribed an official who was in charge of food health and got a certificate saying that the ten thousand tins of fruit he had bought were not past their use-by date. He bought these tins for two *yuan* and sold them for twenty *yuan*. He paid the deposit for a car, a new Honda, and was in and out of big companies to attract attention. He might eat a bowl of instant noodles for his own meal but he would entertain his business partners in luxury restaurants. He bought one tonne of Xinjiang cotton from a textile factory and paid them back immediately. Xinjiang cotton was a special product, famous for its strength, and it had a good market value at the time. The next time he bought two tonnes of Xinjiang cotton and again paid for it in cash at once. The third time he did the same and won his line of credit. The fourth time he used the credit from the textile factory and bought a hundred tonnes of cotton. He sold the cotton, but didn't pay. Taking the money with him, he arrived in Qingdao with a group of men as his followers and a young girl as his mistress. He threw his money around like water, staying in five-star hotels, having lobsters for dinner, drinking French brandy and smoking American cigarettes. Field envied him very much and joined New Man's company. As soon as they arrived in Xinjiang, New Man was arrested.

Field didn't come back until a few months later.

Two days before the Chinese New Year in 1994, Field started a row with me and dashed out of the house, disappearing into the snow and refusing to tell me where he was going. He had been acting strangely like this for a while, doing secret business dealings, busy but never making any money. Three days later the door opened and in came Field. His new suit was neat, his dark hair was shining and he looked content in a mysterious way. I was happy to see him and talked to him excitedly. He said, 'Don't worry about me. Please keep on watching television.' He sat beside me on the couch, back straight, eyes distracted, for about ten minutes and then he stood up and said, 'I must be off now.'

I sensed he was doing something dishonest but nowadays it was the trend for a Chinese man to have a mistress. Wives, especially middle-aged wives, were rapidly becoming a deserted class. This was a lonely era, producing abandoned women. There was a common saying at this time, 'A man in his forties is a flower, a woman in her forties is a burden,' and men were looking for mistresses without feeling guilt.

On the sixth day after Field left, I awoke with a grim premonition. I liked to think I was not a narrow-minded person but I wanted to know the truth. Field owed me an explanation and I wanted it in black and white. 'I have to find out what he is doing,' I told myself and set off to investigate.

I went to his rented place in Licun, but the landlady told me he hadn't stayed there for days. I went to his business partner and found out the man had just married and he hadn't heard from Field for weeks. I went to the post office to make two long-distance calls, one to Shanghai, another one to Sichuan. Both the men, who used to be Field's business connections, hadn't had any news from him for a long time. I went to our city apartment and found it had not been touched since I stayed there the previous week. I went to my friend Big River for help. I told him that Field had disappeared. After we found that Field had left his motorcycle in his rented place in Licun, we knew he was not far away. With the help of a truck driver, Big River managed to remove the locked motorcycle, transferred it to his house and hid it at the back in the courtyard.

Motorcycles were just becoming trendy at the time and Field had sold our three-wheeler to buy it; he looked really smart riding on it, shooting ahead as fast as an arrow.

Giving a speech at Enya and Kerry's wedding, 2001; the speech moved my audience to tears even as they laughed

In the evening I went back to our city apartment and waited for Field's call. I was vexed and anxious and I roamed the room all the time. A few hours later the telephone rang. I picked it up when the first ring had hardly finished. It was Field calling from Dragon Pool. 'What did you do to my motorcycle?' he said agitatedly. My voice was very calm, so calm that it surprised me: 'I know where it is but you have to wait.'

The next morning I met Field at Big River's place. 'Please tell me, Field, where have you been these last few days?' I asked. Field refused to answer.

'You have to answer my questions, my dear, otherwise you'll have to stay here no matter if it is one day or seven days,' I said.

We had lunch in silence; after lunch we sat waiting. I was waiting for him to tell the truth and Field was waiting to get the motorcycle. It was getting dark and a high wind was blowing up outside. Big River's German shepherd was barking fiercely and the horrendous noise was echoing. Field became more and more subdued and his spirit collapsed. At eleven in the evening he decided to confess.

The next morning Field took me to his private love nest. Not far away from the centre of Licun on the second floor of a highrise building I saw a newly-wed's household. The table was covered with new cloth in the dining room and the bedroom was decorated with brand-new bedding.

My new extended family at our home garden 1999, from left to right: Julie, my older stepdaughter; Johnson, Julie's partner; Helen, my younger stepdaughter; Graham, Helen's partner; me; Ian; Nini; my brother, Main; Kerry and Enya

On the lowboy beside the bed there was a tube of medicine, labelled: 'Sex Aid Cream.' I took it and examined it. Field complained: 'It is a poor product. Not helpful at all.'

Field was actually very open and frank about his mistress. He showed me photos of her and he talked about her all the time. He didn't conceal the fact that he missed her very much. He even asked me for permission to let her stay with us. He didn't see what was wrong with it. He said, 'I am not the only man with a mistress. After all, China is a country with a tradition that men should have a wife and concubines.'

It was true that the emperors in history were said to have owned as many as three thousand concubines. Nowadays it was common for a successful man to have a kept woman. Having a mistress showed you had money. Young women offered themselves to rich men for money, houses or overseas trips. The sex industry, which was smothered in 1949, had revived and was booming. Field, once so pure and natural, had become infected by all this and his treachery was very hurtful.

At the same time, the streets in Qingdao were full of flower-sellers. It became so competitive that the profit for my business became negligible. We had built a greenhouse in the flower garden and we rented a shop as a florist, but the profit was nothing compared with the money made by selling flowers directly to the restaurants and hotels. To make a living, I worked in the greenhouse in the daytime and took a bus to the city to teach English at night school. By the time I finished the two-hour lectures, I was exhausted.

Suffering from severe depression, I would cry constantly and couldn't breathe properly. Day and night it felt as though there was a burning wound in my mouth. Every now and again I had to drink cold water to put out the fire in my throat. It seemed that life had thrown me into another dark pit. Could I climb out of it this time? I could. Enya saved me this time.

I was walking through Lying Dragon Village and dozens of children were scurrying around me, yelling in unison, 'Broken shoes! Broken shoes! She's a *liumong!* She has divorced three times!' They threw stones at me and laughed behind my back. I was running like crazy. A crowd of women, old and middle-aged, were mobbing me, spitting at me, their forefingers pointing at me as they screamed and yelled. I stumbled on the kerb and fainted, but I could still hear them gabbling, 'Look how sick she is. It serves her all right! It is the price she pays for marrying a young lad!' I tried to get up and escape the crowd but hundreds of women were spitting at me and shouting, 'You'd better learn your lesson and never again try to break the social conventions!' I staggered home for shelter but found the house even more terrifying. Superb was lying on the floor, her face monstrous. Wearing a dark dress, she was rolling in the dust like an enraged eel, twitching frenetically as she screamed, 'You should die. You wouldn't have suffered such an ill fate if you had listened to me and died earlier! Now you have no way to escape. Kill yourself as soon as possible!' Then I saw my brother looming over me. His brooding features and sombre expression frightened me. I whimpered, 'Please, brother. Don't hit me.' He said, 'You are a bloody single woman again. I am free to hit you. You have nobody but me to teach you lessons.'

When I woke up from the nightmare, I was panting in horror.

Warren Freer had retired from parliament and had become a business broker for companies between New Zealand and China. In early 1995 he contacted me and asked me to find a Chinese company that could buy a wool company in New Zealand.

It took me lots of trips and I talked to as many people as I could about the purchase. At last my hard work was rewarded: I found two companies interested in the purchase. A group of businessmen would go to New Zealand to carry out the investigation and negotiations. They wanted me to be their interpreter for the New Zealand trip and offered me good money and allowances.

As I was told the trip would be no more than a few weeks, I packed my luggage as simply as possible — I carried just a small bag with a few clothes and toilet things in it. I even didn't bring a pair of socks.

On April 12, 1995, I was on an international flight again, heading for New Zealand. Out of the cabin window I could see endless white clouds stretching away to infinity. I felt tranquil and refreshed.

Travel is the best way to fix a lonely heart.

I realised I was walking away from Field.

At the airport in Auckland, Enya hugged me and said, 'Dear Mum, you look sick. Please stay.'

EPILOGUE

In December 1995, I sent Enya back to Qingdao to pick up my mother and Nini. She arrived at Dragon Pool in winter and saw a heartbreaking scene: in the dirty and shabby room, my mother was sitting in the corner, shivering in the cold. The rag-like curtain flipped and flapped in the wind that came through the broken window. Enya called out, 'Granny!'

Mother gazed at her. 'Who are you? I can't see properly. Too many tears have made me half-blind. I miss my daughter so. . .'

Enya knelt down and held her in her arms. 'Granny, it's me, your granddaughter. Mum is waiting for you in New Zealand.'

Thick tears ran down my mother's face. 'Your mother? Where is she? I call her at the road every day.'

Enya burst into tears.

When Mother arrived in Auckland, she had great difficulty adjusting to the different culture. She cursed the radio for talking in English: 'Even this thing has betrayed me.' But she had a wonderful time once she got used to her new life. She enjoyed herself very much, especially after my brother arrived in New Zealand. Main, at the last stage of Mother's life, was free to be close to her and Mother had never been happier now that she was able to be with her beloved son at last. Nine months later, one evening after dinner, she said, 'I want to eat ice-cream.' Main laughed, and joked, 'You forget you've had ice-cream just now. You are getting old and forgetful.'

'I am not old at all. I can carry on for decades. A human being's life

With Ian (front right), Enya (front left) and friends at the Tennis Club of Parnell (back), 1997, soon after I met Ian

span is a hundred and twenty years, don't you know?' Her lovely wrinkled face was smiling like a chrysanthemum blossom.

The next day, while she was waiting for dinner at the table, she gave a short cry and was gone for ever, aged ninety-one.

Mother's easy end — happy at last, no suffering from painful disease — was a welcome contrast with the miserable death of my father. For decades I suffered terrible torment about my father's tortured ending. Now I have some comfort from my mother's easy death. Mother chose a nice time to go. One month before her death I met my present husband, Ian, an outstanding scientist and a professor at the University of Auckland, who offered me love and support during the time I was suffering from my Mother's death.

In 1996, I had begun a new project — to find a nice man to share my life with. Like everything I have done in my life, I approached my search for a life partner with perseverance, unconventionality and a sense of adventure. This search should not be a mere ritual but involves effort. I told all my friends in New Zealand that I was seeking a long-term relationship, but this was not enough. To widen the scope of candidates,

I used every media I knew. For two years, I committed myself to meet, talk and interview tens of men of all types. Using all possible methods I tried to determine each man's habits, intelligence, interests, hobbies, family background, educational level, financial situation and last, but not least, personality. When you meet strangers you take risks, but like everything in the world 'good things don't come easy' — if you are brave, you will win. 'You have to admit an alarming number of men are Princes of Darkness' — this statement from co-authors Joseph W. Rock and Barry L. Duncan was definitely confirmed by my own rich, personal experiences. However, to get rid of that most dreadful emotion — loneliness — it was worthwhile. I dived into this risky matter and worked hard, even though it was like finding a needle in a haystack.

My ample experiences in the past have made me a hardworking person, mentally as well as physically — a good candidate for being a wife. I am a piece of copper pea, uncrushable; a jellyfish, flexible; and a cat, soft enough most of the time but able to extend sharp claws if necessary.

It might sound absurd, but I am sincerely grateful for my past life of adversity, which has made my present and future life — the most vulnerable stages of life — happy and trouble-free.

POST SCRIPT

Qingdao, early May 2004. The chauffeur of the luxury car belonging to one of my former students picks me up from Qingdao Pier Hotel and stops in front of a splendid mauve-coloured building, surrounded by high silver granite walls and a grand gate. It is the Vienna Grand Restaurant.

A cool breeze blows in through the window of the car. The fragrance of popular May flowers, lilac and sophora, mixed with the sea smell is intoxicating. The chauffeur, smartly dressed in a Western suit and tie, gets out of the car, moves to the back door and opens it for me. 'Please, Teacher Liu,' he says as he puts his left hand on top of my head, politely helping me out. I am greeted by the lobby manager of the restaurant: 'I suppose you are Teacher Liu, the guest of Director Yang for Chengyang district? Welcome to Vienna Grand Restaurant. Follow me, please.' He is a handsome man, healthy-looking and well dressed in a royal blue wool jacket, finely tailored.

'Your room is the New Zealand Chamber,' he says to me.

On the both sides of the huge door a team of young pretty girls in scarlet, gold, orange, sapphire and cream coloured *qipao*, Chinese waist-cut robes, are standing and waiting.

The manager says, 'Room New Zealand.'

A wide, rolling staircase made of shiny red wood leads us to the second floor. A long corridor covered with thick, red carpet lies at my feet. I see doors with gold-plated characters: Room America, Room England, Room Italy . . . The waitress pushes the door of Room New Zealand open and I see a splendid room with a huge round table covered with an embroidered

Above: In *Shenandoah* Forest, America, *during our world trip,*
Ian's *sabbatical leave,* 2000

Below: In *front of* Napoleon's *statue,* Paris, 2000

Left: At an evening
party in Paris, 1998

Below: Cambridge,
England, October
2003

cloth, surrounded by fifteen classical European-style chairs. At one of the corner of the room, of course, is the karaoke machine. Every person in the room stands up and bows to me. They are my former students, their wives and children. Most of them are doing well in their careers and quite a few of them hold powerful positions.

This banquet is the fifth, or perhaps the seventh, banquet to which I have been invited during my three-week trip to Qingdao.

In late April, Orchid rang me from Qingdao and informed me that she was going to have her wedding ceremony in early May. I was thrilled by the good news and decided to make the Qingdao trip immediately, even though I had just come back from a five-month trip to Europe and the United States accompanying my husband Ian on his sabbatical leave. Apart from attending Orchid's wedding, I needed to sell Enya's city flat and my own property in Lying Dragon Village.

My house was a brick and granite house divided into four rooms, with a spacious courtyard and a vegetable patch. I had bought it from a friend at a time when houses in the countryside were worthless. Ten years later, people's needs had changed. City residents were fighting to buy houses in the countryside for 'green holidays' — the value of my simple property had increased many times and I had no difficulty in finding a buyer.

Ian and I have been married for nearly half a decade. Ours is a happy, equal, and respectful relationship. He is a very dedicated husband and a great provider. The struggles of the past have been worthwhile as they have bought me a happy and trouble-free life. My battles have also helped me understand life better and I think this has made me a good adviser to my children.

Nini has established a happy relationship with a university classmate and they are working for a television station in Sydney.

Enya got married in 2001 and gave a birth to a baby girl in 2003. From the day after Emily was born, I have taken on an important role as one of Emily's caregivers. Emily is not only a beautiful mixed-race baby but she is also a child with a great future. I believe that she is going to be very successful as well as healthy and happy; after all she is the grandchild of a survivor with a resilient spirit. My loving family has extended to a third

Enya and my first granddaughter Emily, March 2004

generation and I am sure Emily and my future grandchildren will accept me as a true friend.

I am enjoying good health and well being. I have overcome all the pains around my shoulders, back and knees since I started practising the Alexander Technique and learned how to use my muscles naturally. I practise and enjoy singing opera and I no longer suffer from insomnia. I often visit Bruce and his family. He is ninety-two now and is living in a rest-home. In 1998 he went back to China and met, and later married, a young Chinese woman aged in her late twenties.

The banquet starts as soon as I arrive. The host, Yang, my former student at Sunjia School and now a powerful official in Chengyang district government, is sitting at the end of the table, facing the doorway. It is the seat for the host. Opposite him is the deputy host, another former student of mine, who is the head of Wangezhong district, also a very powerful post. He is the only one who smokes — one pack of cigarettes is worth fifteen dollars! My seat, according to the Chinese custom, is beside the host, the seat for a distinguished guest who is always to be served first.

On the big round table there are shining glasses, three for each diner. The small one is for Chinese spirits, the medium one for wine and the large one for beer. The spirit is the best brand, Maotai, brewed in Guizhou, a southern province in China. One bottle would cost the equivalent of one year's income for a Chinese peasant family.

Twelve cold dishes are already on the table. They are like an entrée in a Western dinner but they are in greater variety, from garlicky cucumber and sugared tomatoes, to steamed shrimps and flavoured pig tails. Very soon, hot food on huge plates comes over, one by one. There is abalone, sea cucumber, huge flounder, fat prawns — twenty-four dishes in all. And because this is the 'New Zealand Room', there are Kiwi dishes such as Kiwi lamb and beef.

The host leads toasts for my health and my happy family life, and wishes for me to stay 'young looking' forever. The deputy host leads toasts for my longevity, safe journey, happiness and 'looking pretty forever'. After this, everyone from the table comes over to me with good wishes, admiration and praise. The next step of the banquet is singing. Like most city Chinese, everybody in the banquet is a wonderful singer. One after another we sing, accompanied by the karaoke machine.

The atmosphere becomes hot, enthralling and hilarious. Then it is the time to take photographs. All fourteen guests wait in line to take photos with me, until my smile muscles become sore.

As the banquet comes to an end, I am surrounded by all my former students and their families, listening to their singing: 'Take my song with you, leave your smile with us.' They all say, 'We wish to meet you in New Zealand one day' — the most precious dream you can have as a Chinese.

I am greatly touched and am moved with feelings of pride.